Sung Lee

DR. LEE served as The Director of International Student Education; Chair, Dept. of English Language Studies Program at Biola University, California. She received Ph. D. in Christian Education, Talbot Theological Seminary; MLS University of Southern California; BA, Yonsei University, Korea. She specializes in Christian education, administration, and leadership training, and is actively involved with international students and international ministries. She has also served as a short-term missionary/ educator for the last 30 years in various countries with Grace Ministry International (GMI). She is also an ordained pastor with the United Presbytery in USA served at Grace Korean Church.

Grandchildren

Tom at Israel

President Young Sam Kim

Dr. Corey and Rev. Kil

Dr. Clyde Cook

Dr. Lingenfelter

Moscow Seminary

Kenya Seminary

Cuba Seminary

Biola Commencement

My God

Sung's Faith Story

Sung W. Lee

Recommendations

Rev. Yong-gi Cho
The Founder and Senior pastor of Yoido Full Gospel Church

The letters of the Apostle Paul are often overflowing with thanks toward God. After he met Jesus, he dedicated the rest of his life to preaching His Name. He never ceased his thanksgiving to God even when lonely and cold in a jail. What gave him such devotion? This would be the grace of God. Paul confesses the grace of the Lord as being so active in his life as:

"But by the grace of God I am what I am, and his grace to me was not without effect. No, I worked harder than all of them—yet not I, but the grace of God that was with me." (1 Corinthians 15:10)

As the years go by, I realize myself the great truth that God's grace is big, wide, high and deep.

Author Dr. Lee devoted decades of her life to teaching the Bible and delivering its message. When she was experiencing loneliness from the loss of her beloved husband, she reviewed her life in her diary and put the entries together into a book to share with others the testimony of how gracious God was to her in the "ups and downs" of life.

This book contains her daily joys and thanksgivings. I recommend this book to everyone. It will help you to think more deeply about God's grace toward you, to love him more and to give your faith a revival.

Rev. Ja-Yoen Kil
Senior Pastor of Wangsung Church,
Former President of Chongshin University

There is an old saying (蓋棺事始定) that is completed after the casket closed. We finally know truly who we are after our death. It means the value of a life is not evaluated by an action of a single moment, but rather it is judged by how we lived out the chorus of our whole life.

Such an example is seen in Dr. Sung Lee's life. She was delivered into this world during her mother's life-threatening tuberculosis. She confesses she has felt God involved in her life with His graceful care from her birth until now in every moment and in all circumstances. In experiencing the countless "ups and downs" of life, she felt God's comfort touching her in the sorrow of sending her beloved husband to Heaven first.

Just as Joseph was strengthened by God when He was with him in slavery and in prison, she also found hidden pathways of God's grace and blessings through many difficult times.

As King Solomon says in Ecclesiastes 7:14:

"When times are good, be happy; but when times are bad, consider this: God has made the one as well as the other. Therefore, no one can discover anything about their future."

I have known Dr. Sung Lee to be very honest. She has a soft image but a strong inner person, yet she is a very gentle person who has endured tribulation. She put forth great efforts while she was faculty at Biola University to encourage pastors in Korea to study more in their ministries.

Dr. Sung Lee ruminates on her life as she steps into a senior age and has delivered her testimonies of how God interfered in her past life as a privilege and blessing for us to see.

I recommend this book as a worthy testimony, which will be a blessing of rain upon the churches in Korea.

Rev. Billy Kim
Senior pastor of Suwon Central Baptist Church,
Former Chairman of Far East
Broadcasting Co. in Korea

Those who have received Christ cannot help but preach His name. Dr. Sung Lee provides a life testimony of 70 plus years, from birth to retired faculty at Biola University – and even till now – of the grace of God.

It is a blessing and joyous to encounter the astonishing stories this book reveals, especially since these stories are based on her daily diary. This book truly reflects her life experiences vividly.

I look forward to readers being deeply moved in their faith and for those who do not believe to meet the Lord.

Rev. Jong-Soon Park
Former Senior pastor of Choong Shin Church,
19th Chairman of Soongsil University

This book contains three parts – her family life, her life as a professor, and the story of her Christian life. While the author was working as faculty at the prestigious Biola University (La Mirada, CA), she demonstrated diverse ministry experiences within the wider Korean church, colleges and universities in the United States and within a number of seminaries in Korea and America.

She reveals in this book how she found comfort in her faith when dealing with the loss of her husband, which deeply touched me.

America is a friendly nation to Korea in many ways, especially in welcoming immigrants through past generations. We also cannot forget the American missionaries of the past. They went to the land in the gloomy era of Chosun. The two countries have been a great example of partnering cross culturally in church ministry and will continue to do so in the future.

Author Dr. Lee has done her best to be a faithful role model and example of a Christian leader while she worked at Biola Univeristy. Her testimony points to the phenomenal love and grace of God in her life through the publishing of this book. You will find her story quite touching in its simple but yet powerful message. Readers will sympathize with her testimony and find themselves living it out.

I appreciate the author's heart and give this work high praise. I recommend it with delight!

Thank you!

Dr. Chang Young Jung
15th President of Yonsei University

Author Dr. Sung Lee, a servant of God, has been my longtime friend during our university days in Korea and America. Dr. Sung Lee has received tremendous love and a special grace from God. As a kind Shepherd, our Lord led and worked in her life as He desired. She believed He was with her and kept her as the apple of His eye, so she had no worries and was able to entrust her life to the Lord. She expressed joy on her face all the time.

I received great grace as I read Dr. Sung Lee's faithful story. Her book was written with sincerity, and it truly touched me. She survived a risky childbirth and was raised with marvelous loving care during a sickly childhood. She had a happy family life with a loving husband, Taebum, along with her only daughter, Mina. Her life is seen as being a devoted servant to the Lord.

Dr. Sung Lee traveled to many countries in the world, did mission works, gave speeches with all her heart, and with all her soul passionately served 20 years as a Director of International Student Education at Biola University in California.

Dr. Sung Lee confessed diligently in this book of great works that were able to be done solely by the grace of God, which the Holy Spirit anointed with His overflowing power.

And the reason she wrote this book is to share and bear witness to readers about the limitless grace of our Lord. She desires only that God receive the praise and all glory.

The work the Lord has done in Dr. Sung Lee is the same work He does today. I strongly and gratefully recommend this book and believe readers will receive the same blessings as well.

Rev. Paul Han
Senior Pastor of Grace Korean Church in U.S.

There are many moral lessons we can learn in all life circumstances. Great, faithful Christians learn how to allow God to mold and shape them through any life crisis, as a potter does with clay. They learn lessons from successes and failures, with the sole purpose of becoming a person who follows God's calling. Therefore, as a called people, we confirm and highly value the dreams given by God, and we focus on fulfilling the duties of our vocational calling and not being steered away.

The author, Dr. Sung Lee, wrote in a timeline format in her book about how God worked in her life. She gladly and passionately carried out God's assignment to her as a pastor, educator and theologian. What made her step into an important mission was her dream, not just her experiences but also assurance from God working in other people she met in life. This made her devoted.

The life of a person possessing God's dream is delightful, and there are great expectations of how that person will see God's work being done. Dr. Sung Lee's testimonies are "a story of God's miracles." There is, of course, a cost you have to pay to achieve dreams, no matter how big or small they are. Challenges follow a dream. Dreams have a strong power to turn the course of our lives. They are both a blessing and a risk, because they will disrupt your established way of life.

Dr. Sung Lee possessed a dream and sacrificed much to faithfully march through this race from her mother's womb to now. So, when Dr. Sung Lee talked about her testimony, she was able to say that she is a "blessed, prosperous woman through prayer." She experienced the work of God's grace and achieved victory over adversity.

God speaks through prayer on how to live, giving dreams, and He leads you to achieve it.

Terminology of Go(an abstract strategy board game)

완생(Wansaeng): A stone will stay alive even if it's blocked in every direction with no way to escape.

미생(Misaeng): not complete but will become something, unsettled.

My hope in recommending this book is that readers who desire to become men and women of great belief will be filled with God's grace. And even in a state of "misaeng," the faith of "wansaeng" will proceed under God's providence in every harsh hour.

To My God who has been my lovingkindness and my fortress, my stronghold and my deliverer; my shield and He in whom I take refuge - - - (Ps 144:2)

To Mina and Kris, my daughter and son-in-law,
and my six grandchildren, Caleb, Abigail, Evelyn, Joshua,
Isabelle and Ezra, I love you all

©2020

Sung W. Lee.

Designed by Gina Stewart

Bookbaby

7905 N Crescent Blvd, Pennsauken, NJ 08110

sung.lee@biola.edu

ISBN: 978-1-09831-255-8 (print)

ISBN: 978-1-09831-256-5 (ebook)

CONTENTS

Opening Words

O Lord, in Your strength Sung will be glad, And in Your salvation how greatly I will rejoice! You have given me my heart's desire, And You have not withheld the request of my lips. For You meet me with the blessings of good things; You set a crown of fine gold on my head. I asked life of You, You gave it to me, Length of days forever and ever. My glory is great through Your salvation splendor and majesty You place upon me. For You make me most blessed forever, You make me joyful with gladness in Your presence. For Sung trusts in the Lord, And through the loving kindness of the Most High I will not be shaken. (Ps. 21:1-7)

This Psalm is one of David's songs, but it has been my happy melody to my sweet Lord. I have recited this Psalm every morning as I have my morning prayers, putting my name "Sung" in the place of "king." It was God's grace and His will that my mom did not give up the baby she had in her womb, even though she was suffering from bloody coughing due to her tuberculosis. She ignored the doctor's strong advice that it might cause her to lose two lives, both hers and her baby's. I was supposed to be disappeared before I was born, yet God called me as "you are mine" (Is 43:1) and made me as what I am. God had a special plan for my life before I was even born (Ps 139:16). Before the foundation of the world He chose me (Eph 1:5) according to His will, so I had lots of tremendous, amazing experiences under His miraculous hands throughout my life. I would like to share the story with the world of how God has shaped me, because my life story is His miracle story, a masterpiece written by the Lord using me as its heroine. This is the reason why I cannot boast about anything I have done; my story is only an extraordinary story about what the grace of God has done for a helpless human being.

My God has been with me always wherever I go (Josh 1:9), whatever I do, and He fought for me (Ex 14:14). He has trained me in the necessary things according to his future plan for me without my knowledge, and He always caused all things to work together for good for me (Rm 8:28) and led me to the way of blessings. He has given me blessings upon blessings. As I trust in Him and look upon Him, He has always opened a way for me and accomplished His dreams and visions through me according to His plans.

He answered all my prayers like a caring daddy, but sometimes He never responded to certain requests, so that He seemed to use them to discipline me. However, the Lord who loved me so much always gave the best to me after all. He gives me all His benefits, forgives all my iniquities, heals all my diseases, redeems my life from destruction, and crowns me with loving kindness and tender mercies, and satisfies my desires with good things, so that my youth is renewed like an eagle's (Ps 103:2-5). He has affirmed me in whatever the situation I was in, "I have inscribed you on the palms of my hands and your walls are continually before me" (Is 49:16). Since I have received such an amazing love from my God, I want to tell the world what kind of God He is and what He has done for my life, and how He has made me to be changed from an impossible person to a servant of God for his glory.

PART 1:

Merciful God, My God

The Old Days

The Crying Baby

My mom was seriously ill with tuberculosis when I was in her womb. Because she had a bloody expulsion of phlegm due to her disease, the doctor urged her to get rid of the baby; otherwise, both mom and baby would die. Even though my mom already had three sons and two daughters, my God touched her to keep the baby even though her life was in danger. It was only by His grace that I would be born in this world. Born in such a condition, I was always a sick and crying baby from day one.

I always cried so much and so often that my nickname became "crying baby," named by an old lady, our next-door neighbor. I was born so feeble and sickly that I was crying constantly, and my parents were very much annoyed and concerned about me always. A weak body also brought a feeble mind. When I was seven years old, my parents sent me to an elementary school, but I was still confused and even unable to locate the classroom, so my parents decided to wait for another year to send me to school.

The Korean War

The Korean War broke out in June when I was eight. My father was a high government official at that time, in charge of all the prisons in Korea, so we lived in a government house in Seoul. Fortunately, my family was able to flee from Seoul before the bridge over the Han River was bombed. My mom had a strange dream that night, in which she was terribly frightened because of a burning fire coming toward our home, and then someone told her "a fire is coming from North, flee to South."

Mom got a truck with Dad's help, in which she loaded the children and things needed for fleeing, and we left for Gongju, a city in Choong Nam province where my family owned a small piece of land. We were eight family members including the youngest, Mann, who was less than one year old. We left for Gongju early in the morning and arrived at a house and unloaded there. It was the end of June, still very cold in the morning, but the ondol (온돌), a traditional heating system of the room in the country house warmed up our frozen bodies. Dad dropped by as we arrived at Gonju on the first day but soon left. As he was leaving, he promised us that he would be bringing back another truck in case the situation became worse.

Our area was becoming more dangerous. People were in a commotion and started bustling, moving and trying to flee south, and soon we were hearing sounds of bombing. We were so frightened and worried that Mom was unable to eat or sleep; she only waited for Dad to come. Five days later, Dad came to us bringing a truck. I still remember vividly the day Dad came to us with the truck; we were so happy and grateful to Dad.

The war became serious, and the Han River Bridge was disconnected just one hour later, as my dad along with other government officials crossed over. Our side's army bombed the bridge to block out the North Korean Army coming down to the South. Due to the broken bridge, so many innocent people who were on the bridge without knowing its condition fell into the water and drowned, for they were unable to go back or move forward because of the tremendous crowds on the bridge. When that happened there, it was the most fearful tragedy on Earth! I believe that war is the most miserable, awful and sinful thing in the world.

Our truck went down to Daejun, and the Daejun prison office had arranged a house for our family, but we had to pack again in a couple of days and leave for Masan via Taegu. We eventually settled in Pusan.

Refugee Elementary School

I started to attend a refugee elementary school in Pusan, where was awfully crowded at that time, because thousands of people from all over Korea had gathered there. We studied outside on a mountain side from the late spring to the early autumn. They had set up several rough wooden tables and long benches at a plateau between big trees and set up a chalk board for the classroom. We were able to see villages far away below us from the school, which was situated in a wood that did not have many trees. The boys were delighted to dig the ground to search for chick roots; the girls were picking wild vegetables in the field near the school, and the birds kept singing in the trees around us.

I was still very dull and confused in those days, and my brain was not functioning well, so it was still hard for me to locate any places even if I had been there previously. My school ranking was the last place among students in the class, and memorizing anything was an especially impossible task for me. At the end of our second year at elementary school, the whole class was able to memorize the Multiplication chart. One day, the teacher told us, "Today, we are not going to study, but every student will come to the front to the teacher and recite the Multiplication chart. Whoever can recite them without errors, you may go home, but if you are unable to memorize the whole chart, you cannot go home until you can recite them all correctly." I was quite frustrated, because I worked so hard, but my brain was unable to memorize the chart. I was scared and started crying, for it was getting dark and I was still unable to memorize them. Eventually, the teacher had to give up and comforted me by holding my hand and another poor child's hand, and we came down from the mountain.

Because of the war, people were continually dying, but the spring had come, and spring in Pusan was warm and mild. Herbs and wild greens spread all over the bald hills, where we were still excited and happy to be picking up dandelions, burdocks and barley leaves. I still remember the mixed smell of those spring grasses and earthy soil on the tip of my nose.

Often, as we were picking up those herbs on the hillside, a big truck which had full loads passed by us bringing dust. The trucks were covered with hard tent materials, and the loads kept dancing as the truck went along the unpaved rough mountain road. I heard later that the loads on the truck were all dead bodies. Every night, many people inside the jail died, so every morning, they gathered them up and brought them to the back side of the mountain. They dug huge holes in the ground and put the bodies together in the holes. I remember those trucks passing by us as they climbed up along the winding road to the back of the mountain. Yet, this side of the mountain was still warm and peaceful with the green barley fields.

The Chief Prosecutor's House

The next year, during my third grade, our family moved to Kwangju, Junra Province, for my father was appointed to be the Chief Prosecutor of the Kwangju District Prosecutors Office. The government house for the Chief Prosecutor was an amazingly huge mansion for a young child. The house was built in the middle of a huge yard; my mom made most of it into vegetable gardens, except for one side of the yard which had bamboo and other big trees. Our garden had a variety of vegetables, with garlic, lettuce, cucumbers, eggplants, peppers, pumpkins and others. A giant persimmon tree near a well next to the kitchen bore yellow fruit every fall; we also had five pomegranate trees around the house that were bearing fruit early in the fall.

I liked cherry trees most among the trees; two of them were next to the hen house, and one big tree was at the front of the house. When the cherry was in full blossom, the whole house was brightened, and when the flowers were gone, tiny fruit appeared in their place, which gradually turned into a dark color with sugar. Children loved to pick them up and eat them until their mouths turned black. I loved to watch the goats while they were feeding on the leaves. I always got some leaves of evergreen that had thin and soft edges for the goats that they liked so much. I could enjoy the smell of the leaves as they chewed them, and whenever I visited them, they were always calm and relaxed, busy chewing the cud.

That winter, I caught a cold and coughed endlessly; it lasted for almost 100 days, and the doctor said I had a disease called "whooping cough." I coughed so much and was so sick that I was eventually diagnosed with tuberculosis, which meant I had to receive a shot every day. I was so annoyed and hated getting the shot so much that I always ran away from the nurse who was ready to give me the shot. Then my dad always followed and caught me.

At the end of my 5th grade in Kwangju, my father was appointed as Prosecutor of the Supreme Public Prosecutors Office, and we moved to Seoul. I entered the 6th grade class of Ducksoo Elementary School, one of the most prestigious elementary schools in Korea, and it was very hard for me to catch up with the school work. I had to work very hard; fortunately, I was able to pass the entrance exam for Ewha Girls Middle School, but that obviously affected my health condition, and I started to get sick again, and my tuberculosis recurred.

Memoir of Jeju Island

Mild Jeju

Sickness was all that I could remember when I was young. The doctor advised my parents that I should stop attending school and needed to rest. For this reason, I was sent down to Jeju Island where the weather was warm and where my dad would stay. My father was a prosecutor in the Supreme Prosecutors office in Seoul at that time, but due to his honesty, his conscience would not follow the unethical business practices of the Liberal Party. He was naturally against them; thus, he was demoted to become the Chief Prosecutor of Jeju Island's Prosecutors Office, which wrote one page of my life story in Jeju Island. Later my dad resigned that position and opened his own law firm in Seoul.

The Jeju Chief Prosecutor's house we lived in was a nice Japanese- style home that had a small porch overlooked the back yard that was warm and cozy from the mild and soft sunlight. A lazy cat always fell asleep in the corner. The sun was bright, and the air was clean, and I was happy watching the bright yellow flowers with amethyst color around their petals lined up near the floor, and Cosmos flowers were all over the place as autumn had come.

I was admitted to the 8th grade class at Shin Sung Middle School, and on the first day, I met a pretty girl with huge, beautiful eyes who was kind to me. Soon she became a good friend of mine for four years until I left Jeju Island. Later, after I graduated from college and came to America, she became a very famous TV anchorwoman in Korea.

Shin Sung High School presented a play every year; the stage director was our math teacher, who cast children from the whole school. The season came, then, and he was busy, always foppish, wearing a small round hat on his head with serious facial expressions. His plays were always successful and loved by the whole community, both students and parents. I envied those children acting in the plays, for the teacher never cast me even in the smallest part of the show during the three years I was there. Sometimes I was wondered why he never chose me and was sad, but what part could he use someone like me in, who was always sick?

Romance in the Old Days

I attended the Dong Bu Church Youth Group near my home, where I met a boy there who gave me a kind of love letter, as I was in the 8th grade, soon after I got there. For the four years we stayed on the island, we made so many memories, some were beautiful, but others were sad. Winter sea! Summer beach! The lonely pier with flying gulls! We often went up to the Sara Bong, a small mountain towards the ocean.

The elder in charge of our youth group was not strong and healthy; rather, he was a small, feeble man, but he cared for us with love, and we greatly respected him. He often invited our entire youth group to his house and fed us with delicious food and gave messages in our youth services. Then, one day, we heard he became very sick and suddenly passed away. We grieved so much, and they said that he had sung the hymn, "Rock of Ages, cleft for me, let me hide myself in Thee," just before closing his eyes on his death bed, so we loved that hymn for a long time. His casket went up to Sara Bong, where he was buried in a cemetery on that small mountain. Oh, Sara Bong! We often climbed up there, where we could see a huge block of rock down below covered with creamy white bubbles smashed from the wild waves that were dancing under the blue sky that was pouring soft sunlight, like a fantasy world.

Our youth group went to Hamduk Beach for summer retreats every year. There was an elementary school next to the beach, so the church borrowed some classrooms for the retreats. The back of the school was on the beach, and the front had a huge playground that led to a narrow country road into a wood, but if we turned right from the end of the playground, we could get to a spring that had icy cold water. The people who went there to spend their summer camping would wash things to prepare for their meals and clean their dishes; further down, they washed their clothes with the spring water. They made two big deep-water pools beside the main stream and used them as a public bath, one for women and another for men. When we passed by the place and took a trail toward the mountain side, we could see watermelon fields everywhere, as most of the straw-thatched houses owned the fields, and each home had one room packed with the harvested watermelons. We visited one of the cottages and made a bargain for one, and cut it there and ate it up, it was so fresh and delicious.

When I was in the 9th grade, my health condition became even worse. One day, I went out to the pier with friends where I loved to go, because I would see divers who brought sea cucumbers, abalones, sea shells and many other fun things up from the water.

I enjoyed watching them and really liked the ocean smell! On that day, I suddenly broke out coughing at the pier with my friends; at the same time, I realized that blood clusters were coming out of my mouth. I was so scared and frightened that I covered my mouth with my hands and ran home, and from then on, my condition became worse and more serious. I became bedridden, coughing up blood, with no hope. There was no good medicine for tuberculosis in those days, so I had no other way but to wait for the day of my death.

Healing God

However, my God did not forsake me. There was a church near my home called the "clapping church" by the children, because they clapped hands during their worship services. There was a rumor that an interim pastor of the church had a healing gift from God and could heal sick people by laying hands on them. My father, helpless in such a situation, invited the pastor to our home and asked him to pray for his dying daughter. He came and sincerely prayed for the healing of my disease, and my God heard him and brought a miracle on my body.

Since I had lived in Jeju, I had been sent to a doctor's office in Seoul every six months for new chest X-rays. The doctor always took my X-rays and gave me additional medications, and I would return to Jeju. But this time, my doctor was unable to find any trace of tuberculosis in my chest X-rays, which did not show even any shadows of it. My God had healed me completely from the incurable disease and saved me from death.

From Jeju to Seoul

Following four years of life in Jeju, I returned to Seoul so that I could re-enter the Ewha Girls High School in the 12th grade class. The school was beautiful, and everything looked fantastic with its nice-looking, white high school building, many gardens with all kinds of trees and flowers, the shining amphitheater's stone steps, and the dune located between the middle and high school that had many Wisteria trees with purple flowers providing shadow for the students resting under the trees. The teachers were kind and taught well, but the year at Ewha was so miserable and hard for me, because all the friends I used to know before I left the school now had their own tight circles, and none of them invited me into their group, so I was always alone and lonely.

It was very hard for me to be alone without friends. Sometimes as I walked the corridors or the playground, I felt that everybody was watching me, that I did not know how to behave, and I was so frustrated and sad. It was a miserable and unbearable experience, but as time had passed, I was able to overcome the situation and then those experiences made me a stronger person, and I could well understand how to help other people in such a situation. I believe that the experiences also contributed later to my Christian life in that I was able to concentrate on the Lord rather than on being influenced by my circumstances.

The study at Ewha was not easy at all. Many girls' high school graduates in Jeju were not interested in going to college in those days, so the subjects taught in Shin Sung were to help them become good housewives rather than prepare for college entrance exams. However, when I returned to Ewha, it was like a battle field for the college entrance exams, and I was very much behind in the subjects of English and math. I had never heard about algebra, and chemistry was also new to me, because at Shin Sung they taught biology in 10th grade, physics in 11th and chemistry in 12th.

Even under such an impossible condition, God still enabled me to enter Yonsei University, one of the most prestigious universities in Korea, which was another miracle for me in my life. That year, very unusually, Yonsei accepted students with the entrance exam along with their high school grades, so I wondered if my grades in 10th and 11th may have contributed to this. Since then, by God's grace, I was continually the top student of the class in our department at Yonsei for my four years there. Consequently, I attended the school without paying any tuition until I graduated, and I was the representative of my graduating class at the commencement.

Yonsei University

Yonsei University became a great blessing to me, who was lonely without friends, but coed Yonsei gave me a chance to receive mental healing. The number of female students was small in our department, so we would always get together and were close to each other, and I had no time to be lonely. Every day after school, we went to music halls or watched movies, but the place we loved most was Yonsei Woods, our favorite place that seemed like a jungle in those days. We used to go inside the woods and had endless happy chats from spring to autumn.

One day, as we lay under the Acacia trees and smelled the flowers and the blue sky peeked between the Acacia leaves, I heard a familiar sound coming through a speaker. It was my essay, "Gray Weather," that I had written sometime ago for the school newspaper, and today the school radio station broadcast someone reading it on the air during lunch hour. A half century has already passed since then, but I can still sense what I felt when I heard my own essay on the air.

My loneliness disappeared because of Yonsei Woods and the companionship among our department friends. Moonja was my best friend during the four years of my college days, and even today we meet whenever I visit Korea. Several years ago, when I mentioned something about the needy pastoral students in my

Biola program, she gladly donated a large amount of money for scholarship purposes.

I met my husband, Tom, in the spring of the year I graduated from Yonsei University, the season when pink peach blossoms were in full bloom along the path through Yonsei Woods. He was handsome and fresh looking, like a spring fragrance, and was often humming the song "Who lives over the Southern land." One rainy afternoon, as he and I walked on the wet path of Yonsei Woods under an umbrella, we followed a trail covered with fallen flower petals of cherry and peach blossoms, and we passed through Yonsei Woods at the back of the Ewha Girls University buildings to my house at Chungpadong. Oh! Those Yonsei woods are forever unforgettable even in my fading memory! I long for those days passed away like a stream of water, that makes my heart sad, for the vanity of life is like a lifted fog on the hill (Ps.16:11). My beloved husband went to be with the Lord last February.

My Father, Love Giver

Soon after I arrived in America, I heard the sad news about my father's passing. My dear father went to be with the Lord on December 4th early in the morning of the year 1966. I could not accept the news when I first received it, for the thought of his passing alone broke my heart. Years later when I went to visit my dad's graveyard for the first time, I was unable to look at it, so without a single look, I sat down there and turned my head in the opposite direction, looking at the far away mountains, and wept bitterly. After returning home, I saw Dad's tomb clearly for the first time through the pictures Tom took.

Oh, how much I loved him! My mom was afraid to let me know the news of my dad's passing, and eventually two months later, when I received a letter from my mom notifying me of his death, I fainted on the spot. The reason my heart was so deeply tormented was because my dad had sent me a letter and Korean foods the day before his passing. Today, in America, if I go out to a Korea town, I can see so many Korean restaurants and Korean markets, but no such things existed in 1960th. Hence, Dad sent me Korean delicacies, such as hot paste sauce, seasoned kimchi, roasted seaweeds and others, by airmail. Later when I found out his letter was dated December 3rd, I could not stop crying, because he sent the food package to me on that day and he passed away the next day early in the morning. For the 24 years since I was born, Dad, who spared no pains in taking care of me and gave me his love, had been a model of Jesus Christ to me.

Father's Golden Teeth

All of my dad's front teeth were capped with gold, but I did not know the reason why for a long time, because no one ever told me about it. I heard the story for the first time from my sister when I was grown up, that an accident had occurred in Suwon, a remote countryside, when I was a toddler. One very cold winter night, the house maid brought a fire pot with burning charcoals into the room, and the fire pot accidentally touched my left cheek. I screamed at the top of my lungs as the side of the fire pot touched the skin on my cheek. There was nowhere they could get medicine in such a remote countryside! My mom and dad did not know what to do, and they almost lost their minds. My dad knew about a medicine called "Ajjingko" that was known to be best for burns, but there was no pharmacy or hospital in Suwon in those days. At that time, our family was hiding in this countryside to avoid the Japanese people's tyranny at the end of the World War II.

My dad had to go to Seoul to find a pharmacy, but it was already dark and there was no transportation from there to Seoul, so he decided to use his bicycle to go there. Dad found a pharmacy at sunrise and knocked at the door, and he was able to obtain the precious medicine. He was so anxious for me and in a hurry to return that his bicycle's tire got stuck in a gap of the city tram's railroad track. He fell, and his face hit the concrete ground so hard that all his front teeth were broken out, and blood was gushing out from his mouth, but he saw only the ugly scar on my face if I was unable to be treated in time. Dad forgot all his pain. Enduring the pain with a clenched mouth, swallowing the blood in his throat for so many hours, he returned to Suwon, and upon arriving, he handed over the medicine to mom and went to a clinic for himself. When I first heard about this story, my heart ached so much that I was speechless and just wept silently. My dad! How happy to be a child who had such a dad! I was really a child blessed by God.

Genius Dad

My dad was a genius whose formal education ended by middle school graduation. However, he was able to play the organ, violin and trumpet, and at one time, he dreamed of becoming a writer. Yet he had to give up all his dreams, because he needed to take care of the family and help his mom as the family's eldest son. His father was always away from home, engaged in working for Korea's independence from Japanese control. His family was always badly off, and my dad had to earn his living, so from a young age he had a hard life taking care of daily living with his mom.

He eventually thought that there was no other way but to take the higher civil service examination, so he went to a Buddhist temple to prepare for the exam. A few months later, he took the exam and, amazingly, not only did he pass the exam but he was also in first place, including all the Japanese candidates taking the exam. The newspaper reported it as a top article with Dad's huge picture, and they wrote that it was the first time a Korean passed at the top for this exam when competing with Japanese candidates. Soon he opened a law firm in Hamhung city, but it wasn't easy for him to continue successfully under Japanese control. Fortunately, he received a scholarship from *Chosun Daily News* and went to Japan for further study in journalism. He returned to the Daily News and became the newspaper company's manager for a while. During the difficulty at the end of World War II, Dad took his family and fled to Suwon, a remote place from which our family received the news of Korea's liberation from Japan.

The newly established Korean government announced over a nationwide radio broadcast that it needed to locate my father to join them and pleaded with him to appear at the court. The new country needed someone who knew the laws, so Dad responded to the call. Soon, he was appointed as the prosecutor of the Seoul District Prosecutors Office and, at the same time, as the chief of the Seoul Prison for Seung Man Lee's newly established regime.

The Meaning of Korea's Liberation

Korea's liberation from Japanese control was an extreme joy and an unforgettable event for all Korean people, but it was a real blessing from God, especially for our family. My grandfather was wandering from China to Russia to fight for Korea's independence, and he was repeatedly imprisoned and sent into exile on remote Korean islands. The following clips are from the book, "Hold this Rope (Sul Woo Sa, 1982, p. 19)," written by my uncle, Choong Yon Won.

> One of my brother's nickname was "island boy" because my dad was banished to a solitary far away island, Uchung Do, Okgugun in Junra Province when my brother was born, and my nickname was "prison boy" because my dad was in prison when I was born. The police were keeping an eye on my father and he was always detained at the police station near March

1, so that he was unable to participate in the independent marching of March 1. The Japanese police always kept a close watch over the movements of my dad. When the Japanese police took my dad to put him in jail, my mom gathered my older brothers and neighbors, and they secretly made Korean flags all night long. They brought out the flags to the street in the morning of March 1 and distributed them to the people and they shouted together "Hurray, long live Korea!" Eventually my mom and brothers were taken into police station, the neighbors took youngsters to their home and took care of them until my mom was released.

We saw all the bruises and scars on his whole body at the dead bed of my father. They were too awful to look at, that was a silent prosecution on the brutal tortures of Japanese secret police. I never received a single pencil from my dad, but I was always proud of him because I believed that he was a "patriot for our country."

One of my brothers, a high school student was arrested in charge of involving in "Kwangjoo Student movement," and they put him in a prison for 7 years without any trial, until he was very sick due to tuberculosis, so he died soon after out of the prison. Since I was grown up in such a family, I had to walk on the thorny path of life in both emotionally as well as materially. However, I was always proud of myself that I am a member of such a family because I believed that our family devoted to our country's independence.

My mom was the person I was most proud of and respected, who had a hard life, as a devoted Christian, she had responsible for raising her many children as well as taking care of the financial matters of the family. However, she seemed not lost joy and peace in her mind, and she always encouraged us and taught her children with a Chinese old saying, "The person who works for saving the country, does not concern family affairs."

Our family was now recognized as one of the patriotic families responsible for Korea's independence, so that our family received the special award, "Aejokjang" and a pension from the Korean government. I am proud of my grandparents whenever I visit their graveyard; they are buried at the Daejun National Cemetery.

My Father as a Model

My father was an elder in a Presbyterian church and an honest man. Dad seemed to support the Democratic Party because of the injustice of Seung Man Lee's Liberal Party regime. Consequently, Dad was demoted to the Chief Prosecutor of Jeju District Prosecutors office for his hatred of the Lee government. Dad resigned the position right away and opened a law firm, but he understood the importance of the work of a prosecutor to protect and help poor and unfavorably treated people. So, he decided to go to Jeju Island.

At the same time, I had to go to Jeju due to my sickness. Dad seemed to have more spare time than when he used to work at the Supreme Prosecutors Office, so he became a model to many young people around him. He gave messages frequently at churches and was invited as a guest speaker to youth at their retreats and influenced many people. He was in Jeju almost four years, and then he resigned and opened his own law firm in Seoul.

My Mother

As we may say, love is a word that is reflective of mothers, and there would be no one in the world who received their mother's love more than I did. My mom gave up her life for me from the moment my life started in her womb. She was strongly advised by the doctor to get rid of the baby to save her own life during the last stage of her tuberculosis. But she decided to die with the baby, and since she had me, she showed a tremendous love for me and seemed to feel a strong attachment to me.

I was always sick as I was growing, and mom was always worried about whether I might die, so she searched for all kinds of good medicines to improve my health. She tried to obtain various private traditional medicines, such as snake juice and fire ants mixed with honey; of course, I hated to take such horrible things, but I swallowed them with my eyes shut for my mom's sake. I still remember her staring at my face with smiling eyes that just followed me from one room to another. She always encouraged me and repeated saying to me that a woman could become a congresswoman or a president of a college.

I am still wondering how she could allow me to leave for America, for strangely enough, both she and I accepted my going to America as a fact without any doubts. It seemed clear that it was done just according to God's will and His plan toward me.

A Fortuneteller's Divination

Mom and I went to the East Gate Market two days before I left for America. We walked down the street toward the marketplace, where we saw a blind fortuneteller doing his fortune telling on the street, and mom wanted to consult the fortuneteller about my fortune. Even though she had not shown much of her feelings about my leaving, she must have been very frustrated and anxious about sending her favorite daughter to a foreign country, and I understood her heart. Of course, we were attending church on Sunday, but we must have been nominal Christians. Usually my mom and I did not believe anything like fortunetelling and regarded such things as mean conduct, but my mom seemed very much scared and worried about my going. Mom sat down in the front of the blind man.

"How will be this child's future? Please tell fortunes about her. She will leave for America tomorrow."

Suddenly, the blind man turned his body toward the back with shaking, and then slowly moved his face trying to see me with his white filled eyes. He seemed very annoyed and frightened, gesturing with his hands.

"Go, go. I don't do fortunetelling. Please go away!"

For a while, there was a strange scene between mom and the blind man arguing about do's and don'ts. Then the fortuneteller told mom, "Well, then give money first."

Mom put a bill of 5000 Hwon in the front of him, and then he quickly snatched the money and shouted to us.

"She is God's servant, a servant of God! All well! Everything will be fine!"

Even today when I recall the scene, I feel a chill creep over my back. Many years have passed now, but still as I reflect on that incident, I found out that the devil, the evil spirit, also knows our future. The fact that I will become a servant of God was destined by God's plan that He decided probably before the foundation of the world. Oh, what an amazing grace and a privilege! After I left for America, mom had an opportunity to be born again and completely changed. She became a woman of prayer and prayed for me so much every day until she went to the Lord.

It Started in America

When I Met My Husband

Strangely enough, I began to have so many dreams related to my future husband, Tom, starting from right after I met him. The place of the first dream I had was at Daechun Beach where our family vacationed every summer. I was with him at a certain bungalow, and I held him in my arms, then suddenly he turned into a skull. Upon awakening from sleep, I was so frightened and scared that I ran to Dad and told him about my dream. Then he stared at me with a funny expression in his face and said, "You may marry him. The two of you might live together to an old age." I thought it was an awful and ridiculous dream, but I was surprised by Dad's interpretation. Next night, I had another dream about Tom's death, that he was laid down in an open coffin, and I was crying so bitterly, rubbing his face with my hands. It was so absurd, because I had met him only two times so far, and I could not understand my feeling toward him in the dream, but this time Dad also told me that it seemed like I will be getting married to him.

I had another dream the next night, in which he and I were swimming down to a very broad road filled with crystal clear waters. We were so happy and kept swimming down the waterway for a while, then, we flew up to the sky and continued flying with the swimming gestures. We had so much fun and were so excited that I still remember the feeling even today.

I began liking him soon, probably because of Dad's silent support of the dream interpretations, and his handsome looks and his moderate family were attractive to me. Since he planned to leave for America as an international student sponsored by the Korea Education Department within a month, we dated every day from the first day we met. He came to Yonsei every morning, and we spent the whole day together, since I was working as a research assistant at the Yonsei Education Research Center after my graduation. We had a relatively a short time to know each other, but we went to many places, like the mountains, beaches and amusement parks, and he started to steal my heart. We had a sweet time together, and I wanted to follow him to America.

To America for Further Study

I came to America as an international student sponsored by the Korea Education Dept. in August 1966, and I received a full scholarship from Brigham Young University at Utah. It was because Tom was attending this school, and his two brothers had already graduated from there. One of the brothers had at that time already finished his Ph.D. in psychology from the University of Southern California (USC). Brigham Young University is affiliated with the Mormon Church, but I did not know about Mormonism very much at that time, and I was not interested in any background of the school. Soon we were married. The church members were very kind and generous, for they prepared everything for our wedding free of charge for the poor foreign students from a poor county. They lent me a wedding dress and even arranged a small wedding party, too. We were so grateful for that, and I would not forget their generosity and kindness.

Tom had many thoughts. As we came to America, each of us was able to bring only $100 per person, because in those days, whoever was going out of country was not allowed to take with them more than $100 from Korea. In the 1960s, Korea was so poor that the government was very strict about American dollars leaving the country, so they thoroughly searched everyone before they were allowed on the plane. Since it was impossible to get any supports from Korea, we were very concerned about covering our daily living expenses, so during vacation time, Tom worked at a restaurant as a bus boy, and for a better job he worked as a Keno writer at a casino in Reno, Nevada.

I went to Brigham Young with a full scholarship, but I had to keep high grades in all subjects to keep it. Even though I came to America having passed both the Korea Education Dept. exam and the difficult English exam given by the Korean-American Foundation, it was not easy for me to get high grades for my school work, for listening and speaking in English was not easy for me at all. But Tom seemed to handle English much better than I did, probably because he had the experience of being the English instructor to train Korean soldiers at KATUSA (Korean Augmentation Troops to U.S. Army) when he served in the Korean Army in Korea.

Upon starting a new semester, Tom told me that it seemed impossible for both of us continue to study together due to cost concerns and that he should look for a way to make money. He left for Los Angeles, California, where his two brothers were living. When I finished the semester and returned to Tom, he was settled in Van Nuys, California, working at a medical laboratory as a lab technician, and he had applied for the Permanent Resident card (green card). He had worked a lot in L.A. during the semester.

Receiving a Green Card

By the Grace of God, getting the Green cards was solved very easily for us, because at that time, according to the John F. Kennedy Special Law, there was an easy way to get the card for international students if they are qualified. If any leading American university recognized the foreign university that the candidate student graduated from, the Green card was issued easily, and we received our cards by sending a copy of diploma of Seoul National University Tom graduated to California State University in Long Beach.

I moved to USC for the fall semester in 1967, and Tom also moved to a hospital lab near the school. I received my Master's Degree in Library Science at the end of summer 1969, but it was hard for me to get a job at a library, because I did not yet have U.S. citizenship, and my English was not good enough. However, I was able to get a job at the Blue Cross Insurance Company, so we moved near my work place.

We lived there for around three years. We often went out to the seashore at Palisades Rocky Cliff with Mike, our next-door neighbor. We were equipped with snorkels and flippers and went down under the water, not going too deep, but we enjoyed so much investigating the gaps between the rocks under the water. We would see various tiny living things busily moving around the rocks and often found good-sized abalones. Tom and Mike always measured the abalones they caught and sent the small ones back out into the water. Meanwhile, I looked for a flat place and prepared a couple of abalones to eat. I used a spoon to take out the meat from the shell and cut them into pieces. Then the three of us enjoyed chewing the meat and dipping them in the sour red pepper paste I had prepared at home. I still can hear chewing abalones and remember the strong ocean smell.

The Bronchi Operation

On that day, we again went out to the ocean to enjoy watching the living things under the water and to catch some abalones. Then I suddenly felt a sharp poking pain in my left chest, so we hurried back home. It was not severe, but the pain continued coming and going. The Blue Cross company I worked for was a health insurance company, and the coverage for employees was excellent, covering almost 100% of medical costs. I saw a doctor, but he did not help me much; thus, the company introduced me one of the finest lung specialists in the L.A. area for a second opinion. He was a preeminent doctor in this field, who charged $80 per hour for a visit.

He was calm and gentle. When Tom and I entered his office, he was waiting for us with my X-rays placed on a very bright screen. He said that there are many pockets at the end of my bronchial tubes in the left lung, because I had lots of coughing experiences during my childhood from the whooping cough, tuberculosis and other ailments. He said that presently it seems okay, and the pain will go away, but in case a cold virus or any other bacteria get into the pockets, they could turn into pneumonia and other serious conditions, even causing death. Therefore, the best solution is to have an operation now, while I am still young and strong, and cut off those pockets. I was so scared and frightened, for I had never received any kind of operation before. The doctor finally told me his opinion.

"If you were my wife or my daughter, I would definitely let her have the surgery."

"But, would it be possible that I wouldn't awaken from the operation?"

"Of course, it's possible. When you came to my office today, did you take a freeway?"

"Yes," I answered with a small voice, wondering why he is asking such a question.

"Then, probably you will take the freeway back home, too. On the way to home, would it be possible that you may be involved in a car accident? The percentage for a car accident is higher than if you were unable to awaken from the surgery."

The surgical operation was performed at Mt. Sinai Hospital, one of the top hospitals in the United States, where most patients were Hollywood stars who resided in Beverly Hills. Due to the good insurance coverage, I was able to get the best surgeon without paying any hospital expenses, even though it was a major operation to cut off 1/3 of my left lung. The cost ran into astronomical figures, but by the grace of God, all of them were taken care of by the insurance company. I believe that it was God's miraculous blessing that I was employed at Blue Cross at that time rather than a library, and my God caused all things to work together for good to me (Rom 8:28). It happened that as I was still recovering in the hospital bed, while asleep with a pain shot, I saw a huge dusty table in the front of me and a bright, new golden spoon and golden chopsticks on the table. Someone spoke to me saying they were mine, so I wiped the dust from the table and then it was a shining, beautiful marble table. I was surprised and awoke from my sleep. "Hurray! I am going to be healthy from now on, just like the marble table, the golden spoon and golden chopsticks." I felt so delighted and encouraged.

Moving to Orange County

We unexpectedly moved to Orange County in 1972. We stopped to go out to the ocean after my surgery, and one day, we just wanted to drive southward bound, taking the 405 freeway towards Costa Mesa. After about 30 minutes on the freeway, we saw lots of houses under construction in the broad fields on each side of the freeway, and soon we were able to see more houses, including beautiful model homes with many banners and lots of people around them. As we drove further, we also wanted to see those model homes that seemed well built with fancy styles. The interiors were beautiful, decorated with gorgeous furniture we had never seen before. When we drove down to Fountain Valley, I saw a really beautiful and lovely home like I would dream of in a fairy tale. It was a two-story home with four bedrooms and three baths, and from the window of an upstairs room, I could see over the downstairs living room. The purchase price was $30,000, and if we had 20% down, we could easily get a loan from a bank. I had fallen in love with the house so much that, no matter what, I wanted to buy it.

Tom worked at a hospital lab during those days, but he did not seem to enjoy it much, saying that the job at the lab was boring for him and did not fit his personality, yet the pay was too good to stop. In America, if you want to become a lab technician, you must graduate from a four-year college with a Lab Tech major and also get a license. Tom was lucky enough that he could take the license exam, with his chemistry major from the Seoul National University he had attended in Korea. When he had overtime work, he brought home almost $2,000 cash per month. That was an amazing income, for those days, and we lived in a decent apartment with a swimming pool, but our rental payment was only $189 per month.

We had saved some money at that time and were planning to buy an eight-unit apartment building in Korea Town where we would live in one unit for ourselves and rent the other to the tenants, so those savings helped us easily buy our first dream home. We moved into the new house one month later upon closing the escrow. Tom had no problem getting another job, for he had a plenty of lab tech experience, and most of the hospitals in those days were suffering from lab technician shortages, so it seemed any hospital wanted him.

I was the problem, for I sent out my bios to many libraries, but public libraries were requiring American citizenship and no positions were available for school libraries. One day, Tom suggested to me carefully,

"Honey, if you have nothing to do at home, why don't you get a real estate license?"

It was not a difficult task for me to study and take a test, so soon I was able to pass the agent exam and received a real estate license.

"Sung, what are you doing at home? You know, just next block, the Red-Carpet office. I talked with Mary, the owner of the office, who seemed a very nice lady. I mentioned her about you and she said that she will provide a desk for you. So, whenever you are bored at home, why don't you go out to the office and meet the people and chat with them?"

Having some ideas in his mind, Tom had gently persuaded me. Tom seemed recognize the hot situation in the real estate market, because so many houses were under construction everywhere, and new or old, their prices went up sky high every day. I began to go out to the Red-Carpet office according to his advice, and he started to advertise some sale items in a Korean newspaper. In 1972, none of the Korean real estate offices or even real estate agents could be found in the Orange County area. Upon advertising in the newspaper, many Korean buyers called and showed their interest in buying houses.

Saja Real Estate Company

Tom's style was as a freelancer, and he would enjoy a real estate agent job. He did not like to work staying at one place all day long and hated working at the lab. I sold a few houses, and while they were in the escrow, Tom gave up his lab job to become a freelancer and received a real estate license. Soon, we opened "Saja Realty," our own real estate company in Fountain Valley. The real estate market was continually hot, and the house prices were going up so fast that, for example, if you buy a house and close the 30 days escrow, the house price already went up by 20% easily. Saja Realty did really well, and we became prosperous; we made a fortune, but at the same time we did not spend our money sensibly.

In less than 10 years after we came to America with just our bare hands, we owned several houses and a small motel located in Redland. Later, Tom bought eight houses in Santa Ana, demolished them and built a shopping center on that spot. That brought him a large amount of money. He was working hard and busy making money, but at the same time, he spent money without consideration. We seemed uninterested in saving or managing our money properly, probably because we were young, and he was able to make so much money so easily in a short period of time in America.

Tom liked people and made many friends and was also involved in a variety of organizations, for which he lavishly spent lots of money. It would be a correct expression to say that we squandered money everywhere. We ate haute cuisine at expensive restaurants with wine or even margaritas for lunch and visited Las Vegas so often. We were spending money like using water, without thinking.

PART 2:

Graceful God, My God

Meeting the Lord

The deacon, Man Young Han, the brother-in-law of David Kim, seemed like man who received power from God, for his testimony at a recent church evening service had greatly impressed me, though I who went there only out of curiosity. He shared about how he had cancer of the esophagus and how he was healed and received the Holy Spirit. The time had probably come for me, for God opened my ears to hear, for as I listened to his story, every piece of his words came into my heart with a tremendous touching.

I felt a strange feeling the next morning that I also wanted to receive the Holy Spirit that Han had received. I remembered in his testimony that he experienced the Holy Spirit's touch after he had repented of his sins, so I also wanted to repent of my sins to receive the Holy Spirit, and I knelt before the Lord.

I realized I was such an ungrateful wretch who had lived far away from God. Of course, I attended church on Sunday, but that was just for social purposes. We attended Bethel Korean Church in El Toro those days, gathered in an old building before the Saddle Back Church moved in. My husband and I enjoyed playing poker games with a couple of church families at each other's house by turns after church service on Sundays.

I repented that I had lived according to my flesh and about my worldly life. I had been such a selfish person! I loved only myself and my family, and never loved any others; little by little I was able to see myself and started repenting with tears. I was crying for a while and asked the Lord to forgive me, and then I felt my heart was emptied, and I was anxious to receive the Holy Spirit. I had a strong sense that I could receive the Holy Spirit if Han would pray for me.

Receiving the Holy Spirit

Han was staying at David's house, where Tom and I visited around 10 o'clock in the morning. Han shared with me and Tom about the love of God, the Cross of Jesus and his saving grace, along with casting out demons, and he began to pray for me, laying his hands on my head and shoulder. Strangely, the wordings of his prayer sounded true to me and pierced into my heart, and every word from his mouth became a fact to me. I was filled with an excitement and strong emotion, and I started to weep. He prayed like this,

"Dear God, thank you. I am so grateful that you brought me here to L.A. to save Sung Lee. Because Jesus died on the Cross, and by his blood, Sung's all sins are cleansed and forgiven. Now she became a new person, a child of God, and she is now belonged to you. Thank you so much that her name is now written in the Book of Life. Help her live only for you from now on."

It did not seem to me that it was a great or a special prayer at all. However, each word of the prayer pierced into my heart and became a truth in me, so that I seemed to become completely a new person within a second. I cried for a while, calling the name of my God in uncontrollable emotion and unspeakable joy. When I came out of the room, I saw some people seating in the living room, and I shouted to myself, "Oh my! how they could be so beautiful!" I felt as if I never had seen people before, because their faces were like angels shining as bright sunlight. I tried to calm myself down and looked outside through a window through which I could see far away a small spot of ocean between the trees in the back yard. The whole world in the front of me was surprisingly in yellow color. Everything I saw was literally in the color yellow and mysterious. That was an unbelievably dramatic scene, and it was impossible to explain the situation. My heart was filled with true joy that I was unable to explain with the words of my mouth; indeed, I really became a different person.

Oh, what a marvelous experience I had! When I returned home, I was unable to do anything all day long, for I felt as if I were in a dream, and I could not forget all the experiences I had in the morning. My name is recorded in the Book of Life. I did not know what it was and how it had happened, but I knew that clearly more than I saw it that my name is written in His Book of Life. My heart was continually getting nearer to God.

I felt something was peeling from me during the evening service, I was not sure what it was, but it was something like dead skins or something like a covering on my eyelids. I sensed the Holy Spirit was continually touching me, and something covering me was peeled away, so my conscience seemed to appear transparently, and the word of truth was smearing into my heart. The time had come: My God opened my heart and gave me the saving grace to make me receive the Holy Spirit. Praise the Lord!

The Words of Truth

I never knew that the Bible is so interesting and filled with the whole truth. As I read the Book of Romans in the past, I was unable to understand so many parts, but now those parts are understood by itself. Strangely, as I tried to talk about the Lord to the people, the words of God automatically popped out from my mouth. I liked the Bible so much that I always kept it beside my pillow as I slept, and I read it even while waiting for my turn in line at the bank. The sweet and eternal words of God came out of the Book and completely captured my consciousness.

My heart was full of joy every moment of the last month, and at the same time, I was in tears everyday out of endless gratitude to the Lord. My heart was melting and aching, and tears were running endlessly, because for someone wretched like me, Jesus suffered the painful death on the Cross! If someone lost one of his hands because of me, I might live in debt to the person throughout my life, so I would do anything for him, but Jesus gave his life to me!

"My heart is aching, Lord, my tears are running continually. I want to give you all of me. I want to die for you too!"

Yes! "I have been crucified with Christ and no longer live, but Christ lives in me. The life I now live in the body, I live by faith in the Son of God, who loved me and gave himself for me." (Gal 2:20).

I was born in a Christian family and attended mission schools from middle school to college, so I knew the Bible a little. If someone had asked me, "Are you a Christian?" "Definitely." "Do you believe in Jesus Christ?" "Of course." However, when I was listening to a hymn like "Gold jewelry loved ones and the decorating at home--," it sounded so silly, and I was unable to comprehend it. But now I clearly know that I will live a glorious eternal life in the Father's house decorated with gold and jewelry when the time has come.

Zeal for the Lord

All of us were planning to go to Deacon Yoo's house for dinner after the evening service. We gathered together for a Bible study until the evening service after the main worship on every Sunday. Our group consisted of David Kim and his wife, Sam Kim and his wife, Han Sung Yoo and his wife, and me. (David Kim had a born-again experience one day before I had. After he graduated from Talbot School of Theology, he started Grace Korean Church in Fullerton, California and presently he is the CEO of Grace Ministry International (GMI). Sam Kim also had a born-again experience on the same day as David, and upon graduating from Talbot, he served as a CM&A missionary to Japan and China for a while. After that, he served as one of the associate pastors of Seoul Onnuri Church, but soon he went to the Lord to be with Him. Han Sung Yoo also had a seminary education and was ordained as a pastor who worked as the associate pastor of Bethel Korean Church in Irvine and served as a missionary in Guatemala.)

All of us left for Deacon Yoo's house, and I rode in David's car. We were about to pass over the bridge over the freeway toward Lake Forest Street, when I told David:

"David, you know how much I love the Lord - - with such a heart, with such love - - I can't ask the Lord right now because I am so undeserved - -, Maybe one year or so later, I may go to a mountain and pray so fervently that I might pull out a palm tree, then God may give me any kind of gift or any power?"

"Oh, yes, of course."

My God heard our conversation, and He seemed to receive my heart as faithful.

"My dear child, it's not one year, just one week, no, not even one week. I can give you anything at any time if I want to."

"Oh, what an amazing God He is!"

Receiving Tongues

This day was another historic day for my life. My God is truly too good for me. He poured on me the Holy Spirit in August, and then he gave me his gift, "speaking in tongues," with the Fruit of the Spirit this night. I did not know what it was, and I did not ask for this, but my dear God gave it to me.

I was busy and very tired all day long, but I went to church for the Friday choir practice. It was a cloudy and gloomy day, and we would likely have a shower. Since not many choir members came, the practice was cancelled, and we wanted to sing praise songs from the hymnal to the piano played by elder Dong Back Kim. We sang together many hymns of praise to God, and I suggested the hymn "While the Lord is My Shepherd" (in those days I loved this hymn so much) and "Since Christ My Soul from Sin Set Free." It was about time to go home, and someone suggested, "How about we go to the other room and pray before we leave." Nine of us went into the room.

Our prayer meeting started with David's Scripture reading, and Elder Kim was praying for us. In the middle of his prayer, I suddenly heard very strange noises like a train passing by. I was startled, and I realized that they were the voices of both our Senior Pastor's wife and Song Suh. I stopped praying out of curiosity and turned to look at them carefully, and I saw both kept making funny noises and the pastor's wife was kept rubbing her opened Bible with her right hand. I felt ashamed because I did not pray and was watching other people.

"Oh boy, what am I doing? I should pray, but why are they doing that?"

I did not know and hardly dreamed about what would happen to me just one second later. I was praying and kneeled down on my knees on the carpet and put my face on a chair, so I turned my face back on the chair and tried to continue praying, saying, "Lord!" The moment I called the Lord, my tongue was turning itself, and a strange sound like "Woodada Doodadada" came out of my mouth. I had been very calm and composed that evening, but suddenly I became very much excited by a strange power. Very unfamiliar sounds that I could not comprehend continually came out of my mouth, and at the same time, I felt a cool wind flowing out from deep inside of my stomach that kept touching my face. I was practically shouting with funny sounds like a crazy woman; my hair was disheveled, and my two hands, locked with fingers together, were continually tossed up and down.

Then, I clearly realized that we, the human being, are composed of spirit, soul and flesh. My spirit was madly longing for the Lord and shouted in the full of joy and excitement with a very strange, heavenly tongue, such as, "Woodadada duda, thank you Lord! Woodaduda dada, thank you Lord." Meanwhile, my soul was watching over the phenomena and saying to me, "This must be the speaking in tongues," and I thought, "People surely think that I am really crazy." My flesh was sitting there worrying about my worldly appearance, that my hair was messy and that my nose was running with tears. Now, besides the Pastor's wife and Mrs. Suh, Mrs. Yoo (Han's wife) was added and all of us together were making funny, strange sounds. I knew soon that I was "speaking in tongues" and let it go according to my heart's desires (Acts 2:2-4). That started around 9:30 p.m. and continued to until 1:30 a.m. the next morning.

Waa woos! I received "speaking in tongues!" My God had loved me so much that he poured on me the Holy Spirit the other day, and then today, he gave me the gift of speaking in tongues, a proof that my spirit now absolutely belonged to him. I truly became his property, Halleluiah!

"Fear not, for I have redeemed you; I have called you by your name; you are mine" (Is. 43:1).

Oh, what a fascinating glory! I received unspeakable blessings from my God!

God's Discipline

I was joyous and happy every day in love with the Lord, continually reading the Scriptures, praising him and praying, but why was the reality so hard and painful for me? For the last year, since I had the born-again experience, I have had a period of wrenching discipline from the Lord. I had been living in my own ways like a prodigal son for a long time, but now that I had repented and returned to the Lord, then, why does God give me such painful lashes on me?

It was raining every day. I had been suffering with tearing pains in my heart during the past months of December, January, and until now February. I have held on to the Lord desperately like a drowning person is hanging on to a straw, praying and crying out to the Lord.

Tom was lost in gambling. Of course, we used to go together to Las Vegas and the Casino in Gardena to play pokers, but not like this. I was born again and loved church activities, while he did not have that kind of experience so that he seemed completely alienated from us. All of us who had received the Holy Spirit, so often gathered together to worship, praying and praising the Lord, and our hearts were burning in love for the Lord, yet Tom, who had not received the Holy Spirit, was unable to mingle with the group. Tom did not stop me from being with them, but he did not go to the office to work and indulged in gambling as a professional gambler. He seemed to lose around $500 to $1,000 every night, and so often he played overnight and came home the next morning. We owned some rental houses, so he sold them one by one and put the money in a checking account and used the money until it was all gone; then he sold another house. Bounced checks were returned every day, and I was afraid soon nothing would be left.

Endure, again endure, but it was too hard to bear. Why does the Lord forsake me? Now I have really come to love the Lord, then why does my God allow me having such a temptation? I had never seen Tom behave like this before. Why could not Tom be born again? Last Thursday, it was around 2:00 a.m. in the morning when Tom returned home, and he seemed frustrated and was regretting a lot for what he had done. He must be unable to control himself, and it seemed the Devil was working on him.

The Presence of the Lord

Is it a temptation from the devil or a discipline from the Lord? Whenever I had any opinions different from Tom's, he became upset and angry with me and threatened to throw away all the money we owned through gambling. Then, he would go out to go gambling, like yesterday when we had argued about something trivial; he was very upset and angry at me for that and went away from home. Why I am good and faithful to the Lord, when he is becoming worse? Did not the Bible say, if you believe in Jesus, you and your family will be saved (Act 16:31) and be blessed? "Lord, how long should I wait?" (Ps 43:2) It may be because my God loved me so much that He let me walk through the fire to make me shine like gold and silver.

"Oh, my Lord, I want to be freed from this world. I would be truly happy if I can go to you leaving this world. Lord, I want to be with you in heaven. No fun in this world."

I decided to empty myself to die with Christ and entrust everything in His hands. "I have been crucified with Christ and I no longer live, but Christ lives in me" (Gal 2:20). The Lord said, "If anyone wishes to come after me, he must deny himself, and take up his cross and follow Me" (Mk 8:34). Once I decided to die, I was so sad, and a wailing came out of my deep inside. I cried bitterly. I was weeping sorrowfully by calling on my God, then suddenly I felt the presence of the Lord was upon me, a feeling of something like a soft and huge cloud covering my whole body. I could not see His body or face, but it was the Lord. I knew it, because He covered my shoulders with His right hand and stroked down my back; it was so gentle and tender that I could feel the touch even today. My icy cold heart was melting away and His peace and joy were filling my heart. "Oh Lord, how it could be! Oh, my God!" My eyes shed tears of joy this time, because of His loving kindness and tender mercies. "Dear Lord, I love you. Really I do love you!"

From that day, I started praying for my husband's salvation every day. Although I do not know God's plan for me, I am inscribed on the palms of His hand (Isa 49:16), and surely my present situation and my life are given by Him. So, in any circumstances, I just look upon Him and do my best, because the Lord might have a plan to pull something good out of my agony and my painful situation. He might want to give me more blessings by allowing me to go through such disciplines. Just let me die every day to reveal only Jesus Christ in me, and then I may become a worthy vessel to receive more blessings. The presence of the Lord and His touch gave me a new enlightenment in my life.

It had been one year since I received the Holy Spirit and was transformed, but it has been a really hard and painful year for me. Probably it was the most difficult year in my whole life, I was in a terrible pinch, and it was so urgent that I was never away from my God even one second during the year. I prayed without ceasing for the whole year, and whenever I awoke in the middle of night, I ran to church to pray. Oh! Who would dare to comprehend the Lord's unfathomable thought and His amazing plan? Who am I that the Lord had so much concern for me and disciplined me so harshly? Was that His plan for me -- to make me a woman of prayer?

I went to church to pray every morning upon opening my eyes from that day on, and it became my daily routine. For the last 36 years, every day, I ran to church to pray even at 1 or 2 o'clock in the morning, and if I was unable to go to my church for any reason, I went to another church. This practice has been a tremendous blessing to me throughout my life, and it will be continued until I see Him in person.

The House in the Wood

After one year had passed since my born-again experience, I started to feel that the Lord was releasing me from His discipline. Tom did not go out to play gambling, as if gambling was no more fun for him.

At the same time, the Lord gave us a beautiful new house in a eucalyptus wood. We moved into a gorgeous new house that was built inside of a eucalyptus field covered with sky-high green trees. The builders cut down some of the trees in the wood and built the house like a house in a fairy tale. Whenever we drove into our tract, the year-round green eucalyptus wood refreshed and relaxed our minds, which seemed to me like a gift from God, for I endured well the past one year. We took a pledge to each other that from now on we will start a new life with everything in this house.

The Calling of the Lord

Tasting Heaven

One week's fasting was not easy for me, but when it was over, that was worthwhile and joyful, and I felt nearer to God. He gave me a taste of a tiny piece of Heaven in the morning of the 5th day of fasting. I was not sure whether I was in a dream or a trance, but I saw a bright and brilliant scene covered with sparkling crystal glass from one end to the other. As I looked at it carefully, the whole scene was composed of one huge flower shape, and very bright lights came from inside of the flower. Then, I heard a voice saying,

"These are all diamonds."

It was unspeakably shining, sparkling and bright. The moment passed, and the scene slowly changed to the world where we were living, inside of rich and fancy houses in Orange County, where all of us wish to live. But all the rooms of the houses were so dark, dirty and gloomy, something like when the curtains are down in the evening of a rainy day. I would not know the reason why the insides of all those houses were so dark and dirty. Then I heard another voice saying,

"They are just like dust cloths. If you get anything in this world, that would be a piece of a dust cloth, but what you get from Heaven would be diamonds."

I awoke from the sleep. The dream was so vivid that I could not forget the scene I saw comparing Heaven and Earth. Yes, I got to choose the heavenly works, for I would receive rewards from the Lord, because the heavenly rewards would be like shining diamonds people could hardly even imagine.

Elder Son's Dream

5/4/1980. We held an El Toro cell group retreat at Arrowhead Mountain from Friday, the second, for which I planned and arranged all the programs turned out to be more interesting than I expected. "Subject Presentation Seminar" was particularly well received. It was prepared and presented by group members, since they were directly involved in the seminar as speakers, and they were all positive and excited. We also had recently finished the book of Genesis for our weekly cell group Bible Study, so we had a Genesis Quiz Contest with questions that I had prepared.

Elder Son, the father-in-law of our Sr. Pastor Yong Oh Yoon, called me today after the Sunday worship service. He knew me well, because he lived in Pastor Yoon's house in El Toro, so he always participated in the El Toro cell group meeting. He took me to the corner of the sanctuary and told me about his amazing dream about me.

> "I had a dream about you which was so amazing that
> I have to tell you. it was the Saturday morning after
> you guys left for the mountain and when I came back
> home. I was sleepy, so I took a nap and soon I had

a dream, in which you were preaching in the front of a huge crowd, and you laid hands on the people and you were praying and healing the sick people. It was really an unbelievable scene, and as I awake from the sleep it was almost noon. I was very thirsty, so I drank a cup of water, and then went back to bed and again fell in sleep, and the dream was continued. This time I saw a cross on your forehead and so many people over there also had crosses on their foreheads. You laid hands on them and were praying for them, who were all the servants of God, the pastors. Mrs. Lee, I think God is going to use you in a great way, no matter what, he will use you tremendously. I want you to know this. Then I awoke from the sleep and it was almost evening, well, for all day long, I had dreams about you!"

I was so embarrassed and ashamed of myself that I said, "Well, God can do anything he wants to. I don't know." And I departed from him, but I could not erase his dream from my mind for a long time.

"Lord, I don't know anything. Only Your will be done in my life."

A Dream Given to Me

1/4/1981. God gave me a very strange dream early in this morning. Even a fearful dream! I was preaching on a stage in a huge school auditorium where I was able to see hundreds of faces looking at me from under the pulpit. I was casting out the demons and healing the sick, and I suddenly saw a crippled man on my left side who was healed and standing up straight on his own feet. I was frightened and awoke from the sleep. This dream strangely touched my mind, because it seemed somewhat linked to the dream Elder Son had last year. Although Elder Son's dream seemed to have more story than mine, it was strange that both dreams were so similar. Does this mean that God is sending me a message to become His servant?

1/6/1981. If the Lord wants to use me, then, what can I do for Him? Does He want me to go to a seminary? How could I go to seminary in my present situation? Tom is against the idea that I go to seminary, and who can take care of Mina? This is an impossible thought, because I cannot do anything in my present circumstances. I really do not know God's plan, and I wonder how He is going to handle this situation for me. However, is not He the one who can make impossible things being possible? Is it not He who gives life to the dead and calls those things which do not exist as though they did (Rm4:17)?

The Third Dream

1/8/1981. I prayed to the Lord in the evening,

"Lord, I will set one week, from tomorrow morning I will start fasting until next Wednesday, if you give me the same kind of dream one more time as a sign, I will go to seminary despite any kind of difficulties. Just give me the same kind of dream one more time that you did for Gideon who asked you to show him a sign with a fleece of wool, first he asked dew on a fleece of wool only and dry on all the ground, and then, dry only on the fleece, but wet on all the ground (Judges 6:37-39). You answered him with the sign. I want you give me, too, a very clear sign by a third dream if I have found favor in Your sight and all these dreams had come from You."

1/11/1981. Following the worship service, most of the church members were about to leave church, in which Deaconess Sookja Kim, the president of the Women's Group of the Church, talked in a quiet tone about something with Deaconess Haeja Chang. I passed by them and told them with a light jest, "What are you chatting about without me?" and then Sookja gestured at me to come near to her. She said to me that she was talking to Haeja about a dream she had last night, and the dream was about me. That made me be somewhat surprised, and my heart was alerted in expectation of hearing any messages from God.

Sookja's dream was something like this.

She was on the way to go to a certain place, where she saw a group of people in white clothing, holding baskets by their sides, picking something from a field which was already finished its harvest. "Well, is anything still left in the field? The harvest was all over?" Then, someone answered to her, "Of course. Lots of them are left." As she walked a little bit further, she saw a big pile of straw bags like an open-air stack of rice straw before her eyes, so she looked inside one of the bags, and she was able to see so many large, fresh turnips. Besides the pile, she saw wide fields stretched out in the front of her eyes, and a hoe was in her hand, hence, she dug out the dirt with the hoe and found many more good big turnips buried under the ground. "Oh boy, how could so many large nice turnips still be in the dirt!" Then, I appeared there, and Sookja gave the hoe to me, but her dream was not over yet.

In the scene, Mina was following me crying and in tears. So Sookja said to Mina, "Don't cry, Mina. Mom has a lot of works to do." Then Deaconess Sooki suddenly appeared on the scene and told Mina, "Come, Mina, l can play with you." Then, Mina followed Sooki with a smile on her face, and the dream ended there. While hearing the long story about her dream, it was obvious that this was the third dream I had requested from the Lord as a confirming sign from Him.

4/2/1981. I have often thought about those dreams that God gave me and wondered about what the Lord is asking of me. I will go to Talbot School of Theology this fall, which happened without my efforts. Sam Kim brought me an application form from the school, and I told Tom that I need his signature. He said, "You are going to seminary!" I had no chance to talk to him about my going Talbot, but somehow, he knew already about my going. He signed the sheet without a word to agree with my attending the seminary. (In those days, Talbot requested a "spouse agreement" sheet to be signed by a student's spouse as one of the conditions for admissions.)

When David Kim and Sam went to Talbot Seminary two years ago, I wanted to join them so much, but Tom was strongly against the idea. He did not want me to go to seminary, but today, he signed the agreement sheet without any objections, and everything went smoothly as though done by itself. I hope only that God's will be done in my life.

4/10/1981. I was shocked by a thought last night that was about the dream Sookja had last January. The dream was the one I had requested to the Lord to show me one more sign by a dream within one week, and God gave it to me during the week. Altogether, I accepted it as the confirmation of His calling to me, yet I was unable to understand the part of the dream in which Sooki appeared and Mina followed her. The scene had given me a big question, because in the dream, Sookja told Mina, "Don't cry Mina. Mom has lots of work to do," then, Sooki said to Mina, "Come, Mina. I will play with you," and Mina followed her. The reason I could not understand the scene was because I already made a promise to Deaconess Okran Yoo, Jungju's mother, who would take care of Mina in case I go to seminary, so that Mina should follow Okran instead of Sooki in the dream. Jungju and Mina were both attending the same preschool, and Okran had already promised me to do babysitting for Mina if I go to school. However, one month ago, to the dismay of all of us, Jungju was involved in an automobile accident and was killed. In such a sad and painful situation, I had to consider looking for another babysitter, and happened to unexpectedly meet Sooki a couple of days ago. She asked me if I am planning to go to seminary this fall, and if so, she is willing to take care of Mina, so I don't need to worry about finding a new babysitter for Mina.

Now my question from Sookja's dream was solved. Sooki will do babysitting for Mina from this September, when I go to school. This astonishing incident was telling us that our future is already all set up and shaped according to God's plan. I was fearfully amazed how a dream could be fitting like this! I felt awed and scared. Sookja had the dream before Jungju was involved in the accident, but the Lord, who knew the future, showed in advance through the dream that Sooki will take care of Mina instead of Okran. God only knows our life from the beginning to the end, and our future is all in His hands.

Encouragement from God

9/1981. These days, Tom was busy with outside activities, meeting with so many people almost every day, and he was eventually elected as the president of Korean Association in Orange County. His name has been in the newspapers every day and he's spending money like using water. "Oh Lord, hold him and give him your wisdom."

Our church held a mountain retreat for three nights and four days during the Labor Day weekend. I had so much stress from the beginning of the year from many small and big issues, and eventually I had severe back pain, making it too painful to walk, but I went up to the mountain, taking Mina. During this retreat, I received tremendous blessings that filled me with joy and peace, and my back was also completely healed. I met Rev. Tae Hae Yea, the retreat speaker, through whom God healed me and touched me greatly.

He used an illustration from "The Pilgrim's Progress" by John Bunyan in his sermon. Christian stumbled along a thorny path and at last he arrived at a mount where he saw the cross of Jesus Christ. As he looked at the cross, the heavy load on his shoulders fell to the ground and was buried under the cross. He became so light that he could even fly like a butterfly. That kind of miracle happened to me on the mountain. I was clinging to the Lord with all my strength and wept bitterly. When I came down from the retreat, all my burdens were carried away by the Lord, and I was so light. All the conflicts and struggles in my heart had entirely disappeared.

> "Come to me, all you who are weary and burdened, and I will give you rest. Take my yoke upon you and learn from me, for I am gentle and humble in heart, and you will find rest for your souls. For my yoke is easy and my burden is light." (Mt 11:28-30)

It happened on an early Saturday morning after I had returned from the retreat. I was still in bed, half asleep, when suddenly a very bright golden lay was poured on me from above, and then it was smeared onto my body! Time has passed since I came down from the mountain, and my heart has started to become heavier. Then I felt a huge wave come into my heart, and all the debris inside of me was cleansed by the wave. Unspeakable joy came in and covered my heart, and the words of God started filling my heart.

"Be joyful always; pray continually; give thanks in all circumstances," (1Th 5:16-18)

"Cast all your anxiety on him because he cares for you." (1Pe5:7)

"If you believed, you would see the glory of God." (Jh11:40)

Startled at the words of God, I sat on the bed shouting "Whoa!" Too gracious, my God!

I began to study for the Master of Divinity at Talbot School of Theology this fall semester. David Kim and Sam Kim encouraged me greatly.

I saw a big snake in my dream that night, and upon taking the neck of the snake with my hand, the snake fell dead. God seemed to be giving me His power, and I had a feeling that I would do well in my studies, too. The Lord is with me, so "I can do all things through him who strengthens me." (Phil 4:13)

First Israel Trip

1/1982. The Lord gave me an opportunity to take my first Israel trip in the beginning of this year. Seminary students from all over the U.S. participated on this occasion, and I was a member of the Talbot team. We were planning to study about the geography and history of Israel that appears in the Bible at the American Institute of Holiland Studies (AIHS) in Jerusalem for one month.

The school was located on Mt. Zion next to the wall of the old city, looking down the Kidron Valley. When we walked out of the school's gate, we could see a nice, wide, stone road that spread downward with a spectacular open view. Along the right side, the Jerusalem wall kept going all the way down, and the Kidron Valley was spread out on the left, and we could see Mt. Olive across the valley, and further on, the modern buildings of the new city. All the houses and buildings here were built with pink-colored, original local stones. Old stone tombs were everything in the valley.

It was very cold at night, but the morning air was fresh, and the sun was shining bright every day. There was a small country- style garden outside the back door of our room, from which we were able to see the Hinnom Valley and stone buildings in the southwest direction. The final fight of the Six Day War with the Arab League in 1967 occurred on this hill where the school is now located. The Israeli army at last defeated the Arab enemies, so that they managed to regain the huge lands they had lost before. The garden was deco-rated with roses and many colorful small flowers unknown to us. Although it was January, tender green grasses sprang out all over the ground, like spring time in Korea.

1/2/1982. How does such a small country have such varied geographic characteristics! There were high hills and plateaus, desert and oasis, and plains and seashores. One side was like summer time, another side had snow, and wherever you go, whatever you see, there was history and meanings.

At a small Arab town, Ako near Mount Carmel, we ate dinner at a youth hostel with chicken fries, olive pickles and soup, which were so delicious. Especially the taste of the green olive pickles was too good to forget, because it was less salty, but so fresh and full of fragrance, hard to find in America.

We had drinks at a coffee shop after dinner at Ako near the beach, and then we went up to the ancient city walls built on the water in the 18th century. We walked along the city walls, hearing breaking waves under us and watching the ocean sparkling in golden colors. The soft waves of the Mediterranean Sea in the sunset brought brilliant colors on the water and a fresh ocean smell. The top of the walls was speechlessly romantic.

Stars soon appeared in the sky, and the myriad of them were shining brightly, mingling with the moonlight. We walked on the wall under the night lights until we reached a ruined citadel standing on the water. We turned around at the citadel and kept walking on the wall to eventually reach a stone stairway that descended into the water. I felt as if I were in a different world under the gloomy moonlight.

I Heard a Voice of Calling

1/13/1982. Since I was longing for last night's beautiful scenery, I climbed up to the ancient citadel early in the morning before the sun rose. I sat on one of the inlets looking toward the ocean, where, far away, the horizon was starting to appear between the dark sea and sky. But soon the rising sun brought a fancy colorful sky and water with rapt colors. It seemed like an announcement that a bright, new day was advancing with the songs of sea gulls and the sounds of tender waves.

"Oh, Lord, how glorious your creation is!"

Then, I heard my dear Lord's clear voice in this ancient place.

"Be strong and courageous, my child. You only trust in me. I will do it for you and accomplish all for you. You will fly like a sea gull, so you may soar up high in the sky like the rising sun. You will become a servant for my servants, and you will be used for the world. I will do it for you. You only trust in me and believe in me!"

Because the words from the Lord were so clearly heard in my heart, I was startled and thrown into a state of feverish excitement. My God put wings on me. "Shaa – shaa," I heard the waves constantly dashing against the wall of the citadel down by the water. My heart was beating fast and trembled violently with intense excitement, and the tears were running down my cheeks.

Time for Disciplines

God's work is to believe in Jesus

4/10/1982. I felt avoided in the church from the beginning of last March. When I returned from the Israel trip, they said that the system of church had been changed, and the cell group Bible studies will be conducted by cell leaders from now on. I was not a cell leader, but I had led the El Toro cell group Bible studies until I went to Israel. The number of the group members had actually increased from 5 to 25 since I began teaching the group's Bible study.

I lost interest in the church. I had nothing to do at church this year, for no works were given to me. I must work for the Lord, then, so what shall I do? But I suddenly remembered, "The work of God is to believe in the one who has sent by Him (Jn 6:29)."

That is right. Why have I been thinking the teaching at the cell group is the work for the Lord? Did I want to show up myself? Did I really want to teach at the cell group because of the glory for the Lord? The thought came right into my heart and brought tears in my eyes before my God.

The work for the Lord is to believe in Him. What I should do is only to believe in Him with all my heart, with all my strength and with all my life. I will only believe in Him and love Him, and I will follow Him. I will just look upon Him like sheep are looking up at their shepherd! He will call me and use me in His time when He needs me. I gave thanks to the Lord and praised Him who always let me realize the truth.

Presentation for Israel Trip

4/17/1982. I was unable to sleep at all last night because I felt so much self-pity. How could I have given the presentation so badly?

I had an Israel trip presentation at Pastor Yae's church yesterday, for which I had prepared a lot, but the presentation was a failure, and I felt ashamed. Tom's elder brother and his wife, my sister and Tom came to see the presentation. Had I not given the presentation already two times at our church as well as at other churches? However, today was horrible, although I had prepared well, more than other times, yet, strangely, the proper words did not leave my mouth.

Why did that happen? Were my expectations too high? Did I try too hard to do well to show myself off to them, or have I become arrogant somehow without knowing it myself?

> "Oh, save me, Lord. I am such a helpless and naïve person! If you don't work for me, I can do nothing and be ashamed for everything!"

4/27/1982. I had another presentation today titled, "Report on Israel Trip" at the Orange County Korean Lions Club as a guest speaker. Reflecting on the disappointment of the last presentation at the Pastor Yea's church, I went to the meeting without any special preparation. I decided to speak impromptuly, only relying on the Holy Spirit and doing it in an easy way without stress.

The presentation went unexpectedly well. Everyone came and commented something to me after the meeting: "You are better than a pastor." "I have never seen anyone who knows the Bible that well." "You are the number one among this year's guest speakers." They were unbelievable responses, and I even had an interview with a reporter from "Dong Ah Daily News." I received the best response out of all my previous presentations, and four elders from different churches participated in the meeting. I gave all my thanks and glory to my God.

English Ministry

6/27/1982. Frank McCallum, the Wycliffe missionary, had been the 7th grade class teacher until he left for Seattle to learn the Indonesian language, so I had to step into teaching the class. It already has been four weeks since I took over the class, which was too hard for me, and I was disappointed with today's Bible study, too. The students did not seem to learn anything.

> "Lord, I can't do this. Please send someone else to take care of this class. For you took away from me the opportunity to teach the cell group Bible study in Korean, and I complained that I have nothing to do, is that you gave me such a hard job? Teaching in English is too difficult for me for this age group. It's really too hard for me."

I was so frustrated that I went to the empty church early this morning and cried out to the Lord asking to let me know His will. Since I was so miserable and felt myself abandoned by the Lord, I wept bitterly for a while, and then I suddenly felt the presence of the Lord holding me in his gentle arms.

> "Am I not with you? I will help you and keep you. You can do nothing without me!"

Ah! What a joy I felt! Now, because of the amazing joy, I cried so hard.

> "These have come so that the proven genuineness of your faith - of greater worth than gold, which perishes even though refined by fire - may result in praise, glory and honor when Jesus Christ is revealed. (1Pe 1:7)

The El Toro cell worship meeting was held in combination with the Irvine group this evening. Cell leaders had always led the cell Bible studies from the beginning of this year, but tonight we were going to have a combined group, so they asked me to teach. There were around 40 people because two groups were together. The Lord was with me and he used me beautifully as His instrument.

> "Lord, thank you that you hold me in your hands for the Bible study which you made it to be turned out great. Everybody felt the Holy Spirit was with us and worked for us, because I saw sparkling lights in their eyes. It was so good when I pleaded on our faith in your saving grace. Lord, I realized again today that you are the living God and you love me. I felt so weak and helpless in this morning, but you made me to be exulted before your people this evening. I do praise my God forever!"

Be More Faithful

11/22/1983. Although I was appointed as an assistant pastor in January, I struggled so much to escape from the work assigned to me. I was trying to avoid teaching in English; it was burdensome because my English skill was not good enough, but the Lord seemed to force me to do more teaching in English. From last June, the Lord made me lead the morning English worship service for college students and Sunday school teachers. I did this reluctantly for the last six months, and my English seemed to improve a lot. Yet I still wanted to escape, saying "Get rid of this cup, Lord."

Several months ago, a pastor visited our church and conducted a special service. As she prayed for me, she told me that she had seen a vision that the Apostle Peter ran away from Rome to avoid persecution, then she told me, "Don't leave Rome." What would be the meaning of her vision? Would it not be that I should not run away from the work I am doing now?

> "Lord, help me. I am your bond servant, only your will be done for me. Just help me that I would die every day for your sakes."

Seeing Visions

11/15/1983. It happened last Wednesday night, when I awoke from sleep around two o'clock in the morning. I had such a strong desire to pray that I went to church, and as I was crying out to the Lord for about one hour, it happened when I was going to continue another prayer. Suddenly, the left side before me became very dark and at the same time the right side was very bright. Then a bright light like sunlight from the left side high above came down toward the pulpit, shining on me. I was startled, and as I turned up my face, I was able to see the cross of our Lord Jesus Christ standing there in front of me! I clearly saw Him wearing the crown of thorns, but the shadow from the bright light behind the cross made it impossible to see his front. The thorny crown was so vivid that I was able to see even a very tiny sharp thorn on it, as if seeing dust floating in the air in the sunlight. The crown did not look like I was used to seeing it in books or pictures.

The thorns on the crown were so precious and glorious! They were the proof of the true love of my God who had given me his only begotten Son to save my life (Isa 53:5), to get rid of all my diseases (1Pe 2:24), poverties (2Co 8:9) and curses (Gal 3:13) and for my forgiveness, holiness and eternal blessings, as well as blessings on the earth. The unspeakable glory of God appeared on the cross! I did not know how to stand the strain from God's amazing love, and I cried so much bitterly.

I saw another vision four days after I saw the Lord's cross. I was alone in the church praying for a while, and it became 7 o'clock in the morning. These days I was the one who came to church earliest and left church latest. It was when I was praying about our family financial issues that suddenly a blue sky with white clouds was spread out before my eyes! I saw a faucet from which water was running down toward me that did not gush out, but water from the tap was continually falling on me.

Soon an interpretation came to me. Whenever the Lord gave me any dreams or visions, he always gave me, right away, very clear interpretations in my heart. Today was no exception. My God will provide all my necessary financial needs, so that I do not need to worry about financial issues any more. Praise the Lord! He will continually supply whatever my family needs from above, like running tap water. Praise the Lord!

God's Intervention

Early Morning Prayer

9/20/1984. A quiz for the New Testament (NT) Survey class was given to us last Thursday. I awakened at 3:00 a.m., but I wanted to sleep more, because I had a class until 10:00 pm. However, I was forced by the Holy Spirit, against my will, that I had to run to the church and kneel on my knees to pray at my place in the front of the pulpit.

I returned home at 6:30 a.m. and wanted to have a little bit more sleep, but Mina was busy preparing for school. I was able to close my eyes for only about 10 minutes to doze, and I was frustrated because I had to take a quiz in such a condition at the evening class. Since my mind was vague and drowsy, I drank a cup of coffee before the class that I usually do not, because it makes my heart beat fast.

Unexpectedly, I knew the answers to the quiz questions, so I received 9.5 points. The score was even higher than last week's quiz when I missed one question. But I decided that I would skip the early morning prayers on the days when I have the quizzes.

Today I skipped the early morning prayer and slept late into the morning and went to school. When I received the quiz paper, I felt as if something was covering my eyes and head, so that everything was cloudy, and I missed four questions. That was an unbelievable happening. I had studied more, conditioned better, slept more hours, and all together prepared much more, so then, why? What was truly happening?

That moment again when I was realized how much the Lord loves me and cares for me! The Lord hated most when I was lazy about praying, which I knew through the hundreds of incidents he had shown me. He let me know the fact again this time.

The Lord, My Love

10/1/1984. I was enjoying life these days in peace from the Lord. For the last year, since he gave me the vision about the running tap water, our family had had no financial concerns at all.

I felt every day that my heart is filled with full of love. When I think about my husband, my heart was aching out of a sentiment of pity, and when thinking about Mina, I felt I had not given her all my love. My heart was burning with fervent desires for giving them all of me.

A couple of days ago, I felt a strong compassion as Tom sat next to me, who seemed so good and lovely as if I was falling madly in love with Him. I did not know how to handle my heart, so I ran to church and cried out to the Lord a fervent prayer with loud wailing.

"Oh Lord, I am truly in love with you. Whenever I kneel before you, my running tears are a proof of my love for you that I haven't given you enough. Lord, I love you, really, I do. My tears are pouring like a rainfall. I

know the feeling for Tom and Mina is because of you.
I truly want to give you all of me. You are my true love,
my lover, my Lord Jesus Christ!"

Old Testament Survey Class

2/5/1985. I walked into the OT Survey class today, which was one of the core classes for the entire Masters program students, and around 100 students were packed in a huge classroom. As I entered the room, Dr. Ends welcomed me with a kind gesture, since I had taken his New Testament Survey class last semester. When I had the NT class, I missed only one question out of 50 for our first exam, so I received the highest mark among the students, and because of that, he seemed to remember me.

Dr. Ends was a new professor who came to Talbot last semester; He had the experience of pastoring a church for a while in Florida and had been a Dean of a Seminary. He earned his Th.D. from Dallas Theological Seminary, and he was a very scholarly professor.

However, when he taught about the "Book of Acts," my heart was so aching that I prayed in tears for him at my Morning Prayer time. He had limited the power of God. He told us that the powers that appeared on Apostles Peter, John or Paul would not be expected from us living in today's world. For the age of "Acts," a special dispensational era, God worked in a special way to spread the Gospel, but those miracles would not occur today.

Why did he not know that God is the same yesterday, today and forever (Heb 13:8)! I was so sad. Why did not he completely believe in the power of God?

Dr. Ends gave us today the same assignment to make a research note just as I did for the NT Survey class.

"It seems hard to make, but it isn't that so. I gave the same assignment last semester at the NT Survey class, and some students did well even adding charts and maps. Among them Sung did the best (he pointed me), so you may ask her while you work for the home-work if you have any questions."

I was startled hearing my name was called. Faces of all the students were turning toward me, and I was embarrassed. The professor said with a smile, "Did I make you be embarrassed?" Due to this incident many students asked questions, and I let them look at my NT Survey note in turn.

4/9/1985. I was shocked and repented a lot to the Lord today when I received my quiz answer sheet back. Although the professor mentioned that I had the highest point, my grade was 23.5/25 out of 50 questions, so that I missed many questions.

The day I had the exam, I was so confident, for the 50 questions were all easy except just one question. The test was the issue in this class, because the professor usually did not tell us the scope for the tests and it covered the entire Old Testament in most cases. Did not I give answers with such confidence to those American classmates who asked me for answers to the questions after the exam? As I gave them my answers, some were pleased and others disappointed.

Today when I received my answer sheet back, I found out that all the answers I missed were ones that I already knew the answers to. I even received a traffic ticket on Beach Blvd on the way back home out of excitement on that day. I saw myself to be broken before the Lord.

Arrogance and pride always cropped up in my heart silently and accumulated inside of me without any warnings. If I knew 'this is arrogance!' from the beginning, I would not do that. Am I not praying to be a humble person every day? This must be the work of the devil. The devil prowls around like a roaring lion looking for someone to devour (1Pe 5:8). I should truly be alert and humble to accomplish my salvation with fear and trembling.

"He mocks proud mockers but shows favor to the humble and oppressed (Prov 3:34)"

I knelt again before the Lord and repented in tears. Knowing God hates and despises most those who are arrogant and proud, how would I be so rich in mind! I was deeply ashamed of myself as I reflected what I had said to the Korean students, although half in joke, "These are Biblical common sense, and you should know at least these things to become a pastor." I was so regretful and sorry for my attitude for such a saying, rather than the foolish talk itself.

> "Lord, I am a foolish woman. I am the most naïve person in the world, who doesn't know anything pitifully. Lord, forgive me, just pity on me."

> "- - - God opposes the proud but shows favor to the humble (1Pe 5:5)."

God's Odd Method

8/11/1985. It was truly a strange and mysterious happening. Why does my God love me so much and was so carefully watching over me always and intervening in my life?

After I moved to Grace Korean Church, a couple of Christian friends of mine mentioned to me that they wanted to start a new church in this El Toro area and were planning to invite a spirit-filled pastor. What they wanted from me was to lead the group to have worship services on Sundays until they would search for one, so until that time, they want me to help them.

I told them that I am not ready for such a ministry, and I cannot do it. But they pushed me hard, and it was not easy for me to reject their strong request. What they wanted was only to gather together to worship the Lord, and how would I know that their request was from the Lord and would be the will of God? We eventually decided to have the first meeting at my house on the 13th of this month.

Truly an unbelievable happening occurred on that day. I put a boiled egg in a microwave oven for warming up at lunch time. The moment I touched the heated egg with a tip of my chopsticks, it blew up with a terrific explosion with a bang. Those broken egg pieces hit my lips, and they were spreading out and stuck fast to all over the kitchen walls. Oh, what a disaster!

Of course, my lips were burned. I just finished my cold noodle (Nangmyon) without any egg in such a disaster. The people were supposed to be at my house at 7:30 p.m., but I started to feel bad with a splitting headache without reason, even feeling nauseated from around 7 p.m. I was getting worse, felt myself sinking down deep, unable to speak and it was even harder to move my body. I was unable to stand and I felt fuzzy.

I heard the phone ringing a couple of times, probably people asking for directions to my house, and soon I heard noises as people were entering my living room, but it was impossible for me to talk or to move. I never had such an experience before. People were gathered in the living room, but I was still throwing up in the bathroom. People seemed to pray for a while, then an Elder told people to dismiss today's meeting and they were quietly leaving my house. Only the Deaconess who arranged this meeting and the Elder remained and helped me to get into my bed to lie down, and then they, too, left my house.

Truly more odd and mysterious incidents happened upon their leaving. I felt my body was rapidly recovering. Like a lie, 30 minutes later after they left, my body was restored completely to its normal condition. It was truly an amazing and awful happening, and I realized that God does not want the gathering. Then, my question was why God used such a strange method to prevent the meeting. Could he not tell me "don't do it" in my heart or in my dream at night? My God has such a strange sense of humor! He always seems to use a funny and miraculous method at the last minute.

I called the Deaconess again today and reminded her of the day's happening and told her that this gathering is not pleasing to the Lord. I do not know what is not right, but what I know clearly is that the Lord does not want me to be involved in this gathering. God really used a very peculiar way to lead me.

The Disease of Arrogance

5/12/1986. My God is so good, so considerate and loves me so much! He always intervenes in my life and lets me follow only his ways in all my affairs. I recently received too much praise from groups of people, such as my fellow program candidates talked about me as "a smart student is coming this semester for our doctor's program." Whenever the Korean students saw me, they mentioned to me about Dr. Ends' class story. Also, the praising words from Dr. Fred Wilson, the Director of the Doctor's Program and my Committee Chair. All these sweet sayings made me to be spoiled, very arrogant and proud of myself. I felt as if I were the best, and whenever I went to school, I was joyous and delighted, and life seemed so good and I was happy to live. I pretended not to, but I was indulging in an awful arrogance and pride.

Soon, no need to wait longer, I felt God's whips on me. The study was not that hard, but strangely I thought I was disgraced in front of my peers, which hurt my pride and frustrated me. Class discussions also were not so hard, but sometimes I hated myself because I was humiliated due to my lack of preparation. I began to lose my interest in studying and wanted to give everything up.

In such circumstances, I started to re-evaluate myself. As I felt my weaknesses and limitations, all the pride I had at the beginning of the semester disappeared, and I began hanging on tightly to the Lord.

> "Lord, why should I need to have a doctor's degree?
> I can't do it. I want to stop it."

As I started to become more humble, the situation began to change. A few days ago, I gave a 15-minute message titled, "What are you looking for?" for my turn at the devotion time in the Integration class. The Holy Spirit was with me and gave a great touch in the hearts of the students.

Dr. Brooks praised me so much on the message that I felt even embarrassed.

> "Sung, I know you are using a different language, but the Lord may call you as a preacher for American people. In the future, if American people invite you to give them a message, you must say "yes." I mean not for Korean churches, but American churches, that may be your mission."

It seemed clear that most of the students were blessed during this devotion. Unusually, all the students stood up and held the shoulders of the person in front of them and went around the class singing praise songs and glorifying the Lord as we never had before.

The event brought me tremendous encouragement, and from then on, very strangely, the studies became easy for me as well as the class discussions and unexpected presentations. I realized again how much my God really loves me!

The Grace of the Lord

Tom's Activities

8/11/1985. These days, the newspapers and TV were showing huge announcements for the fund-raising concert that will be held at Disney Concert Hall, sponsored by the Orange County Korean Youth Foundation. Tom was the president of the foundation, so he seemed very busy.

The first part of the concert was dedicated to a devotion arranged by the Orange County Men's Evangelical Association and was followed by a short ceremony, then the concert. Everything went so well in the Christian environment, and it was especially great that the former famous comedian, Pastor Kyu Suk Kwak, was the MC for the concert.

Tom was concerned about the number who would attend, but the concert hall was packed with around 1,300 people. The entire music program was excellent, as well as Tom's welcome speech. It was a successful event.

I was usually not much interested in Tom's outside activities, but this event opened my eyes and brought me a new meaning. We Christians who received the Holy Spirit should not be staying inside the church; rather, we should go out into the world to give ourselves to the lost people to help them meet the Lord. The Moon Church pulls those young people out of drug addictions and has them sell flowers in the streets for their church. We must take them to meet our Lord Jesus Christ as their Savior. The Lord seemed to give me a new vision and another prayer request.

> "Lord, pour on Tom your wisdom, brightness and power. The most of all, he needs a personal encounter with you. Help him to invest all of his strength, his talents, his time and materials, and even his life in eternity which will receive heavenly heritage, not in building a tower of Babel for his own glory in this world."

Dream for Tom's Salvation

11/19/1985. I had been praying to the Lord for Tom's salvation every day, even several times a day. The Lord gave me a dream last night that seems an answer to my prayers.

"Did I not say to you that if you believe, you will see the glory of God? (Jn11:40)"

Maybe not now; however, I believe that the Lord will save Tom in His time. I went to the Irvine Baptist Church for my morning prayer yesterday. Since Tom left for Korea with a one-week schedule last Saturday, I have prayed harder for him, and the Lord gave me a dream this morning.

Our house had a huge patio at the back yard. When I looked from the patio in my dream, a calm, blue ocean was spreading out from the patio! People wearing white clothes sat on the patio, and the patio turned out to be a raft departing from the house and went down to the water. The people on the raft started to sing a praise song.

I was also sitting on the float, and then I saw Tom coming toward me in the clear water with no clothing on top. I held his hand, and we went down together; since he was under the water, holding his hand was not hard for me at all, and I was extremely happy. As I awoke from sleep, I felt so happy and my heart was indescribably refreshed and grateful to the Lord. It was already 6 a.m., but I wanted so much to pray that I went to church and knelt before the Lord.

> "Oh Lord! Thank you. You answered my prayers. Thank you so much that you led us to a sea of grace and led him to sink in your grace. God to be glorified and honored! I am so grateful to you for the saving grace for us."

> "Believe in the Lord Jesus, and you will be saved – you and your household. (Ac 16:31)"

God's Warnings through Dreams

8/25/1986. The Lord often spoke to me and let me know what I should do through my dreams; for example, whenever I skipped my morning prayers, he always gave me warnings through my dreams. My God always receives my morning prayers and is pleased with them. In fact, no matter how much I prayed, why would my God in His abundant glory need to like my prayers? That was only because He loves me so much that He wants to hear my confession of love for Him and my childish effort to make myself agreeable to Him. In addition, He enjoys conversing with me.

If I miss prayers for three days in raw, I usually get a signal from my God. He is letting me know through the dreams that devils are attacking me, because the devils are approaching me whenever they seize a vulnerable moment in me. Since last Wednesday, I was too busy to go for prayers for a couple of days, so I repented today and kneeled before the Lord. As I returned home after praying, I took a short nap in which the Lord gave me a dream.

It was my house in the dream, which had a high wall around it and a huge gate in the middle of the wall that was supposed to be locked always. I felt some bad people were pushing the gate to get into the house, so I ran toward the gate, shouting "Who is there? Who is this?" When I neared the gate, I found out all the gate bolts were unbolted, so if anyone pushed the gate it would be easily opened. I felt a chill up my back, and I rapidly latched the door bolts one by one. As I looked outside over the gate, four men wearing black suits with short hair cuts were trying to get into my house. I was so relieved because I had barred all the gate bolts.

When I opened my eyes, love of the Lord smeared into my heart. How great God he is! He gave a warning to me who was lazy for the morning prayers. The devil enters us to devour us as a roaring lion if he seizes a moment when our mind is disarmed. I skipped my morning prayers for a couple of days, then all the door bars were loosened like that!

20th Wedding Anniversary

9/8/1986. Today is our 20th wedding anniversary. Now 20 years have passed, and we see each other as individuals who have changed so much. He is not narrow minded and is generous, big in scale and acts magnanimously without calculation. Even though he would not have enough money, he gives anyone asking for it without calculation, and buys expensive things without hesitation. Saving money is not his style, but still he wants to make money and go in for speculation with awfully risky investments according to his intuition.

Of course, I had been the one who received the benefits, but I was afraid of and hated to get big money from risky investments. Saving is a must for me; I prefer to be small in scale and hate to invest in something just with guts. My desire is to live a simple normal life peacefully. Then why did God allow me to meet a person like Tom as a husband? How I would know my Lord's deep thought! Only I shall give thanks to my God for Tom is my husband.

He would like to live in his own way, his own life style that pleases him. So do I in my own way, but in such circumstances, I have tried very hard not to be hurt and must look for something that may please me. He often mentioned to me,

> "I am happy now. Life is so good to me, so just leave me alone. Please don't ask me to live in your life style and try to put me in your shape. Aren't you doing whatever you want to do? You are going to seminary and going travels if you want to."

He asked me to leave him alone, and he loves to be outside and often came home late after dinner. Almost every day he goes golfing and enjoys being around his friends, even though he does not drink. Hence, I am now used to him being what he is and have not been bothered too much. I have learned how to enjoy my own time alone, so I am pleased to study, love to read books, and enjoy watching TV dramas.

Yet, I love Tom whom probably I might marry again if I have another chance to be married. He is a comfortable man who does not bother me much, and in almost all cases, he allows me to do what I want to do. He especially encourages me to spend money for myself, such that I wear expensive clothing, have name-brand bags and drive a good car. He is the one who has trusted in me, supported and encouraged me the most in all the situations.

He mentioned to me that he is a normal person and happy to live, but to my eyes, he has seemed always insecure and lonely because of an emptiness in his heart. He needs to meet the Lord personally. The Bible says believing God is a gift from God (Eph 2:8), then why does not my God quickly give this gift to him?

> "Lord, I implore you. Quickly give your gift of salvation to Tom for I want him to be happy. I truly want him to live in your peace and joy."

Mann Went to the Lord

10/31/1986. My dear brother, Mann, died unexpectedly early this morning. Startled by the news, my heart sank down and I was dumbfounded, even though I know that a single sparrow would not fall without God's permission.

All our family members were gathered together for lunch after last Sunday worship service, so that was a farewell lunch! He was too young to go so early, leaving two young sons, 2 and 4 years old; that was tearing my heart into pieces with pain. How could such a thing happen?

He worked so hard to make money for all those years, and was now about to live in comfort, and then God took him. What was wrong with him before the Lord? If the Lord did not love him and he was an abandoned child, God would not call him. There are so many children of the devil in this world, but my brother was God's child, so the Lord took him in the best time for him, because it definitely worked together for good to him in certain ways.

My heart was aching because I had not given him enough of my love, and I was regretting so much. I thought about him a lot and loved him so much in those days when he stayed in Korea, he had just come to America, and he got married. I wanted to give him anything I had, and I always had a feeling of pity toward him. But I thought recently that he had been too stingy, and I judged him and did not love him as I did before. I used to love him without reservation, but I had been developing a feeling of disappointment on him in my mind.

> "Oh, Lord, can I be forgiven? You died on the cross to redeem the wretched like me from destruction with your unconditional love. I received such a great love from God, how would I looking for a reason to love my brother? Why can I love him only when he has a condition to be loved? The Lord loved me without condition, then why should not I love my brother without condition?"

> "Lord, it seems too costly for paying to learn a lesson. Is there no way to return? Forgive me Lord. I will be a woman of love from now on, only giving without condition. I will never anticipate anything from anyone, and deal only with you, so if someone hurts me you comfort me by pouring your blessings. I will never calculate with a person, so in my life there will be no more disappointments on any one!"

"The Lord said, 'Greater love has no one than this: to lay down one's life for one's friends (Jh15:13)." But no matter how much I love anyone, yet still I have my life that I cannot give up for the person. Then how can I say, "I am disappointed with you!" Lord, now my heart is going to burst out because of my love and compassion toward my brother."

I remember the church mountain retreat last summer. Mann confessed his faith in front of the congregation with a loud voice, "I believe in Jesus Christ, I believe in Jesus Christ."

"If you declare with your mouth, 'Jesus is Lord,' and believe in your heart that God raised him from the dead, you will be saved. For it is with your heart that you believe and are justified, and it is with your mouth that you profess your faith and are saved (Ro 10:9-10)."

I believe he is now resting under the wings of the Lord in Heaven.

11/2/1986. Before the main funeral service, a small family service was held at Rose Hills Memorial Park at 5 p.m., and I saw his body for the first time in the coffin.

I was scheduled to give an Israel presentation at Big Light Church at 3 o'clock today. My situation was too hard to do both things, and I wanted to cancel the presentation, but the church had requested me for the presentation several months ago, and I had already changed the schedule twice. Besides, the church had announced the occasion for a long time, so it was hard to request another schedule change. I went to the church in difficulty, but I finished the presentation well in God's grace and returned quickly to Rose Hills Memorial Park.

When I approached the building's 2nd floor, I heard Pastor David Kim's voice praying in the corridor. As I heard the noise from the weeping and morning of my family members and Pastor Kim's prayer, I felt again that I was losing all the strength from my body, thinking, "Ah, it was true!" Since we had heard the news of his passing only from the Police Department, we had probably hoped that the message would not be true.

My dear brother was only 37 years old, the youngest among our siblings, but now he is laid down in a casket like this! "Oh Lord, I implore him into Your hands." I was unable to deny a smearing fear of death within me, but rather that he was looking down at us from the Lord's bosom.

Assistant Teaching

5/25/1987. A great distress to all our doctor's degree candidates this semester was the Research Design class based on statistics, which was not easy. It was a difficult job to put data into a huge computer, which often did not work well, to analyze the outcomes. We had an individual research with Dr. Fred Wilson instead of the class gathering from the last part of the semester, and according to Dr. Wilson, I was the only one following the class schedule.

He asked me if I could help the statistics class as a teacher's assistant for the next semester. This teaching assistant position had been posted for any student who would do well this semester. I told him that I will do it and praised the Lord. He said that the school will pay me out of the scholarship fund for the Doctoral degree Program.

10/28/1987. Since Dr. Reuben Brooks had to participate in a conference held in Boston, he asked me to cover his graduate class, "Research Principle 655," for both last week's and today's lectures. They were my first lectures in English for graduate students, so I was worried and concerned, but it seemed to be turning out all right. After my 2nd lecture, I received an evaluation of excellence as a teaching assistant.

I have a strong desire these days that I would like to teach at Biola upon receiving my degree, so I have been praying every day for this. The Lord has put this desire in my heart and let me have fervent prayers every day, so I have believed that the Lord will answer this prayer request.

Lectures and Translations

First Interpreting at Grace Korean Church

1/17/1988. It was raining cats and dogs today, and Pastor Kim went to Japan, so Dr. Brooks was invited to give the sermon at both the first and second Sunday services. I interpreted for both services, and many people, including Tom and Mina, mentioned I did well.

> "Lord, help me that I wouldn't be proud of myself. If I become arrogant, I will be end of it. Help me that I can be cool on other people's opinion and not like to be praised by others."

We went to the Velvet Turtle and had a delicious lunch after the worship services.

Worship led by the Holy Spirit

3/19/88. A devotion meeting was held, sponsored by the Woman's Association of Woodland Hills Methodist Church, at the house of Chang Won Ahn, Tom's high school classmate at Hidden Hills. His wife, Seung Ja, the president of the Association, asked me to give a message for today's service from last December.

People gathered there not only from Ahn's Church but also from our Grace Korean Church and other churches. It seemed that more than 50 people were together. We began the worship service by singing praises led by the choral conductor of the Methodist Church after a great meal. I strongly felt the presence of the Holy Spirit among us during the opening songs, and I was filled with tremendous joy from the Lord. People told me that they were so much blessed because of my shining face with joy.

My message received a great response with many loud Amens during it, and one lady came to me after the service and told me that it was the first time she ever said "Amen." I felt a great encouragement and gratefulness to the Lord that He used someone like me for His glory.

Although the service was over, people hesitated to leave the place and sat down around me kept asking this and that. Seung Ja seemed very pleased, and I did not know she had such a pure heart like a child trying to be faithful to the Lord. It seemed all together a beautiful picture before the Lord. "Lord, thank you and I love you!"

Interview for faculty position

3/24/1988. I had a meeting today at 3:30 p.m. with Dr. Rob Radcliffe, the Chairman of the Christian Education Department. I told him that I would like to teach a class at the undergraduate level or at Talbot for this fall semester. Since I had taken his Christian Education Philosophy class last semester, he knew me well. He said that it was a great idea, and he was encouraging me a lot, for my situation is favorable because I am a woman and a non-white. I should check the school catalogue and indicate which class I would like to teach.

But he said he had resigned the Chairman's position last week, and now Dr. Michael Anthony is the new Department Chairman, so he was the person to decide on hiring faculty. I was glad because the interview with Dr. Radcliffe went well, and I thought my God had put me such a desire inside of me, and eventually he was going to accomplish it. I decided to send a letter along with my bio to Dr. Anthony, who does not know me.

4/12/1988.

"Well, Lord, I ate my own fruit. How come I was so sure with such a confidence! I was again indulged in arrogance. I always did not forget praying to the Lord to make me a humble person, but the germ called arrogance was so poisonous that it smeared into my heart. Then it settled silently inside of me and controlled my thoughts and behaviors. I know so well that the Lord hates arrogance and it brings the end of everything."

Why did I regard the interview as a trivial thing? Why today, I even forgot to eat anything until noon, so I had no strength at all during the interview, and when he asked me anything, I was dull and unable to give him any good answers at all, and my outfit also looked so ugly.

Dr. Anthony simply told me there was no opening for this fall semester, which was not the answer I expected from him. Since I had believed there was an almost 90% chance I would be hired for an adjunct position, that was absolutely an arrogant thought. On what basis had I thought that I was so great and qualified?

I was sure that God again worked in this situation. As I reflected on that experience, if I were hired as an adjunct, how much more proud would I be of myself? The Lord loves me so much that he causes all things to work together for good to me (Ro 8:28).

10 Deacons Became Elders

4/24/1988. Today, 10 deacons in our church were ordained as elders. Dr. Brooks came to our church again and gave messages at both the first and second services, which I translated for him. I was so envious of those ten deacons who became elders and their wives. How great it would be if Tom were one of them!

> "Dear Lord, I know you are so much concerned and interested in me, and always leading me by your tender hands. I know you love me as apples of eyes, then why don't you make my husband to be changed? Don't I want it so much? Is it because what I want has nothing to do with your plan for him? I know your thought and my thought are different (Is 55:8-9). Is it because of me, because of my certain wrong doing before you? Because of something I haven't yet realized, are you using him for me as a rod?"

I know Tom is saved, through the dream the Lord gave to me sometimes ago. Even though he seems like an unbeliever in other people's eyes, I know the Lord has answered my prayer, because I always feel warmth and tenderness whenever I pray about his salvation. It is truly an amazing and mysterious thing! Only I give thanks to my God.

God Did It All

7/1988. Mina is going to become a middle school student this fall. To help her settle down well in a new environment, I let her register for a summer school class at the school she will attend this fall. Mina was planning to take a keyboard class this summer, so she and I went to the school to register for the class. As we entered the school, which was so crowded with big kids, we saw a completely different world from the elementary school she attended. Most of boys and girls were big and tall and looked like adults.

When Mina saw those tall, huge guys, she became chicken-hearted and started crying! I was embarrassed and led her to a stairway at the corner and let her sit down and cry it out until she could calm down. After she composed herself, we began to look for the keyboard class in the crowds. In the midst of them, we met an oriental girl whom Mina seemed to know well. Mina suddenly called her with a happy, smiling face.

"Jennifer!"

"Hi Mina, you came!"

"Mina, is she your friend?" I asked.

"Yes, she attends our church. Her parents also come to Grace Korean Church. She is one grade higher than me."

"Jennifer, are you going to take this keyboard class, too? Would you go with Mina? This is Mina's first time here today and it seems hard, she knows no one here."

"Oh, yes, I will go with Mina. I will take care of her. Don't worry about her."

My mind was relieved so much! I was so grateful. I found out later that Jennifer is a daughter of one of our church deacons whom I know well, and she is a smart and good student. I praised the Lord! I hope continually that Mina and Jennifer become good friends, because for kids this age, having a good friend is so important for them. All parents should put their best efforts into their kids getting a good friend and letting them to belong to a good friend group. I hope Jennifer will come to our home any time and spend weekends with Mina. I will prepare their favorite food for them and support them all I can. Because of Jennifer, I hope Mina can start her teens without too much stress in her school life; that will probably be the same for Jennifer.

Since I was planning to leave for a trip to Europe on August 1, I had arranged for Jennifer to come over to our house and stay with Mina for one week. I went out to market with the children and let them buy the groceries they wanted for the week. I prepared everything for them so they could have a happy time together for the week. Parents should have concern for and support their children so they can make good friends.

Josh McDowell's Conference

6/1989. A huge Christian Youth Conference sponsored by Josh McDowell Ministries was held at Irvine Meadow Amphitheater. The entrance fee was $37, but a Christian rock concert with Michael W. Smith, Sandi Patty and others, who were Mina's favorite musicians, were planning to perform. I let her go and picked up Mina and her friend, Linda.

Mina is going to become an eighth grader this fall, and today, she seemed to receive tremendous grace from God from the conference. Even though she returned home late, she did not want to go to bed and instead chatted with me in her excitement.

"So, was it good?"

"Yea, Mom. It was awful good. When Pastor Josh had a call for those who wanted to accept Jesus Christ as their Savior and asked to arise, I did, mom. I accepted Jesus as my Savior."

"Wha Woo- - Congratulations!"

"And today, I heard really an incredible story from the pastor. It was so unfair."

"What is so unfair?"

"There was a high school girl who had a boyfriend before she knew Jesus. Then one day, she happened to go to bed with the boy. After the event, she broke up with him, and just concentrated on her study and went to college. She met a good Christian boy in the college, and upon graduating college, they got married and having a happy married life. Eventually she got pregnant and delivered a baby, but sadly, the baby was deformed. The doctors investigated the reason and discovered that the mom's old boyfriend had a contagious venereal disease and transferred the disease to her. Then she had given the disease to her baby and her husband. Mom, how could such things happen? How unfair for her husband and the baby? When I heard the story, I cried."

As I heard the story my heart was aching too.

"The pastor asked us to arise if you can promise to the Lord that you will keep yourself pure until getting married."

"So?"

"Of course, I arose too"

"Oh, I see! You did well. Then, the conference was worthwhile for $37!"

"No, it was not valued at $37, but definitely more than $100."

I hugged her hard in my bosom and told her that I love her very much.

Crushed with a Motorcycle

7/6/1989. The accident was like this. I did not go out much besides going to church and school these days, because I was busy preparing for the coming comprehensive exam for my doctor's degree. Hence, a rumor was running around among Tom's high school friends that we were divorced. Tom was playing golf today with the friends from the morning game, and they were going to eat dinner at Garden Grove after the game, so Tom asked me to join him.

I received a reminding phone call from Tom at evening that he was leaving for Hyungchon Restaurant in Garden Grove, so for me to now leave for the restaurant with Mina. I reluctantly left home with Mina. At the first crossroad with a signal not far from my house, a motorcycle was running toward us as I made a left turn and collided head-on into my car. The motorcycle was driven by two young kids and was running straight at high speed at that moment I was making a left turn on yellow. They said, no matter what the situation was, the party who made a left turn was responsible for the whole accident.

My car was banged up in a collision with the motorcycle, and the impact of the collision threw the two young men off the motor-cycle. I saw they banged into the front part of my car and bounced up high in the air. Mina, who sat on the front passenger seat, hit the front window glass hard with her head, and her forehead was bleed-ing and she was crying, "Mom, my head, my head." My car seemed badly smashed up in the front part, and the wrecked motorcycle presented an awful sight. Just within a second, I found myself in hell, fallen from heaven.

"Oh, my Lord, what was happening? What was happening to me?"

I was not injured at all and was perfectly fine, but I was in hell, and soon the police cars and two ambulances arrived. They moved the two kids on the street into an ambulance and Mina and me into another ambulance and drove us to a hospital. I called Tom and my brother (absent mindedly), to come to the hospital, and they arrived soon, but we did not know what to say each other. Mina's head X-ray was taken; fortunately, the doctor said that it seemed nothing to worry about but keep her from getting into a deep sleep. Oh, what a horrible disaster!

We returned home and went to bed, but Tom did not say a single word. I was also unable to utter anything from fear. I knew what Tom was thinking, because I had the same thought, and both of us were too scared to open our mouths. I felt as if my heart was drying up and burning in horror, and we were unable to get any sleep, even as the night grew deeper. The scary thought pressing us so much was whether the two men, or even one of them, was dead. If it were so, how would I live the rest of my life? Just because of the fearful thought, we were unable to talk or get to sleep.

Around 4 o'clock in the morning, Tom slowly slipped out of the bed and put on his clothes. Soon I heard him starting the car's engine and opening the garage door, and he drove out. Then around one hour later, the phone rang, and it was Tom.

"Ah, we live now, honey. It will be okay. Don't worry. Both were alive!"

As he sneaked into the Emergency Room, a nurse stopped him and asked him where he was going. Tom responded to her with an upset and frustrated voice, "Where are those patients who had the motorcycle accident last night. I am a family member." Then, she led him to their rooms, so he quickly peeped inside one room and was able to see a boy in teens watching TV, putting his left leg in cast on a chair. In the next room, a little older boy was talking with someone on the phone. Oh, merciful God, no one was dead! He eventually heaved a sigh of relief, so he gave me a call.

I was so grateful to the Lord, and I have been able to breathe well since last night. I really appreciated Tom, too, who was always beside me and kept me whenever I was in a difficult situation.

By the Grace of God, no one was fatally injured. Even though the two guys without helmets hit the front of my strong Mercedes so hard that brought smashed it out of shape and bounced them high into the air, they were not dead. "Oh Lord. Thank you again!" The insurance company paid them $100,000 for each and in addition, Tom gave them $3,000 more.

Your Glory or My Glory?

4/20/1990. My dissertation was completed on March 1, and I had the final defense today. The 15 minutes given to me for the presentation on the dissertation was mainly spent chatting with the committee professors, and eventually I became a doctor. God did it all. I truly gave all my credit to my God and all the glory to Him.

I was applauded by all the committee members, and Dr. Fred Wilson, my Committee Chairman, spoke very highly of my work. He said that the chapter 5 of my dissertation is excellent, so he wants to get my permission to use it as a sample for other students. Dr. Don Brown, another member, also sent me a letter asking my permission to use chapter 2 as a sample. He wrote,

> "I would like to borrow a copy of the second chapter of your proposal…. I would like it for three purposes: 1. I would like to use it in the doctoral seminar course as an example of what that chapter should look like, 2. I would like to share a part of your findings with the pastor in my church who has recently been directed to start a small groups ministry, and 3. I would like to share a part of your research with the Mountain Area Sunday School convention. Naturally, I would credit you as the source."

5/29/1990. Upon finishing my dissertation on March 1st, I had been praying fervently, for I wanted to work at Biola to teach at least one class. I mentioned to God whenever I prayed, "Lord, it's for your glory." I prayed that I wanted to teach at Biola for the glory to God.

Then, I heard a tender voice ringing inside of me in this morning while I was praying.

> "Why do you want to teach at Biola? Are you sure it's for My glory? Isn't this for your glory? You want to boast to people about teaching at Biola upon receiving the degree? Isn't that the reason?"

I was stunned because the Lord's observation was right to the point.

"Oh, Yes, Lord. You are right. It was for me, for my glory."

I suddenly felt that my heart had sunk down deep, and I became very calm. Tears began to surge upon me like waves on the shore.

"Lord, forgive me. I truly used the Lord for my glory."

I was slowly and carefully looking at myself and started to empty my heart and entrusted all my life into His hands. My heart was quietly filled with the prayer that the Lord had at Gethsemane, "Yet not as I will, but as you will. (Mt 26:39)"

> "Oh Lord! Am I not your servant? It's not right a servant has any dreams for her own benefits. The servant must have desires only for the Lord's will to be done in her life."

My God's dreams and visions for me have already been given to me, and He is on the way to fulfill them according to His plan. Then why am I entreating Him so hard, asking for my wishes? I repented and made up my mind one more time to surrender completely to Him. I felt as if I was laying down a heavy burden. I truly gave thanks to the Lord this morning and was able to leave the church with a light mind.

6/6/1990. I have been praying to the Lord every morning for only His will and His plans for me to be accomplished. I repeated the Lord's prayer at Gethsemane, "Yet not as I will, but as you will. (Mt 26:39)"

How much my heart was now relaxed, joyful and free! If the Lord does not allow me to work at Biola, it would be fine as I would be following His will, and if He does not want me to teach at all at any place and stay at home, that would be okay, too. I just wanted to entrust everything into His mighty hands and enjoy peace and freedom. I began to comprehend the true meaning of surrender and what trusting in Him meant, that is, peace and freedom, and after all, only His will be done. So, no matter what, I would be happy and rejoice.

Celebrating Event for My Degree

8/18/1990. Our family went to Korea last month as a celebrating event for receiving my degree. We stayed at Seoul Coex Intercontinental hotel for two weeks and met many friends, and Tom spent lots of money according to his style. Mina and I had a wonderful time shopping at a huge mall next to the hotel. I also greatly appreciated that I found a church at the front of the hotel, where I went every morning to have my prayer time while we stayed at the hotel.

Then, we traveled to Jeju Island and checked into the Shilla Jeju Hotel at Seogwipo. The hotel celebrated their opening on that day and gave all their guests a tea cup set as an opening gift. The hotel was very impressive and built beautifully, and our room commanded a splendid prospect of the ocean. The window overlooked some swimming pools with blue water shining like emerald under the sunlight, and the stairways stretched out down as far at the beach through gorgeous gardens with colorful flowers. We went out sightseeing here and there and tasted fresh sea cucumbers and sea squirts that were my favorites, and it was a delightful trip.

Upon returning from Korea, I had another wonderful trip east with my sister, when we went to see the Niagara Falls. Our eyes were opened as heard the thunderous sounds from the great water-falls in the morning. We saw the falling waters through the hotel windows, and we were struck by the grandeur of the falls. In the front of our eyes, a huge stream in flood rushed along exuberantly into the giant falls, which were magnificent. The breaking waters were shining like crystals under the morning sunlight, and clean and bright sparkling waters made huge water bundles and came down in torrents under a bridge. Behind the bridge, it seemed as if the forest, with its various trees and flowers, was playing a grand orchestra with singing birds.

We walked under the falls to be showered with the waters, and we looked down the whole magnificent round fall in one sight from a helicopter. We also enjoyed the scenery by looking around in an excursion boat, and we kept praising the Lord for His amazing creation.

Another Message from God

9/1/1990. I was heading towards home today, after the church service, on the 405 freeway, when I suddenly saw a vision that the Lord showed me about myself before my eyes. I was so surprised and shocked, because I saw something that was fully filled inside of me.

"I can't use you, because you are filled full. If I pour more on you, you may be broken down."

I was startled at the voice that was God's, piercing into my heart, ringing inside of me, and in an instant, an interpretation came into my heart. I had cried out to the Lord so much for becoming a useful vessel for Him every day, but the Lord was telling me that he was unable to use me because I was filled with dirt. I was brimming full of arrogance and boasting, so if He adds more, I would be broken. So how can my loving God pour anything more in me?

How much I had been praying to God every morning to make me a humble person! I was completely broken down before the Lord and cried bitterly. I remember that when I received my degree, I was pretty happy with the praises people gave to me, but I always said to them, "Oh, no, not me, God did it. Yes, God did it." Yet I was filled with pride and arrogance deep inside of me. As I received people's praise, it made me feel as if I had done it well with my own strength, and the thought of pride seemed to grow up in my mind overnight. Then how would God use someone like that?

I had again an experience of feeling that I was crumbling down to dust inside of me. The Lord had asked me two months ago, for whom I wanted to teach at Biola, "For My glory or for your glory?" Then today the Lord said that He cannot use me, because I was filled with arrogance and pride.

"Oh Lord, what shall I do? I will empty myself and die, so that you can use me according to your plan. From now on, no matter how glorious things happened to me, I wouldn't even be happy. I will regard it as if only it was happened to my friend, as a third party I will share the joy. The Lord has done it, so the Lord should be praised and glorified. Why should I? God did it, so the fruit and its glory should go to the Lord."

I knelt before the Lord praying in tears with tearing in my heart. I was hearing something like a sound of shattering icefalls from a glacier while I was praying.

"Yes, I will empty myself, empty completely. I will die, so, have mercy on me and accept me. I pray only Your will be done in my life. You are the only one to receive the glory, honor and praises!"

Calling from Biola University

New English Language Program

9/6/1990. I received an unexpected and strange letter from Dr. Wes Wilmer, the Vice President of Advancement of Biola University. He invited Tom and me for lunch with Dr. Sherwood Lingenfelter, the Provost and the Sr. Vice President, and Dr. Ruben Brooks. They wanted to hear from us about a Korean student exchange plan. We were unable to understand what they wanted from us, because we never thought about such things, and we had no ideas about a Korean student exchange plan.

10/5/1990. Tom and I were thinking every night, "Why is Biola calling us? What do they want from us?" He and I gathered our thoughts almost every evening, but we were unable to find any answers.

"Well, what are we going to lose? Don't they offer a free lunch?"

"Okay, let's go meet with them, and find out what they really want."

We had a lunch meeting at the Biola Board Dining Room (BDR) with Dr. Wilmer, Dr. Lingenfelter, Dr. Brooks and his daughter, Joyce. The menu was delicious papaya salad with the inside of the papayas filled with chicken meats and other goodies.

We had nothing much to talk about and exchanged greetings and meaningless chat. Then Dr. Lingenfelter said,

"I heard, these days, it's very hard for students to enter into a college in Korea. Is that right?"

"Yes, I heard that too."

"Then, how about we bring some students from Korea here to Biola, teach them the English language first, and then, we may accept them to our academic programs for their further studies?"

Dr. Lingenfelter seemed to have studied diligently on this issue. The moment I heard this, an old memory came into my brain as a film strip about the ESL Program I attended at USC when I studied for my master's program there. I took one ESL class along with my other degree classes at that time.

Biola did not have such an English language program. Students, both graduate and undergraduate, were unable to come to Biola at all if their TOEFL score was below the standard. If Biola develops a similar language program to what USC had, we may first accept international students with low English proficiency and teach them English here at Biola. And their English skill has improved; let them take one or two regular degree classes along with advanced language classes. If their proficiency has eventually improved to the required standard, then, let them take all regular degree courses.

Since I had an experience studying in such a program at USC, I was able to tell them of the possible success of such a program at Biola. All of us at the meeting agreed that this English program would be what Biola needs at this time to bring students from Korea.

11/16/1990. I had meetings with Dr. Ed Norman, the Dean of Continuing Education, and Dr. Sherwood Lingenfelter, the Provost, almost every week, and Dr. Surgent, the Dean of Arts & Sciences joined our meeting today at 1:30 pm. Biola eventually made a proposal for the new program, which was approved by the University Curriculum Committee. According to the proposal, this new program will be called "English Language Institute (ELI)," which needed $100,000.00 for start-up costs that they planned to obtain by donations. They said that the director would be a person who has a TESOL Ph.D.

Since this program needs a Korean connection, they asked me if I would help the program on a part-time basis, around 20 hours per week. I was so excited and overjoyed to work at Biola, but that was not God's plan for me, His plan was much more brilliant and unbelievable.

That evening at home, I was still so excited and wanted to read the proposal one more time before I went to bed. When I read the word "director" on the proposal sheet, my heart started beating fast and a strange feeling of electricity was going down my body. It was a strong power that I was unable to explain, and the thought was that I should be the director.

"No, this is not." I shook my head. I tried to ignore the thought, because I knew I was not qualified to be the director. I do not have a TESOL Ph.D. Is not this an English program? I went to bed trying to avoid the thought that was surging into my heart like advancing waves.

Called as a Director

> "Sung, isn't it too much? You have a different degree and isn't teaching what you want eventually?"

> "I know. But still I should become the director. I don't know even myself why I am so anxious for this. It seems the Lord wants me to become the director."

This was the communication between Tom and me during the last week. Time didn't help me, because now this thought that I should become the director pressed me down so hard from morning to night. The thought was growing stronger as time went by, and it became no longer a problem for me that I did not have a TESOL degree.

Today, I met with Dr. Lingenfelter and told him in a trembling voice, but boldly,

> "Dr. Lingenfelter, for this new program, I read the proposal again, considered it over carefully and prayed about it. The Lord wants me to become the director. I should be the director of the program. Is it possible?"

> He seemed somewhat surprised, but he said,

> "Oh - - -, it's possible, but I can't make the decision by myself. We should discuss about this at the Curriculum Committee."

"Yes, of course, thank you. As the director, I would bring a better proposal than Biola's."

I uttered this without thinking and unexpectedly.

"I see. Then please bring your proposal next week."

My mind began to calm down. I knew that the desire in my heart was from God and becoming the director was God's will. I immediately called USC and CSU and asked them to send me their ESL brochures.

However, I already had a complete picture about the program in my mind. At the luncheon during our first meeting, when Dr. Lingenfelter said, "Let's bring students from Korea and teach them English language first, and then let them continue to study their major classes at Biola," I knew already how I would do the program from the beginning to the end. I was able to make a proposal as well as the actual ELI brochure with God's insight.

12/4/1990. Tom and I went to Dr. Norman's office at 1:45 p.m., and upon sitting down, Dr. Norman was asking me for the proposal that I had prepared. I handed it to him, and he opened it and glanced the sheet, smiling, and then he took out an envelope from inside of his jacket, put it on the table and pushed gently toward me.

> "This is a new Biola proposal. We have the same mind. Congratulations on becoming the director, Dr. Lee. Let's do well together."

When I opened the sheet inside of the envelope, I was able to see my name as the director on the top, so that both proposals were identical. God made me the director who wanted so much to work at Biola, and I gave all the glory to my God.

ELI, the Lord's Program

12/14/1990. This event was completely planned and done by the Lord who wanted to train His servants, so God wanted to have such a program at Biola. There must be many of God's servants whom He planned to send out all over the world after their training at Biola or Talbot School of Theology, and God chose me as the program's director.

God did another miracle to show me that the new program was pleasing to Him and that all had been done according to His will. I received a phone call from my Sr. Pastor's office during the same week, to come over to his office right away, so I went to his office without a question. When I entered his office, Pastor Kim stopped talking with a gentleman whom I didn't know, and then he introduced me to the man and told me that he is Elder Kim from Korea, who will help our ELI program.

I told Pastor Kim that this new ELI program had started one week ago and that I became the director. I also mentioned to him that the program needs $100,000.00 for the start-up costs. When Elder Kim heard the story about the program, he was willing to donate $100,000.00 for Korean students with no strings attached. It was a miracle. Neither the school nor I could have dreamed that the money would be given to us that quickly. My God let me know clearly that He was the one who had done it all from the beginning to the end.

Ears to Hear

1/5/1991. 1990 was the year of blessings and an unforgettable year in my life. God made me finish up my 10 years studying at Talbot by receiving a doctor's degree and becoming a director of a Biola program.

As I look back at the last seven months, the Lord gave me two opportunities to hear His voice and to repent. How grateful I am for the grace of God to me! If I was unable to hear the voices, probably nothing would be have happened to me, because God would not use any vessels filled with dirt like arrogance, jealousy, envy or any evil things.

Our merciful God is always speaking to us through the Holy Spirit, but the problem is that we are unable to hear His voice. Our God truly wants us to hear His voice and repent what is not right in us. Did not He tell us in the Bible, "He, who has ears, let him hear? (Mt 11:15; Mk 4:9)"

We can hear the voice of God at any time and at any place, but it is only possible when our spirit is sensitive to hear His voice. Our spirit becomes sensitive through various devices. Prayers have been a tool in my case. When my spirit becomes sensitive because of my fervent prayers and deep conversation with the Lord, my ears can hear His voice. If I pray to God with a sincere and truthful heart, whatever it is about, and even if the prayers are not answered right away, my spirit may build up a special relationship with God. Then I can hear Him and know what is wrong with me, so I can repent.

God does not always give me what I am asking for. As a good father, what He gives me is better and greater than what I am asking for, according to His providence. The Lord said to Jeremiah, "Call to me, and I will answer you, and show you great and mighty things, which you don't know (Jer 33:3)!"

Prayers have been a profitable business for me. I always pray in a loud voice for around two hours every morning, as if I am talking to a friend, because silent prayers are not easy for normal people. Silent prayers often bring wrong thoughts smearing into our mind, and sleepy spells overcome us. As I pray to God in a loud voice with my words and lips, I can be easily all in and able to concentrate on the prayer. Whenever I pray, I remind the Lord about His promises in the Bible as if I am having a conversation with a friend, eyeball to eyeball, telling Him about my heart and trying to read His mind.

I do not make any extra effort to listen to His voice during my prayer times, because He talks to me in His time, anywhere. Of course, He spoke to me during my prayer times, but lots of other times in my dreams at night, at the ocean side, and inside of a car on a freeway. Most of my prayers are composed of desires He gave me in my heart (Phil 2:13) and of those promises in the Bible, which are His assurances and blessings, so I always cling to His words. I long for my prayer time every morning, and my heart is always filled with joy and thanksgiving, and happiness after prayers.

Hired as a Full-time Faculty Member

3/1991. I was hired as a full-time faculty member of Biola University on March 1st. All the faculty candidates must have an interview with the president at the final stage of hiring. My faculty interview with Dr. Clyde Cook, the President of Biola, was held at Los Coyotes Golf Course near my home, which seemed a very unusual case. That day, Dr. Cook, Dr. Norman, Dr. Edwards, Dean of Rosemead School of Psychology, and Tom played golf together, and I had the interview with Dr. Cook in his golf cart moving from one hole to the next. It seemed a special consideration for me, not giving me any stress. I never heard of any other faculty member who had their interview in this way. Since God did it, everything was different.

9/1991. The ELI program of Biola was officially launched starting this fall semester, and Professor Pati Cole joined as the program's academic coordinator. Thirty students came from Korea for this first semester, which was an unbelievable number. We opened a language laboratory named after Elder Kim, the donor. Six students completed their English study and moved to Talbot, and three students moved to their undergraduate programs at the end of the semester.

First Korea Visit with Dr. Norman

11/22/1991. I visited Korea with Dr. Norman to recruit students from Korea for the next semester. When we arrived in Korea, we found out that nobody seemed to know about Biola University, and we did not know where to go and whom to meet for help. Then, I thought about Dr. Chang Young Jeong, the Director of the University Planning Dept. of Yonsei University (later he became the president of the school), who might be able to help us.

I calculated that if Biola and Yonsei would set up a Memo of Understanding (MOU), Biola would be better known in Korea. Someone would say, he does not know about Biola, and then we may say, Biola has an MOU with Yonsei University, then, he might say, "Is that right? I am the one who didn't know the school!" We may start with gums if we do not have teeth. Dr. Norman and I went to Yonsei to meet Dr. Jeong, with whom I had had a good longtime friendship since we attended both Yonsei and USC together. He kindly welcomed us, but his response was the same as others.

> "Where is located the school? I never heard about the school. What do you want me to help you?"

> "Biola is a very good Christian University. We want to have a MOU with Yonsei. Would it be possible?"

> "Well, I think it might be possible. Fortunately, the Dean of Office of International Affairs is my senior of the Yonsei Business School I attended. I will introduce you to him. Let's go to his office now."

Dr. Hak Jong Lee, the Dean of International Affairs of Yonsei, promised us that he will study about Biola and consider establishing a MOU between the two schools. He said that soon he will visit Biola. Yonsei became the first school Biola made a MOU with among the schools in Korea.

In addition to Yonsei, we visited several more universities and introduced Biola to them. We met Dr. Yong Kil Mang, the Dean of Jang Shin University, Dr. Jang Sang, the Director of Student of Ewha Women's University, and Dr. Goo Young Jeong, the president of Seoul Women's University. We also visited Jeon Ju University, as well as the Asia United Theological University.

Minority Conference in Washington, D.C.

6/5/1992. I just returned from a Conference for Minority Concerned held by the Council for Christian Colleges and Universities (CCCU) in Washington, D.C. Glen Kinoshida, the Director of the Minority Department, and I participated as representatives from Biola, but the presidents or vice presidents came to the Conference from other schools.

Most of the participants were American-born, but I was the only one who was a first-generation immigrant. Probably because of Korea's short immigration history, there seemed there were not many who were in the position of president or vice president of a college or a university among Korean second-generation immigrants. There were three Japanese and four Chinese, including one of the guest speakers, who were second or third generation immigrants, in the conference. Glen also was a fourth generation Japanese, and I was the only one who had American citizenship but was not born in United States.

I learned many new things during the Conference about the pain, conflicts and struggles among minorities in America, particularly among black people, and I felt keenly their sad feeling with their dark skins. Public discontent and their dissatisfaction seemed beyond the bounds of my imagination. Since many schools sent black representatives, I was able to learn new aspects about those with whom I had not much opportunity to encounter in my home environment.

I found out that I belong to a minority group, but I am not the one they are talking about. I am an American citizen, yet I seem to belong in an alien category, for I was born in Korea and finished my college education in Korea, and then came to America, and I still think my mother country is Korea. As a Korean living in a foreign country, what kind of complaint I might have! Rather than complaining, I always appreciate America and her people.

I can boldly say that I have never been discriminated against while I was living in this country. Although some people might say that I had been lucky, Americans are very decent people in this regard. Maybe because they also were immigrants themselves from the beginning, they seem more generous to immigrants than in any other countries on Earth.

The coordinator of this conference was a black lady who worked at the CCCU office. She asked me to give a message at the morning devotion for the third day of the Conference. I was somewhat flustered, because I came there without any preparation to give a message, but I could not say no for Biola's sake. I did not know what to share with them, so I had no way but to pray.

My faithful Father was letting me know what to say in the morning, by sensing me to read 1 Corinthians Chapter 13. During the last two days, too many discussions raged about racial discrimination against colored people, everybody's heart was devastated, and particularly those black representatives looked very distressed. Although all of them are Christians, their anger and hatred were about to burst out because of their sad experiences of pain and conflict. At this juncture, it seemed a wise choice to remind them of God's love.

As I expected, upon ending the devotion, many came to me and expressed their gratitude to me, saying that this was the word of God they needed to hear at this time. I was seeing people hugging each other here and there.

"Lord, thank you. I trust that you were glorified through this mean and naive servant."

I met next day the President and the Vice President of Nyack College in New York. As they met me, they seemed very delightful, and they knew me already as well, as they were familiar with my program at Biola.

"How do you know me?"

"We heard about you from President Clyde Cook, who told us that the new ELI program developed at Biola last year is the one Biola is proud of. Is that right?"

The presidents of colleges and universities that belong to the CCCU meet together every year in January, when those presidents share with each other about what their school had accomplished during the previous year, things like new programs or any special events in their school. President Cook presented to them our ELI program as Biola's pride in this year's gathering.

Vice President Mapstone of Nyack came to me after breakfast of the final day of the conference, and said,

"Dr. Lee, when are you able to visit Nyack?"

"Yes?"

"Please visit our school and evaluate our ESL (English as a Second Language) program. Our program seems to have some problems. Please come and see what the problems would be and how we can solve them."

"Well, how can I be a help? Still, if you invite me, I may visit your school at any time."

He told me that upon returning to his school, he will let me know when the best dates would be after checking their school calendar.

7/4/1992. Nineteen students are presently taking our ELI Summer classes. The Biola English Study Tour (BEST), our special summer program, will be held four weeks from today until August 1. Thirty-six students participated in this special program, and Seoul Women's University sent many of their students.

Invitation from Nyack College

7/14/1992. Nyack College formally invited me by sending a round trip airline ticket and an honorarium. I did not expect that they would invite me so soon. Even though the ELI Summer programs went on here at Biola, I decided to accept Nyack's invitation, since I had both excellent academic and activity coordinators.

The Nyack campus in New York state was built on a residential hillside of 66 acres, overlooking the Hudson River and Tappan Zee Bridge. As I arrived at the school with their guide, Dr. Turk, the Chairman of the English Department, received me with a great welcome. The campus was gorgeous, unlike L.A. in high humidity, and all around was a thickly-wooded hill with abundant green leaves and a thousand summer flowers.

I was ushered into Simpson Hall which was, they said, the first building built on campus, built out of stones in 1800th. I saw the Hudson River, which had an enchanting beauty, flowing slowly with a shining, golden reflection from the sunset, from the window of my room under lush vegetation. Dr. Turk took me to a Japanese restaurant where we had dined with Sushi and Sashimi.

7/15/1992. There was some smog, but the morning campus was perfumed with the sweet summer aroma from the abundant leaves and flowers everywhere. I met President Boda again at the Vice President's office after breakfast. Vice President Mapstone handed over to me various documents related to their school, and we had a good time chatting. He asked me to make a written report for a recommendation on the situation after reviewing their program.

They took me after lunch to the Nyack Korea Center located in Flushing, New York. I felt that it was necessary for Nyack's ESL program to become more intensive, because it did not seem easy for Korean students who were going to study their major classes in English at the main Nyack campus after finishing study at the Korea Center. Since they studied their major in Korean language at the Korea Center, although they studied English language along with their major at the Korea Center, it became a great challenge for the students transferring from the Korea Center to the main campus. There must be a big gap in English proficiency between the Korea Center and the main Nyack campus.

I recommended an idea to move the Korea Center to Nyack main campus, because the poor condition of the Center's building would bring disgrace to Nyack College. We discussed closing the Center and using some other methods, but the school had already considered the idea. They seemed concern about the influence of the Korean pastors who were involved in the Center. The Korean professors presently teaching at the Center are respected pastors in the Korean community, so if the Center was closed, it might bring problems. The only solution seemed to be to tighten the existing Nyack ESL program to become more intensive.

They took me to Carnegie Hall that evening, where I enjoyed Tchaikovsky's music with the New York Philharmonic. Its acoustics were so special and different from other halls. It did not have heavy curtains and chandeliers that would impair good sound distribution. The hall's smooth interior, domed ceiling, and the steep design between each row of seats help the sound to sound alike to any location in the hall equally. It brought great sounds even to my dull ears.

Trip to Eastern Europe

8/1992. I was invited as a main lecturer at a Christian Education Seminar held by Budapest Reformed Theological Seminary in Budapest, Hungary. It happened when I met Dr. Ferenc Szucs, Dean of the Seminary last summer when he came to California to visit Union Seminary where I was teaching. He gave our students a special lecture about Hungarian Christian history for 5 days, and I translated his English lecture into Korean for our students. So I was acquainted with him, and he asked me if I could possibly visit to Hungary and come to his seminary to lecture about Christian Education next summer. I received his invitation early this year through Pastor Hee Min Park, the GKC missionary in Hungary.

Hungary has recently gone through rapid changes. Christian faith was dwindling with beautiful church buildings only seating a few elderly people for the last 40 years. With Communism abolished, the government has permitted for the first time that if the parents of high school students so desire, they may have religion classes, namely Bible teaching courses, in the public schools. The response was overwhelming.

However, they were unable to find trained Christian teachers to instruct these young people. Thus, about 200 high school teachers who were teaching regular courses but professing Christianity (they tend to be older) have stepped in. They enrolled in the Budapest Seminary, one of the top two reformed seminaries in Hungary, to receive training in Christian Education.

I left for Vienna on July 31st, one week before the seminar, and joined the Russia Mission Choir of GKC that was planning to tour in big cities in Eastern Europe to perform for evangelizing. We went to Budapest from Vienna and from Debrecen to Oradea in Romania, and from there to Bratislava in Slovakia. Then we were planning to visit Prague in Czechoslovakia and Berlin in Germany. I was interested in this, and it was an exciting opportunity to see those cities in Eastern Europe, but at this juncture, I wanted to have some time alone to pray for the seminar starting from Monday.

So, I left the GKC team at Bratislava. Pastor Park introduced me to Eva, an English-speaking Czech missionary, and he also departed for Prague with the team.

Eva and I tried very hard to locate a good, air-conditioned hotel, but all the hotels in the city seemed to already have been booked up, because of a huge conference in this city starting on Monday. We were unable to find any air-conditioned rooms, so we decided at last on a hotel located upstairs in a restaurant where it was very humid and hot without air conditioning.

Since I needed to pray and prepare details for the lectures, I told Eva, "let's not to call each other until Saturday." After Eva left, I felt thirsty and wanted to drink some water, but no plain drinking water there, and only orange juice or other fruit juice was available, but it was too sweet to drink. They had only mineral water as drinking water, yet the taste was unbearable to drink for me.

The food was unbelievably cheap; no matter how much I ate, including any kind of juice, it was less than $1.50. Most of the menu was cooked with greasy meat. I was unable to read the menu written in the Slavic language of the Czechs, so I had to watch what other people were eating, and I ordered the same kind of dishes. I wished to have some salad without dressing, because it was always mixed with oils, and I wanted to tell them to just give me salad without dressing, but sadly no one in the restaurant understood English.

It was a real agony to bear such high humidity and hot temperature. Although I sat down and did nothing, my body was soaking wet with sweat, and I had to shower at least four times a day with cold water. Since I was sweating all day long without drinking water, severe cramps attacked both of my legs several times at night. It was so painful, I had to wake up completely in the middle of night and massage them. The cramps were terribly severe on the second night, attacking my whole body. I had never had such an experience. My whole body became paralyzed and twisted, and tremendous unbearable pain was in my body. Since the attack came two times that night, I was scared even to close my eyes.

The first thing I did in the morning was to call Eva. The seminar would start on Monday and today was Friday.

"Eva, can you come to me now? I'm very sick. I want to leave for Hungary today and please take me to Dr. Szucs' home."

"What's wrong? How much do you sick? I will be there right now."

I told her that I wanted to leave here right away and go to Budapest and to take me to Dr. Szucs' home. She said that she will find out if any transportation was available, and soon she came to my hotel, and I was so appreciative. We had breakfast together at the restaurant downstairs in the hotel and enjoyed a salad dish without oily dressing, so fresh and tasty. I realized one more time that a human being is such a weak and vulnerable being.

Fortunately, I met a cellist, a member of the Czechoslovakia National Symphony Orchestra, who was tall in stature and intelligent looking, but she did not understand English, so we were unable to communicate with each other. Since the orchestra was not performing during the summer, she was able to ride with me to Dr. Szucs's apartment. I paid her gas fee plus generous tips, and after saying farewell to Eva, we left for Budapest.

When we arrived near the Hungarian border, an endless line of cars was waiting to cross the border. The cars in front and in back of our car were from West Germany, and they were eating apples and cookies and drinking colas. Since we had left Bratislava after breakfast and did not expect such a delay at the border, we were hungry. It was already past 2 p.m., but there was no place to buy any kind of food at the border area, where it was so crowded with the long line of cars and all kinds of people who seemed to be waiting for hours to cross the border. We would have brought something to eat if we had known the situation would be like this.

Those tired looking people who sat crouching by the roadside outside of their junked cars were people from Czechoslovakia who seemed poorer than people from Hungary. They said that many people from West Germany visited Czechoslovakia or Hungary for shopping and eating over the weekends and then return home, so that the border is so crowded.

Apartment of Dr. Szucs

8/4/1992. We barely crossed the Hungarian border by late afternoon and went to a nearby small store to get something to drink and some sweet rolls that we ate inside the car. She suggested we call Dr. Szucs to tell him that we crossed the border. We arrived at the Budapest Seminary almost at dinner time, and Dr. Szucs was waiting for us at the school's gate. He said he had received a phone call from Eva that I was sick.

After I said thanks and farewell to the cellist, I went into Dr. Szucs' apartment. When I finished Hungary sightseeing with the choir team last Monday, I was invited to sleep at Dr. Szucs' apartment as the seminar's guest speaker, so it was very comfortable and familiar feeling, like a homecoming today.

The peaches I had that evening were so delicious, an unforgettable taste I had never tasted before. Dr. Szucs told me that his father lives not far from here in the countryside, and a big peach tree in his yard bears so much fruit every summer, that he picks a full basket for them every year and sends them to his son's family. A full basket was delivered this morning, and Mrs. Szucs made delicious peach pies out of them for dessert tonight. I picked up some peaches from the basket, washed them and had a few bites. They melted in my mouth, bringing sweet juice with very delicate fragrances. I was, eventually, able to communicate with the Dean in English, drink water and eat plenty of plain vegetables and delicious peaches. Lord, thank you so much!

Dean Szucs had a wife, two sons and one daughter. Mrs. Szucs baked pies as dessert for every meal. Their menu was simple, but their table manners were perfect, including the young children. Since the nation's basic wages are low, the Dean's salary alone seemed not enough to support the family, so his wife had to help the family economy by working at school on the staff as well as a janitor. They said it was still not enough for five people to catch up to the soaring living costs every day.

Disputing on Heresy

8/6/1992. On Sunday, Dr. Szucs and I went to his Hungarian church for the morning service, and we visited a Korean church in the afternoon, where the violin teacher of Dr Szucs' daughter was attending. The Korean church was big, gathering around 100 people, for which I was excited and grateful to see Korean people gathering to worship the Lord in such a foreign land. A man came out from the church welcoming us with a bright smile and introduced himself to us as a missionary.

> "Oh, welcome to our church. I'm so glad you are visiting us. Isn't he the Dean of the Budapest Seminary? I once participated in a seminar held at the seminary. We will eat hamburgers together after the worship service, so please join us. I will introduce you to the congregation at the announce time. Did you come from L.A.? Which church are you attending?"

> "I'm from Biola University and attending Grace Korean Church."

> "What? What did you say? Pastor David Kim? Grace Korean Church? Oh no! That church practices heresy!"

I was shocked by his responses and felt as though I had been slapped on the face. I did not know what to say, because I never had such an experience. His complexion suddenly looked like a face biting a worm, and he looked at me as if I am a terrible epidemic or

125

a devil. Of course, he did not introduce us at the announcements time, and upon ending the service, he wanted us to leave them as quickly as possible. I never had such an insult in my life, and I was so sorry to Dr. Szucs. Although he could not understand the Korean language, he seemed to comprehend the situation. I had pity on those missionaries from GKC who had to work in such a condition. What kind of mission work can they possibly do in such an environment?

I tried very hard to convince the Dean on the way back to his house that they have wrong information and explained to him that GKC and Pastor Kim are not heretics. He said that he understands the situation, but I was not sure how much he trusts my saying so. I told him that I have studied at Talbot for 10 years, and I know what heresy is or is not. If GKC practices heresy, why am I attending the church? That night when I went to bed, I was not able to sleep because I was so sad, and my heart was aching. What in the world do those people know about it!

> "Lord, you are the Almighty God, judge the situation. Solve this problem. If you don't do anything on this awful situation, how can we do mission work here?"

We moved to Nagykoros Teachers' Training College of the Reformed Church on Monday morning, after spending two nights at the Dean's house. The scenery of fields and mountains on the way was beautiful, and on either side all kinds of unknown colorful flowers were blooming in the background of dark and light greens all over the place.

This Reformed Church School was opened in 1893 to train teachers for the Hungarian primary schools over 100 years. The school became completely secularized after World War II, so it was closed. The institute was re-opened in the fall of 1990, and it has been used as a place for nationwide pedagogical workshops. I pray the school again becomes a college to train truthful Christian teachers to impact their world for the Lord Jesus Christ.

Budapest Teachers' Seminar

8/20/1992. It was a 5-day seminar, and all 5 day's schedules were covered with my lectures, except for one hour of Dr. Szucs' per day, and he interpreted my English lectures into Hungarian for the Hungarian students. His English was excellent, and around 35 people attended the seminar, including students from both the Reformed College and the Budapest Seminary.

During the seminar, the meal was the hardest part for me. The menu did not fit my tastes, but the students seemed to enjoy the meal and had wonderful table manners.

Eastern Europe, just born into the free world, was a completely foreign world to me. Because of Communism, which had a different ideology, it has been a forbidden world for Western people for a long time. They had lived a different life style due to their poor economy, yet 70 years ago, they were materially abundant and lived well, much better than Korea. One day, I had a chance to go up to a church bell tower and looked down at Nagykoros City. I saw the whole city was packed with houses with beautiful red-tiled roofs. Those people inside the houses lived in poverty, but their life style seemed like simple in its graceful patience, calm and composed.

Since it was my first trip to an old communist country, lots of things were unfamiliar to me. Probably I should have prepared more carefully for the trip. I thought that it would be easy, only for one week, so if it will be hard, "how much would be difficult!" What I had brought with me for something to eat was only seven packs of

Ramen, dried oriental noodles. I had to divide one pack into three pieces for each meal to cover for a whole day. Thankfully, a small store was nearby, so I was able to buy some chocolates from there.

Budapest was a city filled with thousands of graceful architectures, so she was named the Paris of Eastern Europe. I visited the Hungarian Folk Village with Dr. Szucs' son to understand their culture and the Hungarian National Museum to appreciate their arts. We were enjoying the beautifully flowing Danube River from the museum.

When I arrived at the train station in Vienna, Missionary Jung Joon Lee was waiting for me. As I arrived at the missionary's home, an amazing table with all kinds of Korean food was waiting for me. What I had done was just take a train for a while, so how could such a different world be here! It seems truly a crucial issue that where we belong to, that must be the same as in spiritual world. I was again so relieved and glad that I belong to the Lord. A thought that came into my heart and somewhat bothered me was that it would be okay that I eat this well and live abundantly like this! Remembering Dr. Szucs and his family, those teachers who participated in the seminar and the many people whom I met during the last week, made my heart melancholy for a while.

All the delicious dishes on the table were prepared by a Deaconess of Pastor Lee's church, who thought that I had a hard time at the mission field. The table was packed with all kinds of Korean dishes, such as Bulgogi, Jobchae, Baked fish, Joen. . . It was just unbelievable that I was able to eat such Korean foods here in Vienna. I tried very hard to hold back my tears, for the food she prepared was so touching for me who had almost starved for a week.

"Lord, thank you. Only because of you, I'm receiving such a treat."

Japan and Korea Trip with Lingenfelter

10/19/1992. When I landed at Osaka Airport, Pastor Nobumasa Mitsuhashi (Director of Japan Baptist Denomination) and Dr. Kimio Shirai (Biola honorary degree recipient) welcomed me. We went to the Osaka Castle Hotel, where Provost Lingenfelter was waiting for me in the lobby.

The reason Dr. Lingenfelter and I visited Osaka and Tokyo this time was to recruit students for the ELI program's coming spring and fall, as well as to find some contacts in Japan. In addition, we wanted to see about the possibility of opening an ELI extension program in Osaka or Tokyo area, because Pastors Mitsuhashi and Shirai had given us a proposal for this project.

As we considered it in many ways, it did not seem easy to start the extension program here in Japan for several reasons. First, so many ESL programs are already available all over in Japan, so Biola's expensive ELI program would not compete with them. Also, the Biola ELI program is not just an ESL program; it is one of Biola's departments where students can take language classes along with their major courses. Of course, the suggested program would only teach students the English language here, and when their English proficiency has improved to the level to take academic classes, then they would be sent to Biola. It was hard to decide.

After the Provost and I spent two nights at the wonderful Osaka Castle Hotel, we moved to Tokyo by a bullet train. We took our residence at a small hotel, in walking distance from the Ochanomizu Christian Center (OCC), a huge, handsome building located in the middle of downtown Tokyo, where many Christian offices were gathered.

We had a Biola promotion meeting at OCC in Tokyo and, amazingly, I met many pastors who had received honorary degrees from

Biola who helped us in many ways. During the first evening in Tokyo, Dr. Kaoru Kishida (Biola honorary degree recipient), the Director of OCC invited us to a restaurant on the top floor of the Prince Hotel in downtown Tokyo. We had a great dinner while watching those brilliant red lights that filled the streets. I was introduced at dinner to Dr. Koji Honda, the respectable evangelist in Japan who was also the Chairman of the Board of OCC. I was also very pleased to see again my old friends, Pastor Sam Kim and his wife.

10/24/1992. As we arrived at the airport in Seoul, Judith, Dr. Lingenfelter's wife, soon appeared; she had a class to teach at Biola, so she was unable to join us for the Japan trip. The entire itinerary was successfully processed in Korea, and everything went well. My friend Moonja took us to the Korean Folk Village, where we had a fun time, and Dr. Jae Sook Lee (Director of Seocho Hospital), my husband's niece, sent her car and driver whenever we needed a ride.

Dr. Lingenfelter was invited as a chapel speaker to many college chapels and gave messages at churches, so I had to do translations for him more than 11 times. I was delighted to hear from Dr. Lingenfelter that he liked me as his interpreter, and he wishes to use me as his exclusive interpreter.

I was especially delighted when I translated Dr. Lingenfelter's chapel lectures at Yonsei twice. It was at the same auditorium where I used to sit and listen to chapel lectures, and it was the same platform that I walked up for the first time on the day of my commencement.

> "Thank you, Lord. It's all your grace. Those days, I was only sick, no attractive, and in frustrations! Now I feel as if I became a Cinderella. The fairytale now became a reality only because I met you. Lord, I love you."

Merciful Hands of God

Bankruptcy

12/1992. The year 1992 has been a blessed year for me, but it was a hard and painful year for Tom. The Bakersfield Shopping Center that he put his greatest efforts into eventually fell into another's hands, along with other properties, an office building and even the house where we were living! We were unable to escape from bankruptcy after all.

> "Lord, what did I really want? If Tom became a person to be completely dedicated to the Lord, nothing is matter to me. I have nothing to worry about since the Lord has given me already such a handsome place to work like Biola. What does that mean to have lots of money and to own a shopping center? Am I not eating good food every day and living well in His grace? I have no complains. We lost all our fortunes, and even without a house to live in, yet I am okay."

When I thought about Tom, my heart was aching, but I was filled with full of peace given from my God. Has not my God kept us and protected us as an apple of eye in His grace, love and blessings?

I trust in Him, the compassion and mercy of my God who works together for good to those who love Him and who are called according to His purpose. The Lord will never fail me nor forsake me and make me to be ashamed of! He will never allow me to be mocked by people to say, "where is your God?"

> "Because you love me," says the Lord, "I will rescue you; I will protect you, for you acknowledge my name. You will call on me, and I will answer you; I will be with you in trouble, I will deliver you and honor you. With long life I will satisfy you and show you my salvation. (Ps 91:14-15)"

1/12/1993. We finally left, in the rain, the house in the wood where we had lived since 1978 and moved into a small house on a hillside near Biola in La Mirada. It had been 20 years since we moved into a rental house, and the change felt unreal to me. How happy and excited I was when we first bought a dream home in Fountain Valley, when I was only 29 years old! Since then, financial blessings had continued for us, so we had freely spent and were more well to do than any other people around us. In addition, my God met me to be saved! Truly I am a happy person who has no want!

Is my God, who has endured for a long time, trying to whip to call his beloved son, Tom? As a loving father, He lashes him now, and after that, He would recover him in a better shape than ever before. My heart was aching as I saw Tom, because seeing his drooping shoulders made me sadder more than losing all the money and fortunes we owned. I felt endless pity for him when I saw him, who often casts furtive glances at me to read my facial expression in a quiet manner.

"Oh Lord, forgive us. Forgive all of it and have a compassion on him. Please throw away the whip and touch him with your tender hands and heal his wounds. Restore his soul and guides him in the paths of righteousness for your name's sake. I know that we will grow through this trial, Lord, because my God will fight for me, so I shall hold peace in my mind (Ex 14:14). Lord, restore us. Give us your strength to overcome this trial with a best attitude. Help us not lose joy and always stay in peace."

God has always had His special plans and purposes for all things. He causes all things to work together for good to those who love Him and to those who are called according to His purpose (Ro 8:28). We are in His hands, so I entrust my whole life into His hands. Do not be hasty! God will restore all things for us in His perfect time, and the proof that I believe in God is peace in my mind. In any circumstances let us not be angry or worry. I will only look upon the Lord and overcome quietly all the pains by accepting the reality that is under God's control.

4/12/1993. I was so grateful to the Lord that I received today an encouraging letter from Dr. Lingenfelter, the Provost and Senior Vice President of Biola University.

"Dr. Lee;

Thank you so much for the excellent report of your response to the request of Dr. Chung at Seoul Women's University regarding the mixing of American and Korean students in this special summer program. It looks like you have done an exceptional job of planning to meet these expectations and I commend you for your very fine work.

Once again you have demonstrated responsiveness to feedback from others, effectiveness in adapting the program to student needs, and the diligence to plan with care matters relating to the English Language Institute. I commend you for your fine work and thank the Lord once again for bringing you to Biola University."

Treat as Heresy

6/1993. A thought has been growing in my mind since I had the shocking experience of a false charge of heresy about Pastor Kim and GKC during my Hungary trip. That was the thought that I should let Biola know about GKC, because Biola is an inter-denominational Christian University accepted by most churches in the Evangelical Christian community. The school is well known as a model university in its academic aspects as well as faithful to the Christian faith among Christian schools. I was confident that if Biola would accept GKC, the dispute about heresy in the church would be easily dispelled. Biola knew that GKC was suffering from heresy criticism, and Pastor David Kim is a graduate of Talbot School of Theology at Biola, and I attend GKC.

When I started to work at Biola, several people sent anonymous letters to Biola warning them from accepting a person attending a heretical church. Because of that, I had to have a special interview with Dr. Dennis Dirks, the Dean of Talbot, who asked me this and that and, eventually, some core questions.

"Sung, GKC teaches that the church members got to speak in tongues in order to go to heaven?"

"No, the church teaches you must believe in Jesus Christ to go to heaven. Speaking in tongues is just one of God's gifts as a proof that you have received the Holy Spirit. We believe that even though you don't speak tongues, if you believe in Jesus Christ and are born of water and the Spirit, you can enter the Kingdom of God, just as the Bible teaches."

"I see. Then why do many people mention GKC commits heresy? What do you think?"

"I don't know well. But what I know clearly is that Pastor David Kim is not a heretic, as well as GKC. If the church was heretical, why should I attend to the church? I have studied at Talbot for 10 years, so at least I am able to distinguish between what is heresy and what is not."

"I heard you are close to Pastor Kim."

"Yes, we attended the same church for a long time and had a born-again experience at the same time. Even so, if he is a heretic, I wouldn't attend to the church he is pastoring. If the church commits heresy, my life is in danger. Why should I go to the church with such a risk to my life? The church has nothing different from your church or the church Dr. Cook is attending. If Biola asks me to change the church I am attending to work at Biola, I would have no problem to change. I may go to your church or Dr. Cook's church, because those churches are the same church as GKC. The reason I am attending Pastor Kim's church is because we have been longtime friends and he is a pastor who truly loves the Lord. I'm not going to GKC because the church teaches any special things. Pastor Kim is a faithful person and a good friend with my husband, so that Tom and I are attending the church."

The conversation with the Dean ended there, and we had no more to talk about. I was sure that if Biola's President or Vice-President could see GKC's mission work, they would realize that GKC is not a heretical church. Also, if Pastor Kim can receive an Honorary Doctor's Degree from Biola, the false charge on him and GKC will be ended. I had not yet talked to David about my idea, but I felt that God gave me such a thought for smooth missionary works for GKC.

First, I requested that Pastor Kim invite Dr. Lingenfelter, the Provost who is teaching at Biola for World Mission, as the speaker for the 3-day Russia Missionary Conference that was planned to be held in Saint Petersburg at the beginning of June. I heard that the Conference would have around 450 people, including GKC missionaries in the Russia area and the graduates of Moscow Grace Bible College.

Teaching at Moscow Grace Bible College

6/19/1993. Yesterday I flew from LA to Moscow to teach Christian Education at Grace Moscow Bible College (MGBC). I lined up for the entry formalities at the airport, but the line was never shortened because so many people broke into the line. People continually jumped the queue, and it seemed to take almost two hours until all the people front of me left and my turn came. It was raining outside.

The Bible College was located in a deep forest, and I met many missionaries working there and had some unexpected, tasty Korean food. A pot stew with soybean paste and cucumber kimchi was deliciously cooked by a local Koreo (Korean Russian) missionary for me.

It was already past midnight, but the mysterious dim gray light of the white night added a fantasy of a summer night to this strange land. I learned many new things, such as that a small gift, something like a piece of chewing gum or a chocolate bar, could be exchanged with a big love in this place.

6/21/1993. "Lord! Lord!" came from the students' crying out in the early prayer meeting as it seemed the Kingdom of God was penetrating the evil world. Those students were boarding in this place, and all the expenses were covered by GKC. Since my lecture had to be translated into Russian by a Koreo interpreter, some part of the lectures would not be properly translated, but it seemed to go well.

It was still raining in the morning, but it soon cleared out and brought a fresh and sweet aroma from the wet flower beds around the wood. Dusk falls, the deep forest outside the window of my room had a desolate scene and gave me an exotic mood. The sound of shaking leaves of tall and thick trees by the blowing wind made me feel a bleak loneliness, and the wind seemed to pierce through my bones. Strangely, it reminded me of a story in the novel, "Sentience (유정)," written by the famous Korean novelist, Kwang Soo Lee that I read long time ago. The Lake Baikal in the story was an ancient, massive lake in the mountainous Russian region of Siberia, and the story described it as a winter lake, but I wondered how this sound in the wood reminded me of the sound of the lake.

6/23/1993. Today I had only one session to teach, so I was able to go into downtown Moscow with Missionary Hyunja. We had wanted to go into the city to look around for anything to buy, but we were unable to see any stock at all in the stores. We saw here and there long lines of people with stern looks who seemed to be waiting for rations. We were unable to find any restaurants or snack places, except a McDonald's Hamburger place, which was one of two locations in Moscow. That place was packed with people, and the meal was more delicious than I could ever imagine.

The symbolic center of Moscow may be the Kremlin, a fortified complex in which we can see the house of the President and Tsarist treasures, and Red Square where St. Basil's Cathedral and the GUM Department store is located. The whole area was tremendously crowded with people. St. Basil's Cathedral has six onion-shaped domes that are basic pastel, dark green and brick colored. It was built under Ivan the Terrible. This Cathedral, which has a unique graceful elegance in the harmony of its color and patterns, was erected in commemoration of Russia's 1552 victory over Mongol forces. A sad legend related to this architecture had been handed down. Ivan the Terrible lost his mind when he saw the completed, beautiful Cathedral and ordered the architect's eyes to be removed so that he was unable to build the same kind of architectures anywhere else.

We visited Lenin's museum and found out that he seemed still to be an idol to the Russian people. His Mausoleum in the middle of Red Square was guarded by two motionless guards. The frozen Lenin was lying inside the mausoleum on a huge bed surrounded by several armed guards.

6/27/1993. We went to the Bolshoi Theater yesterday evening to watch the ballet, Giselle, which describes the eternal sorrow of a lost love. Outside it was still cold and raining, but it was a fantastic experience. Today, we went out to the Moskva River with some guests after the worship service, and from there, we rode down following the river around the port in an excursion boat, from which the city of Moscow seemed very much in an exotic mood.

Russia Festival

8/8/1993. I landed in San Francisco yesterday, using United Airlines, to participate in the Russia Festival sponsored by GKC. I had planned to take Aeroflot, the Russian airline, from San Francisco to St. Petersburg with GKC members. I was instructed that my luggage had to be checked out at San Francisco and put in Aeroflot, but United Airlines told me that I better get the luggage at St. Petersburg airport without checking out at San Francisco. That caused a huge trouble.

Upon arriving at St. Petersburg, everybody was busy getting their own luggage, and I also stretched out my neck to find mine out of many pieces of luggage, but mine never showed up. Even though every luggage seemed to come out, mine still did not come out. I had no choice but to leave the airport with our team after reporting to the Aeroflot lost and found center upstairs.

The reason I came to this festival was to be a helper for Dr. Cook, who came as the main speaker for the conference. Since I was going to have the trip with the president, I was carefully considering what clothes to wear. I was completely at a loss, because all the clothing and food prepared from my Hungary experience were all gone.

Whom shall I blame? No, before I blamed anyone, I wanted to pray to God for thanksgiving, because considering the situation, all was my fault. How much effort I put on packing the luggage! I did not even pray much for the trip itself or for all those Russian participants who got to be saved. I was concentrating only on my own interests, such as clothing to wear and what I need to eat...that was all I thought about. It seemed the Lord gave me a rod to teach me, because nothing happens accidently to those who love God. If God did not allow the incident, it would not have happened.

I repented in thinking that I might have deserved to lose the luggage. Even though I was in an unspeakably miserable condition, not a single word of complaint came out of my mouth. I felt relief, rather, a feeling as if a misbehaving child might feel relieved after being spanked by her mom.

Dr. Cook, who was unable to comprehend my mind, considered me as very decent and mature. I was not complaining at all even in such a condition, and continually smiled and acted as if nothing had happened. Dr. Cook seemed very much impressed about my behavior and praised me greatly, saying that my attitude was "A+." I responded to him,

> "Dr. Cook, if the Devil brought me this accident, I won a victory, because the Devil definitely practiced this to take away joy from me, but I'm still happy. Also, if it was a test from God, Hallelujah, I have surely passed."

We laughed together. I believe that my God will bless me abundantly.

> "Lord, thank you. People continually lend me their clothes, socks, trouser and T-shirts. I'm grateful because of so many beautiful people, so I have nothing but to give thanks. Everything is good and among them you are the best!"

8/12/1993. The Festival was quite formidable and sensational for the last couple days. It was a precious festival, even if the situation was a bit frenzied. Since the Holy Spirit had worked powerfully, so many people met the Lord and accepted Jesus Christ as their personal savior in tears in his grace. We knew that having such a huge conference would be impossible in a completely different world if the Holy Spirit did not work for the whole situation.

Ten thousand Russian people came to the festival from all over the Republics of Russia. They said that it took one week for those from Sakhalin Island or Khabarovsk located in the eastern part of Russia. GKC paid all the expenses for those 10,000 people for their transportation, boarding and other costs for the conference. Their meals were prepared with the raw materials brought from U.S., Korea and Europe by the team members. Strangely, nothing was literally displayed to sell in any shops in this city. The display stands were all empty in every market. Team members were around 750 people gathered from the U.S., Korea and Europe through several chartered planes. All the team members served sacrificially with all their hearts for the Russian participants, even when they had to skip their own meals.

Twenty-one Hours in a Chartered Train

8/13/1993. Dr. Cook and I spent 21 hours in a chartered train today from St. Petersburg to Minsk, which was tediously passing by deep woods and soon the endless, barren fields. The train had several cabins on both sides of the train cars, and each cabin was given to Dr. Cook, me and Elder Kang, who accompanied us.

Nothing to eat and only hot water were available inside the train, for no one told us the situation in advance; consequently, we had not prepared anything to eat, and we had to starve. Fortunately, someone gave me a snack box that had contained some crackers, peanuts and drinks, so we would eat them with tea.

I was okay, but I was very sorry that I was unable to prepare any meal for Dr. Cook for all day long. He seemed to notice that no food was on the train, so he did not come out at all from his cabin. Someone gave me a cup of ramen, so I made a cup of tea and knocked on his cabin door but heard no response. I asked Elder Kang to try knocking on the door.

"Dr. Cook, Dr. Cook, please open the door. I brought you a cup ramen and tea. It seems good."

> "No, I don't want to eat anything. Just leave me alone. I was always so busy at the school that I couldn't have much time to pray. I want to pray now with fasting. Please, you may leave."

I heard his somewhat irritating voice, insisting that he is praying and fasting, but he did not even open his cabin door. He must be very hungry. Perhaps, he acted like this out of his graceful delicacy and consideration for us. I just entered my cabin to lie down on bed, and soon fell into a deep sleep for several hours from fatigue.

It was not the first time that we had to skip meals. There must be myriads of people involved in preparing for this Festival for a long time. However, in such a different culture in a different world, it was impossible to expect that a conference having 10,000 people would be running smoothly.

The people in this country seemed to be acting all in their own ways and having no rules or laws to keep. So many interesting episodes happened. One morning, a group of our team members was waiting for the bus scheduled to pick them up, but it did not show up on time. They were frustrated, because they had to leave on time for the conference center to prepare for the participants' breakfast to start today's programs on the schedule.

They saw at that moment a public bus passing by them with a few passengers. One of the team members ran to the bus and stopped it. Through our interpreter he suggested to the driver that if he can take our people to the conference, we will pay him $100. Upon asking, the driver ordered the passengers to get out of the bus on the spot and took our people on the bus and brought them to the conference center. It is truly an unbelievable story to comprehend in our common sense. How could a public transportation driver act in such a deplorable way? People here make a promise, but the promise may be broken at any time without any excuse. Perhaps, it was because we were there during the period of confusion, immediately after the opening of the nation to the free world. It was very difficult for me in such circumstances to take care of Dr. Cook comfortably, even providing merely three meals each day, which sounds very ridiculous.

Although it was not easy, the conference became a successful festival which pleased the Lord. It was a festival that God did it all, because we know that it was impossible with our own strength. The grandeur of 10,000 people gathering in one place! It was truly an unbelievable event that we fed 10,000 people for each meal with love and encouragement for one week.

Visit to Minsk Church

8/15/1993. We had a decent dinner at a hotel in Minsk last night, and we moved to Pastor Yay Mitch's church in this morning, where Dr. Cook was scheduled to give a message in their service. Dr. Cook and I were checked into a hotel with Bob, our interpreter who was 19, looked smart and spoke English very well. He was one of the graduates of the first group from MGBC. Dr. Cook's message was translated by Pastor Mitch's brother-in-law, who did it very well.

The fried chicken for lunch at the church was great and delicious, the best taste we had in Russia. We went out for a city tour after a cup of tea at Pastor Mitch's home in the afternoon. And then we moved to the Minsk airport to fly to Moscow. The airport seemed newly built, but nothing was there, no shops, nowhere to eat or to buy anything, nor a drinking fountain. I had never seen any airport like this. They served only salty and smelly water in a shallow small iron, dish-shaped cup in the plane.

Two GKC missionaries met us as we landed at the Moscow Airport and led us to the Cosmos Hotel, which was luxurious and very expensive, and sold colas as well as bottled waters. Downstairs in the hotel was a casino where so many slot machines were lined up under dazzling colorful lights. After checking Dr. Cook into a room, I moved with the missionaries to the cheap hotel where our Korean members were staying. They had come to Moscow directly from St. Petersburg, while I visited Minsk with Dr. Cook. We were planning to pick him up from the hotel tomorrow morning, and to give him a Moscow city tour.

Finishing the Trip

8/18/1993. I have personally learned several valuable lessons from this Russia trip and the festival.

First, I learned the meaning of patience, since I always had to wait, yet nothing had been done that I wished for. I had to wait until Lord's time had come, and He always did it all for me in His time.

Second, lost luggage made me frustrated and extremely uncomfortable, because I had nothing to wear and no way to get the necessary items, but it could not make me sad and miserable. As I clearly understood that I am in His hands and under His control, it became a chance to learn another new thing.

Third, as many people were lending me their clothes and other necessities, I felt their kindness and loving hands; however, nobody was truly able to help me. When someone lent me her clothes, they were almost fit to me but never perfectly. I realized that no one exists in this world identical to me, and nothing completely fills my needs in a perfect way. No one on Earth could heal my wounds completely or substitute my deep sorrows. Jesus Christ only paid it for me on the cross at Calvary, He who had been the substitute for my death, all the diseases and curses on me forever (Isa 53:5)! I praise only the Lord Jesus Christ and bless his mighty name!

8/20/1993. Upon opening a new academic year, Biola starts with a faculty retreat on campus, held at the end of August each year for two nights and three days. At the first meeting of this year's conference, Dr. Cook shared about his trip to Russia for the festival last month, and he asked Dr. Lingenfelter to tell us about his trip story, when he had experienced St. Petersburg last June. The Provost walked up to the front and began to tell us his story, about how he was invited to go there and how GKC is performing missionary work in Russia. The Provost shared some unforgettable experiences he had in the mission field with the faculty.

> "One day a very old man came to me and held my hands with his both rough hands. He stared at me in tears in his eyes, repeating 'spasiba, spaciba,' the word of thank you. He said to me, 'I was a real bad communist, a very bad person, even I killed people. I knew I had no way but to go to hell because I had done too much horrible things. Then, the GKC missionaries came to here and introduced Jesus Christ to me so that I was able to be saved. I don't really know how to express my thanks to them.'"

Dr. Lingenfelter was choked up, so he was unable to continue to his speech. Dr. Cook continued to talk about the festival experience that was one of the most blessed opportunities for him that he would never forget.

Hope for Family

1/5/1994. My God is so good, such a merciful and gracious God! My deep desire for this coming year was also that my family becomes completely dedicated to the Lord.

GKC held a special one-month early prayer meeting called "Dew of Grace" from the third of January. Tom agreed to attend the meetings with me, and he did well for the first two days.

He came home last night around 2 a.m., because he played "Go" at his friend's home and did not notice the time was that late. No wonder, he who was usually apt to doze off during sermon times and started to fall asleep as the pastor began to speak. It would be natural since he did not sleep enough, only three hours last night, because he came home at 2 a.m. I usually sat next to him at church, but today someone else was sitting in between us, and I was unable to wake him up when I saw him dozing during the sermon time. People around him could hear his snoring, and I was really embarrassed and hated him, especially as a young girl in the front raw of us turned her head to see him.

"Lord, what a disgrace!"

I was so frustrated that I did not even talk to him in the car until we got back home, and I felt that I would not want to go to church any more with him. Hearing my murmuring, Mina said,

> "Mom, isn't it still better that Dad goes to church even snoring at church than not going to church at all?"

Like a fox! My heart was strangely melting like snow when I heard her single comment. Yea, Mina is right. What does it matter that I was humiliated! Shouldn't I be grateful that he went to church with us, even though he must be very tired? Surely, it is grateful! Suddenly these thoughts came into my mind, 'Why am I so anxious about him? Why am I so impatient? God knows everything, and is not his whole life in God's hand? The Lord loved Tom so much that he gave up his life for Tom on the Cross at Calvary!'

"Delight yourself in the Lord, and He shall give you the desires of your heart (Ps 37:4).

Korea Visit with Dr. Norman and Tom

5/4/1994. Last October, I went to Korea with Dr. & Mrs. Michael Wilkins, the Dean of Faculty of Talbot, for both his seminar translation and ELI promotion. His seminar on "Discipleship" went great, and we had a fun and profitable time.

It was delightful that Tom was able to join Dr. Norman and me in our Korea trip this May. We visited Yonsei University, and its campus was beautifully covered everywhere with pink colors, from young handsome faces, cherry blossoms and azaleas that brought spring fantasies to a dreaming visitor.

During the last two days, we had a wonderful chance to visit the 6th Infantry Division, called Blue Star, stationed on the front line of the 38th parallel, with whom GKC had a MOU, so the church members had visited the Division every year. Fortunately, our schedule was well arranged, so we were able to visit there having great experiences, such as entering an underground tunnel that the North Koreans had dug and a tank ride. We looked over North

Korean villages from the top of a mountain through a telescope far away across thick green woods.

ELI Became International Student Education

6/1994. Biola University developed a new English language program called English Language Studies Program (ELSP) and ordered me to become the Director of the new program, which combined the existing ESL program in the English Department in the Arts and Sciences School with our ELI program. In addition to the language program, our Department handles the Biola English Study Tour program (BEST), develops sister relationships between international Christian Schools (MOU), and manages students for the International Student Exchange Program (ISEP). Therefore, the Department name had been changed to International Student Education (ISE).

I believe the reason that our Department had flourished so much was that, in addition to His grace, Dr. Norman, the Dean, and Dr. Lingenfelter, the Provost, had always supported 100% my ideas, my judgments and my decisions. The ELI/ESL merger was announced by the Provost to all Biola faculty and staff on February 15th.

By the grace of God, our ELSP program had worked successfully for many years. Most of our students were composed of the servants of God, among whom around 70% were ordained pastors and interim pastors. They normally finished their seminary trainings in their native countries and worked for 6-7 years assisting church ministry in their countries and then, they wanted to have further studies at Talbot in the U.S. However, their English proficiency was not good enough to study at Talbot, so they entered our program, during which they studied the English language along with taking some Talbot courses according to their English skill level.

Second Korea Trip with the Provost

9/22/1994. I took a second Korea trip with Dr. Lingenfelter and his wife. We held a seminar at Taegu, sponsored by a small mission group for whom a Talbot graduate was in charge, and not many people gathered for the seminar. Dr. Lingenfelter worked hard as a speaker all day long, but they were unable to offer any honorarium to him. The Provost handed me a Biola envelope at the hotel corridor that evening.

"What is this?"

"An honorarium for the interpreter."

"No way, the main speaker hasn't received any, then, what is the honorarium for an interpreter?"

"Well, this is a special honorarium from a speaker to the interpreter who did great job. You did an excellent interpretation."

I felt that there would be no such boss like him in the word. It was the same with Dr. Cook as with Dr. Norman, who had been so good to me and never forgot to take care of me. Is it true that all the American males are well-mannered and nice? Is it because they are Christians? Probably they are the servants of my God whom he had prepared for me!

We spent a wonderful time at Jeju Island for two days, for Elder Young Woon Kim, a parent of one of our students, arranged for us to stay at Shilla Hotel at Seogwipo. I stayed at this hotel a few years ago with Tom and Mina, and I had a great impression of its fanciness and luxury. Coming again here made me excited and was a wonderful gift to us for rest and relaxation, and we appreciated Elder Kim very much.

PART 3:

Compassionate God, My God

Lectures in Mission Fields and to the World

Lectures at MGBC

11/25/1994. I arrived at MGBC, which had been moved to Pushkina, the birth place of the famous Russian poet, Alexander Pushkin. I now visited Moscow to teach twice a year, because a new group of students was admitted to the school twice a year. Whenever I leave for mission fields to teaching, I often feel a kind of tension with reluctance because of changing routines and going on long flights alone. But once I get there and meet the students, I forget all the hard things and my heart is filled with joy, because I can think about the amazing things that will be accomplished through the students and the many souls who will be saved by them in the future.

God continually sends me out to the world according to His promise to be used as "a servant for his servants all over the world," so he has planned all the trips and taken care of my health, too. One of the marvelous things is that I do not feel any time differences; in Russia there is a 12 hour difference from LA, but upon arriving at Moscow, I would start a lecture right away according to their schedule. Also, when I return to LA, the next day I have no problem going to Biola for my regular work. I just appreciate my great God.

First Korea Visit with Dr. Cook, the President

3/29/1995. This was my first Korea visit with Dr. & Mrs. Cook. We went out to Itaewon for shopping on Saturday and had a fun time with my friend Moonja, who guided us and treated us to a fancy Korean dinner of 17 courses.

Dr. Cook gave messages at Incheon Soong Yi Church for their Sunday morning service and at Choong Shin Church for the evening service. I had a teachers' seminar at Dong San Methodist Church in the afternoon. We visited Yonsei University on April 3rd, and Dr. Cook gave two chapel lectures with my interpretations. Dr. Ja Song, President of Yonsei, invited us for lunch along with Dr. Chang Young Jeong and other leading school figures.

Following the visit to Jang Ahn Junior College, owned by Jong Wook Ryu, Tom's high school friend, on April 4th, we were led to Dae Rim Paper Co., which he also owned. We watched a wonderful scene in which great mounds of trash were loaded on trucks, went through various machines, and turned out beautiful, hard brown papers that were all rolled and packed by machines. That was a fantastic process. He invited us to a restaurant for dinner of specialized eels, and we tasted many kinds of eel dishes. Tom arrived today from LA to join us.

4/9/1995. Dr. Cook preached, and I translated for a total of around 100,000 congregants at three mega churches today: Young Rak Presbyterian Church, Yoido Full Gospel Church, and Kwang Lim Methodist Church. Yoido Full Gospel, the world's largest church, sent out the message to 22 additional locations, including Japan, through TV broadcasting, in addition to the church's 1 o'clock main worship service. Pastor David Cho presided over the worship service, and as the sermon ended, he praised me greatly for my good interpretation from the pulpit.

Since Dr. Cook had used the same sermon already at many different places and I had also interpreted the message many times, I was able to translate powerfully with emotions. Dr. Cook seemed quite moved today and told me,

> "Sung, it was truly an impossible happening that we were able to speak to so many people in one day. Probably, my mother also would say to me that it must be impossible, however, nothing is impossible for the Lord."

> "Yes, you are right. God did it. I praise the Lord."

> "We got to be continually humble. We shouldn't regard this as easy because we had done it before at other churches. I'm always careful about this. Every time, we got to ask help from the Holy Spirit for renewed fresh hearts."

Trip Around the Earth

5/27/1995. Upon finishing my teaching at Moscow, I left for Sakhalin Island through Khabarovsk. I was invited as a lecturer for a Christian teachers' seminar at Kholmsk (Home Mansiyk City) on the Island. It turned out to be a trip around the earth.

As I landed at Khabarovsk Airport, Missionary Citi Chung welcomed me, and I stayed at her house for two nights. My original plan was to do some sightseeing and resting during the weekend, for the seminar would begin at Sakhalin Island on Monday, but it did not work out according to my plan. Pastor Joon Kyu Chung (Citi's husband), a missionary at Khabarovsk, did not leave me alone. He requested me to speak at a college student group tomorrow, Saturday afternoon, for which I was not ready for anything, but I had to say "Yes." In addition, he wanted me to give a message at his church's service on Sunday afternoon. Not only that, on Sunday morning to give a message at his brother's church. He seemed to charge me a lot for the two day's room and board!

I heard that there was a small island, not far from there, for enjoying scenery by a boat ride, but without sightseeing or resting I should leave for Sakhalin. Nevertheless, my heart was filled with joy. Oh, what an abundant grace of God! How much more worthwhile and valuable hours I had here, hardly compared with sightseeing! "Lord, thank you."

Pastor Chung's church was huge, and they brought all the chairs they could get to add in the sanctuary, which had occupancy for 500 people. The seats were still not enough; so many people were standing at the back and side of the room for the service. It was a great service that lasted two hours long, with praise songs conducted by the Pastor himself and my message. Be glory and honor to my God! Upon ending the service, I saw the church members start an "Evangelism Explosion" to the newcomers whom they had brought for today's service. It was a very impressive ministry.

Met an Angel

5/30/1995. The plane from Khabarovsk to Sakhalin was a small one, like one that I took from Juju to Seoul when I was young. It was a very tiny plane with only one propeller and less than 20 seats. The plane was parked at the runway in the middle of a huge ground, so all the baggage had to be carried individually by the owners to the plane. The problem was that I had three pieces of baggage, because I had already spent two weeks in Moscow, and not only should I bring them to the plane but also put them in the plane as if it was a bus ride. How could I take my three bags of luggage from the airport building to the plane? I did not know what to do, so I was just standing there in despair.

Then, an angel appeared, a Chinese gentleman who seemed like a businessman with a tie that matched his suit. He had no luggage in his hands. He was coming toward me while putting his passport and a small envelope in the inside pocket of his jacket, and he spoke to me,

"These are your baggage. I will carry them for you." He took the biggest package among them.

"Are you sure?" Don't you have your own?"

"No, I don't have any." He was opening both arms with a smile.

"Wow! How could it be! That's wonderful. Thank you."

He took two of the big bags out of the three in both hands to the plane in the middle of the ground and lifted them up to put them in the rear cargo area of the plane. Upon arriving at the Sakhalin Airport, he also took out all my baggage and brought them inside the airport building.

"Praise the Lord, 'Jehovah-Jireh.' Lord, thank you so much for sending me your angel!"

Kholmsk Seminar

6/2/1995. I was welcomed at the airport in Kholmsk by Missionary Yong Bok Suh, who was involved in a Christian school ministry, K-12 (from kindergarten to 12th grade). A local Russian missionary was the principal, and my interpreter was the English teacher of the school, who was excellent in English.

We left Yuzhno-Sakhalinsk Airport going toward Kholmsk, around 50 miles away. The scenery was fantastic all the way to the school, a green land with magnificent blooms of colorful flowers. The splendor spread in front of my eyes was like I had never seen before in my life, where the delicate dunes and small valleys were all covered with dick shot trees, flowers and shrubs that I had only seen in the world of fairytales. All the leaves of the plants were huge, and some of them opened like umbrellas. When the Jeep turned a corner on the road around the dunes, the blue sea was shining with brilliant lights under the sun between green woods. The old roads had thousands of holes without any repairs for a long time, and the cars passing there were dancing and getting dirty from the muddy waters in the holes. We would see some traces left over from the WWII which were half-burned house skeletons and ruins of rusted debris of old warships in shallow water on the seashores.

Those toddlers who had come to this remote island holding their parents' hands were now grandpas and grandmas and lived in Koreyo villages. Their houses in the village seemed old, probably built 70 years ago. The outside of most houses was covered with a black tent kind of material, but the inside of the houses kept the heat well and were warm.

Most houses had their own well and a vegetable garden inside of their house. When spring came, they would get all kinds of wild edible greens and mushrooms from the dunes, and they gathered young brackens all over the place. The stalks of the plant which had umbrella-sized leaves would be also used for several different dishes and for making pickles as winter food. They were able to get a plenty of various fish, all kinds of shell fish and salmon from the sea.

The seminar finished well, by the grace of God. Because of the small number of teachers, we could hear individual teacher's experiences and had group discussions to solve the students' problems, instead of my one-way lectures. The teachers opened their minds and sincerely presented problems they had encountered that seemed to be on a serious level. As I go around the world, the pains of teenagers are exiting, especially the discrepancy between the outside world and the local conditions that looked like they make the youth frustrated. The fast-developing modern conveniences made them behind and separated from the outer world, since their environments did not seem to be easily changed. In such circumstances, the key issue was how we help our youngsters grow up as happy adults. We had heard and discussed about many incidences of juvenile delinquency. We concluded that there would be no special way to help our youth to prevent them from straying, except to give them plenty of our love, forgiveness and grace, and let them have personal encounters with the Lord Jesus Christ.

Picking Up the Sea Snail

6/10/1995. Following the Sunday worship service, we all went out to the beach, for which everybody had prepared a pair of long boots, and someone lent one for me, too. Wearing the boots that reached up to our hips, we went into the water, but it did not become deeper even when we walked far into the water. Someone told me that Japanese people had put cement concrete structures under the water for a certain purpose during the WWII, but no one knows the reason.

As I went into the water following them, I saw many treasures under the water all around me. Countless conches spread out around my feet, and everybody was busy to picking them up. They gathered them and boiled them in a big pot at the beach. Meanwhile, someone cooked a stirred fry dish with mushrooms picked freshly from a hill near the beach. Everyone had brought something to eat from their home, including rice, kimchi, mixed vegetables, salmon boiled in soy sauce and other leftovers. It looked like a feast with all kinds of delicacies and, honestly, I had never tasted such tasty food in my whole life. Especially the kimchi taste was extraordinary, perhaps, because they used fresh-cut baby cabbages from clean nature.

One day, we visited a "Dacha," a weekend cottage on a small piece of land in the countryside, which was given as an award from the government to selected people from state-owned enterprises and industrial workers. Those who received such land usually built a small cottage on it and cultivated vegetable gardens to solve their winter food shortage. The Dacha we visited belonged to an old couple who had a pretty cottage with a magnificently bloomed flower garden, and behind it a small water stream was flowing. It seemed quite deep, so that they could catch some small fish from there. It was superb!

We went out to a big stream to see salmon coming up from the ocean next day after dinner. They said that myriads of salmon were coming up to lay eggs at this stream that was connected to the sea this time of year. Constant loud noises of the salmon jumping deafened my ears in the white lights after sunset. I told my interpreter next to me,

"There must be thousands of salmons!"

My interpreter replied, "In July and August, thousands of salmon are coming up to many streams like this around this area. However, the government banned people to catch the salmons here because they must spawn. $200 per fish will be fined in case anyone is caught fishing here. Still everybody comes bringing buckets, not one or two, but a couple of them to fill with fish at night."

"What? $200 per fish! Then what are they going to do if they got caught?"

"Well, still people come at night and catch them. As myriads of salmon are continually coming up, people can easily catch them and cut open the abdomen of fish to take out the eggs and put them in a bucket, and the rest of fish into another buckets. They preserve them in salt and eat through the year."

"I see."

"But people don't stop there. They catch more salmons for one or two bucketful and use them as fertilizer for their vegetable gardens."

"Ooh! Isn't it too much? Eventually there will be no more salmons left. Because of this, was the taste of kimchi that good? Used the best fertilizer in the world?"

Korea Trip with Dr. Dirks

9/11/1995. I visited Korea with Dr. Dennis Dirks, the Dean of Talbot, and his wife. We arrived yesterday here at Daejun from Seoul and visited my grandparents' tomb at the National Cemetery on the way to Hannam University. Dr. Dirks gave a Seminar at Hannam for a pastors' gathering of around 200 people, and I interpreted for him.

9/19/1995. I had a special seminar for students at the Teachers College of Juan Presbyterian church at Incheon City on the 17th. It was the third step of an educational program for the students who want to receive a teacher's certificate from the General Assembly of the Presbyterian Church in Korea. The seminar went well by the grace of the Lord.

Dr. Dirks spoke at the chapel of the Full Gospel Yongsan Seminary this morning, and I had a Teachers' Seminar at Doklipmoon Church for their Teacher's College students in the evening.

Seminars in Bulgaria and Romania with Dr. Cook

10/9/1995. In support of GKC, Dr. Cook and I went to Sofia in Bulgaria and Bucharest in Romania to give seminars to the local pastors and church workers.

Dr. and Mrs. Cook and I landed in Athens via Paris. Missionary John Park from Sofia met us at the Athens Airport and guided us. We went sightseeing today around the city of Athens and the ancient biblical site of Corinth, located on the isthmus that connects Greece with the Peloponnese. We looked at Athens around the Parthenon, the Temple of Athena on the Acropolis plateau, the market square, and the Areopagus Hill where the Apostle Paul debated with those Athenians. Wherever we went, we saw so many ruins of temples and debris of idols, which had been made only by artisans' hands from the beginning, so they were nothing but toys that had now turned into pieces of stone debris everywhere, trampled under the feet of people, wild dogs and cats. It was interesting and made us laugh to see dogs lying on quiet roads with closed eyes, like ancient philosophers meditating.

We left Athens in Missionary Park's station wagon and headed north towards Thessalonica via Meteora and slept at Thessalonica. Outside the hotel where we stayed was what seemed a market place, so we heard the noise of a thousand voices until late night. We left for Sofia through Nilopolis and Philippi early in the morning, and Pastor David Kim and his wife joined us at Sofia.

Dr. Cook had a seminar for local pastors at Sofia in the morning on the 12th, and I had a seminar for pastors' wives and Sunday school teachers in the afternoon. Approximately 500 people participated in both seminars.

10/14/1995. We were taken to a huge cabin that was used as a church, located deep in a forest in Bucharest, Romania, on Saturday. The cabin was built in a deep valley with a very steep, high mountain behind it that was magnificently covered with autumn leaves glowing red. A stream with a lively current flowed in the front of the cabin. We had a worship service there, after which we had a time of fellowship eating local food that the church members prepared. The day's special menu was a dish of barbequed trout they had just caught from the stream.

10/18/1995. We had seminars for around 800 local pastors, their wives and church workers all day long on the 16th. Dr. Cook held a seminar in the morning, and I held one in the afternoon on the topic of how to raise our youngsters into happy adults.

Yesterday and today, we had city tours and sightseeing in the mornings, and two huge crusades for local people in evenings, for which around 5,000 people were gathered for each crusade, and Dr. Cook gave messages for both. Many people walked down to the front and accepted Jesus Christ as their personal savior.

10/19/1995. We moved to Vienna, Austria, where we had a city tour and went to a lake with beautiful scenery where the movie, "The Sound of Music," was filmed. For lunch we went to a small, cozy restaurant that overlooks a peaceful, blue lake, where we enjoyed a fish menu of, they had caught in the lake and freshly prepared. We had a Vienna sightseeing tour, looking around the Central Cemetery of Vienna where famous musicians are buried and where we saw immense monuments and many unique shapes of the tombstones. We visited Salzburg to see Mozart's birthplace and house museum and enjoyed shopping there all evening.

We traveled toward the direction of Poland the next day, while enjoying picturesque mountains and fields with autumn colors, beautiful streams and lakes in Europe's quiet countryside. As the car turned a meandering mountain road of Switzerland, suddenly our eyes caught a fancy slide running down and following the mountain ridge from the top. The slide had bright red, blue and yellow-colored round containers in which each person can slide down on it. I wondered who had built such a slide in a remote deep mountainside like this, as no one was sliding there. We became children again and got out of the car.

"Let's rest here for a while."

"Then are we going to slide?"

"Gee! That's great."

It seemed very fun to me, but the two wives wanted just to watch the others who were sliding down. So, Dr. Cook, Pastor Kim and I took a cable car going up to the mountain top, and from there we slid down all the way. Inside the car it was kind of stuffy and choky for a long drive, but after shouting and laughing for a while on the slide, I felt refreshed and relieved.

We continued driving to drop by the Auschwitz Concentration Camp Memorial near Oswiecim in Poland, where the German Nazis massacred Jewish people during WWII. We saw many personal items belonging to the victims and walked inside the gas chamber that the Nazis used to kill thousands of lives. When I saw the actual place, I realized how man could become extremely wicked under the Devil's control. Still, I wondered: if God did not allow it, such happenings could not exist in human history.

First Taiwan Visit with Dr. Norman

11/18/1995. Dr. Norman and I visited Taiwan with Angela, a Biola Taiwanese student who had prepared all the itineraries for this trip. Her father graduated from the National Taiwan University and was presently a Taiwanese consul in an African country. We were able to meet a group of influential people in Taiwan because of the many friends of Angela's father. Dr. Samuel Chang, the President of Chung Yuan Christian University in Chung Li, was especially one of her father's best friends, so we visited the school, and he promised to send students to our BEST program. We also visited Providence University, Tamsui Oxford University, Eternal-Life Christ College and Taiwan Baptist Seminary.

The Second Korean Pastors' Conference

2/1996. Our International Student Education program held the second Korean Pastors' Conference. The two speakers were Dr. Gary

McIntosh, who was known as a specialist in church growth, and Dr. Donald Sunukijan, well known for expository Bible preaching.

When I consulted with Dr. Michael Wilkins, Dean of Faculty at Talbot, about recommending any Talbot faculty to speak at our conference, he suggested I meet with Dr. Sunukijan, who joins Talbot this semester and is well known for Biblical preaching.

> "Sung, today, he is going to leave for Texas after his final interview, so before he leaves, you may meet him. I have already told him about you and the seminar. You now go to Talbot building, then, you wouldn't miss him."

I met Dr. Sunukijan at the front of the Talbot building entrance.

> "Welcome to Biola, Dr. Sunukijan. I believe you have heard from Dr. Wilkins."

> "Yes, I did. I will take the part of the seminar, Biblical Preaching. Stragely enough, when I decided to move to Talbot, the Lord told me that when I go to Talbot, I may work a lot for Korean people . . . yet, I didn't expect that is happening so fast."

It was such great timing. My God had prepared for those perfect speakers for the seminar. Glory and Honor be to my God!

Second Korea Trip with Dr. Cook

3/20/1996. I went to Russia to teach at the MGBC last January, and this month I visited Korea with Dr. and Mrs. Cook.

Pastor Jong Soon Park took us to lunch at a very fancy restaurant on the 55th floor at 63 building, and he was always generous to us as a friend of Biola. The outside view from the glass window of the restaurant was tremendous. The Mayor of Anayang, the husband of my high school friend, came with her to the Hilton where we were staying and bought us Korean cuisine at the Sura Restaurant for dinner.

3/25/1996. Dr. Cook gave a message at Onnuri Church yesterday afternoon and at Myung Sung Church in the evening. We visited Soong Shil University this morning and signed a MOU between the two schools, then we gave a Biola presentation at Anyang University at 5 pm.

3/31/1996. Elder Young Woon Kim, our student's father, again invited us to a trip to Jeju for two nights at the Shilla Hotel in Seogwipo that helped us to be relaxed and rested. We enjoyed the quiet beach until Saturday afternoon and had a Jeju tour, too.

The Mayor of Anyang City had arranged for us to visit some churches in Anyang. We visited both Anyang Jeil Church and Anyang Methodist Church, and Dr. Cook gave sermons and I interpreted. Dr. Cook usually preferred my interpretation for his messages. Sometimes the pastor of the church we visited wanted to interpret Dr. Cook's sermon, but he was usually reluctant, probably because I had already done so many for him. He especially did not want his sermon, "No Way," to be interpreted by anyone else if I was available. Often when a different person had to translate, then he switched to another sermon.

BEST Program

9/1996. A total of 87 students participated in this year's BEST program in July. Chung Yuan University in Taiwan sent 49 students according to their promise, and others came from Seoul Women's

University, Kae Myung University and Soong Sil University. Professor Karen Bauman worked as both Academic and Activity Coordinator for this special program. We had a total of 46 students for this fall semester for the ELSP program from many different countries, besides Korea, Hong Kong, Japan, Thailand, Russia, Indonesia and the Philippines.

Korea Trip with Dr. Sunukijan

10/3/1996. I visited Korea with Dr. and Mrs. Sunukijan. When we arrived at Taegu Airport, many people were there to welcome us, even though it was late at night. We found fruit baskets in our hotel rooms that were from Elder Kim, who cared us in genuine love, so we deeply appreciated him.

We were very busy visiting four churches on Sunday, starting in the morning: Soe Bu Church, Han Saem Church, Sa-Weoul Church, and Nae-Il Church. Dr. Sunukijan gave messages with my interpretation to all the churches.

10/9/1996. We left for Young Ju through country roads to go to Dong Bu Church, after the 11 O'clock chapel at Taegu Theological University. The car was running on country roads with golden fields on both sides, continually passing by mountain paths, rice pads, apple orchards and vine groves crossing a railroad. The scenery of the Korean countryside under a clear blue sky with soft sunlight was friendly and affectionate, quite different from my old memories.

We eventually arrived at So Baek Mountain Hotel after crossing over some green hills. After unpacking, they took us to a church member's home where a well-prepared dinner table with delicious local delicacies waited for us. A beautiful evening service was given to the Lord with all our hearts.

Love of Elder Young Woon Kim

10/10/1996. Elder Kim came to our hotel around 7 a.m. to suggest that we drive up following the East coast to enjoy the ocean and relax. He drove us through An Dong to Young Duk, famous for king crabs, and we tasted crabs, sashimi and row octopus at the place. Elder Kim had been always generous and gave abundant love to me and Biola people whenever we visited Korea, and we deeply appreciated him. After we went up to Kyung Ju, the old capital city of the Shilla Dynasty, and saw the famous Bulkooksa Temple, we returned to the airport via Po Hang to leave for Seoul.

10/14/1996. Dr. Sunukijan held a Biblical Preaching Seminar yesterday for the pastors at Soong Shil University to celebrate their 99th anniversary. Then we visited Anyang University to set up an MOU signing ceremony for a sister relationship in the morning, and gave a Biola/ELSP presentation at the Korean Christian Centennial Building of the school.

China Visit with Dr. Sunukijan

10/15/1996. We left Seoul to go to Yanji, China, and on the way, we spent two nights sightseeing in Beijing. We visited Ming tombs, the Forbidden City, the Chinese imperial palace, the Summer Palace and the Great Wall; through them I realized that China is truly a huge country, and the people's scale is big. I saw extraordinary things from a king's mausoleum that was able to be reached by a long, underground tunnel, to a palace that was too huge to see all of them in one day and to the endless steps on the Great Wall.

We flew from Beijing out to the Yanji Airport to get to Yanbian University Science and Technology. The airport was very crowded, although everywhere in China is always full of people. As we arrived at the airport, waiting for us were Dr. Joong Sup Kim, one of the school's vice presidents, and one of my classmates in the Doctor's program at Talbot. We unpacked at the school's guest house.

10/17/1996. We ate breakfast at the school restaurant, with a great menu of bellflower mixed with dried pollack dish, turnip kimchi, tofu soup in bean paste and duck bulgogi. The students were eating three meals here, and I wondered if the menu was always good like this, or was it a special for today because of the visitors to the school?

The classes started at 8:00 a.m., and my main job was interpreting. We had an MOU signing ceremony at 11:00 am. President Jin Kyung Kim gave both of us letters of appointment for Visiting Professor and asked us to come to the school at any time to teach their students. Lunch was also very good with a buffet style, and we ate with students. We were invited for dinner to Dr. Joong Sup Kim's home, where we received an amazing dinner table with all kinds of delicacies that his wife had prepared. She said that except for butter and cheese, they can obtain any kind of food materials here at a very low cost.

We went to the border area between China and North Korea the next day, divided by the Du Man River. I walked on the river bank to get to a bridge over to North Korea. The river had not much water so that a rower or a boat would not be necessary like the old days, and some part of the river was dried up enough that people may cross over the river by walking. I was able to see factory-like buildings far away on the land of North Korea. Many souvenir stores around the border area were selling North Korean handcrafts and stamps.

Second Korea Visit with Dr. Sunukijan

4/1997. I had been to Moscow to teach in January, and I again visited Korea with Dr. Sunukijan this time. The Lord's prophecy seemed to be coming true that he will work a lot for the Korean people.

The seminar at Shin Ban Po Church, which gathered around 100 pastors, received a good response. I usually had a Biola/ELSP presentation at the end of all the seminars, so that we were not only providing pastors with a continuing education opportunity, but we were also introducing Biola as an outstanding Christian University and its ELSP program to the Korean Christian community.

Another Preaching Seminar was held at Soo Young Ro Church in Pusan arranged by Pastor Su Young Oh of Shin Sang Church. Around 130 pastors and church workers participated in this seminar, and we also received good responses. We stayed at the Hyatt Hotel in Hae Woon Dae Beach, and it had a fantastic view of the beach and ocean under the blue sky. It was another fun thing to look at and to taste sea squirts and sea cucumbers inside the carriage on the beach under the sunset.

The 21st was Tom's 60th birthday, so we planned three nights and four days for a Hawaii Trip using a tour company. We had an exciting rendezvous at the Honolulu Airport, as I was coming from Korea and Tom came from America. We had a wonderful time there watching a Polynesian Show, shopping, enjoying dinner on a boat on the ocean, and snorkeling.

Third Korea Visit with Dr. Cook

10/22/1997. I visited Seoul and Po Hang this time with Dr. and Mrs. Cook, and we stayed at the Hilton Hotel near South Gate in Seoul. We went to the Lottie Department Store yesterday and toured them around the fancy and busy food court downstairs.

10/26/1997. Dr. Cook preached at the Main Service of Onnuri Church today and I translated. The secretary of Yong Jo Ha, the Sr. Pastor of the church, called me last night.

> "Dr. Lee, Pastor Ha said that Pastor Samuel would be better to interpret Dr. Cook's sermon tomorrow."

> "Ah, yes…, but Dr. Cook wanted me to translate his sermon tomorrow. Who is Pastor Samuel? Can he interpret without any preparation?"

> "Pastor Samuel Kim! I heard you know him very well too."

> "Well, I really don't know any Samuel Kim at Onnuri Church. I will discuss about this with Dr. Cook tomorrow morning."

Dr. Cook always preferred that I translate his sermons and did not like especially when anyone tried to interpret without reading his manuscripts in advance. As soon as we arrived at the Church, Dr. Cook asked Pastor Ha.

> "Is there any problem if Dr. Lee interprets?"

> "No. Of course not, she can interpret."

Dr. Cook wanted me to translate his sermon this morning, and Pastor Ha seemed a bit embarrassed to say "No" to Dr. Cook. So, I translated, but the situation was somewhat awkward to me. It was a contrast to the situation at Yoido Full Gospel Church when Pastor David Cho led the worship service, and he wanted me to translate Dr. Cook's sermon. Upon finishing the sermon, he praised me a lot to the congregation that I had made a great interpretation. If any church does not want me to translate, I have no reason to do so.

I found out later that Pastor Samuel Kim was Pastor Choong Mo Kim. I never thought that he was working at Onnuri Church, and I also never called him Samuel. We knew so well each other, and my husband and I always call him Sam Kim. I really would not think about that he was the same person. When I met him after the service, I understood the situation. Pastor Sam Kim would surely translate without reviewing manuscripts, even though I would not know Dr. Cook's opinion on it.

Upon finishing the service, we moved to Choong Shin Church for the one o'clock service, and after the service, we went to Kwang Sung Church to preach. We ate dinner at the Chinese restaurant in Walker Hills, where the shark fin soup was so delicious.

My 55th Birthday

10/28/1997. Today is my 55th birthday, and I received very special congratulations from Dr. Cook who sent me both a beautiful flower bouquet and a fruit basket. We were scheduled to have dinner with President Yei Hwan Kim of Chong Shin University and Dr. Chi Mo Hong in the evening. Dr. Kim came with his wife and Dr. Hong was accompanied by his wife and grandson. The dinner was delightful with laughter at Dr. Cook's endless humors and jokes.

Dr. Cook gave a sign to a waiter near the end of dinner, and then a big cake that was fancily decorated with many candles came into the room with many waiters. I was greatly surprised and very touched. For Dr. Cook had carried a big box from the hotel, so I thought he was taking a gift for President Kim, but it was a cake box for me that he had ordered to the hotel bakery in advance.

"Thank you, Lord. What am I, so that I receive such love? You love me, so they do!"

Invitation from President Young Kil Kim

10/29/1997. We left Kim Po Airport for Po Hang to go to Han Dong University early in the morning. The school campus was excited because their Fall Festival was starting today. It was windy, but the campus was beautiful with a full view of ocean.

Someone told me that Han Dong may be Biola in Korea, because it has the highest Christian student rate among Korean Christian Universities. It was good to see Dr. Kim's smiling face again; he had visited Biola several times before, and he gave us the school tour. There was truly a precious Christian school in Korea emphasizing intellect, spirit and morality. We checked into the Chil Po Beach Hotel following the evening service at Po Hang Joong Ang Church.

We ate dumpling soup at breakfast the next morning after watching sunrise over the ocean. Then we returned to Han Dong to bid a farewell to President Kim. He asked me to visit Han Dong at any time and give a special lecture to the students.

Moscow with Mina

1/3/1998. I accompanied Mina this time to visit MGBC for my teaching ministry. The reason I go to Moscow, the cold and icy land, in January was to use my winter vacation. Because I had been too often out of the country, four to five times per year, I had to consider Biola work as well as not too much off teaching the classes at Grace Mission University.

Although I gave Mina the Moscow city tour of the Kremlin and Red Square, I wanted to show her St. Petersburg. We left for the city by a night train on the day of my last teaching in Moscow, which had two bunk beds for four people in each cabin without any separation between men and women. Soon two young men came into our cabin, putting their luggage on the upper bed, and went outside. Since I did not know when they would return and what kind of men they were, I was unable to sleep. They came back to the cabin in the morning and seemed to have stayed in the dining car all night long.

We were welcomed at the St. Petersburg train station by the son of the Gymnasia missionary whom I met in L.A. sometime ago. The Gymnasia in St. Petersburg was a Middle School sponsored by GKC to bring up gifted children to impact Russia in the future for the Lord Jesus Christ. I had a chance to look at several places here during the festival in 1992, but this time I was able to see more places in this historic city.

The city situated on the bank of the Neva River was founded in 1703 by Peter the Great and had been the imperial capital until the capital was moved to Moscow. The city had played the country's central role for politics, economy and cultural aspects. The Winter Palace, the three-story, Baroque-style building has more than 1,000 halls and rooms that were lavishly decorated with all kinds of marbles, gold-plated ceilings and walls, and chandeliers were enchantingly beautiful. The facades were richly and elegantly decorated. The palace is now the Hermitage Museum, which has 3 million collections, and is one of the three largest museums in the world.

Near Gymnasia, the Summer Palace is located in the northeast corner of the Summer Garden, which sat on an island by the Fontaka River, Moyka River and the Winter Carnival. The palace was closed for renovation when we visited. We saw only the thousands of frozen fountains and icy tracts in the Garden. We returned home safely, bringing with us wonderful, but cold and freezing, memories.

2/17/1998. I received the President's Award today, "Award of Excellence" along with a monetary prize that was given to a person who had contributed to Biola. It must be a reward for my best work during the last seven years. Glory to the Lord!

I received a letter from Dr. Sherwood Lingenfelter, Provost and Senior Vice President, who wrote,

> "Dear Dr. Lee:
>
> - - - It is through this award that we wish to express our deep appreciation to you for your leadership, and for your extensive service in the development of the English Language Studies Program here at Biola. - -
>
> We thank you for your faithfulness to our Lord Jesus Christ, and for your diligent efforts to add this new dimension to the educational programs of Biola University. May God bless you as you continue to serve Him, may the program flourish under His guidance, and may your work to bring many more international students to Biola be established through His hand."

Trip to Brazil with Dr. Sunukijan

3/27/1998. I heard that the Korean communities in Brazil have been developed greatly through the clothing business, and Christian parents are looking for good Christian Universities in the U.S. to send their children. Thanks to a Talbot student from Brazil, I was able to plan to visit Brazil with Dr. Sunukijan. All the arrangements for churches to visit, preaching at seminars for pastors and other preparations went well in order.

Then, an unexpected accident occurred suddenly just two weeks before leaving. Shocking news came to me that the pastor who prepared for our visit to Brazil cancelled all the arrangements he had made, because I, the interpreter, attend GKC, which is a heretical church. It was an awful happening like a bomb to me because I thought all arrangements had been finished smoothly, and besides, the heresy charge on GKC had been all solved. But they said that still in some remote places people think GKC is heretical. I was so discouraged that I did not know what to do and was just sitting in despair for a while talking to the Lord, "Lord, what shall I do?"

It was around 8:00 p.m., and I wanted to make a phone call to Pastor Yong Jo Ha at the Onnuri Church in Korea. It was because last week I had a chance to speak with him about this coming Brazil trip over the phone, and he told me that if I need any help, just let him know. Maybe my God already knew about this happening, so let him to mention like that to me? I made a call to the church and surprisingly he was there, and I was able to speak with him.

> "Pastor Ha, what shall I do about the Brazil trip? The local pastor who helped the arrangements cancelled all the schedules because I am attending a church of heresy. I'm so frustrated that I am calling you."

> "Gee, is that right? Well. . ., I may check to Brazil right now. Un Chul Hwang, the Sr. Pastor of East Mission Church in Sang Paulo was one of my associate pastors of Onnuri sometimes ago. I will check with him what he would help about this situation. I don't know what time Sang Paulo is now, but he may be in church praying. I heard he and his wife are always staying in

church for overnight prayers. I will make a phone call now, so just wait for my returning call."

It seemed such an impossible situation, but Pastor Ha was going to help me, so I was somewhat relieved. I knew that if the Lord is pleased with this trip, then, he will take care of it. After 20 minutes had passed, my phone rang, and it was Pastor Ha.

"Fortunately, I was able to speak to him. It was night over there, but as I told you, they are always at church for praying at night. I explained to the pastor that you have only two weeks before departure. He said that it wouldn't be much problem to arrange churches to speak and a seminar for pastors. So, call to Pastor Hwang right now, he is waiting for your phone call."

Oh, how grateful! In His grace, all the itineraries for church visits, seminar for pastors, Biola/ELSP presentation were rescheduled. They prepared everything so well, even without enough time, that all the church visits were gracious, and the Preaching Seminar for pastors was successful.

I had a great impression when I visited the East Mission Church in Sang Paulo. The pastor was filled with the Holy Spirit, and so was the whole church in which every member seemed to love the church, the pastor and his wife. I had confidence that God will continue to bless and use this church in great ways for the Kingdom of God.

We visited Rio de Janeiro, known as one of the most beautiful harbors in the world. We took a cable car going up to the mountain top and watched a giant loaf-shaped monolith called Sugarloaf far in front of us, and took pictures under the huge statue of Jesus

Christ, Christ the Redeemer. From there we would see the picturesque beauty of the ocean down below.

10/22/1998. I went to Korea to visit Seoul and Daejon with Dr. and Mrs. Clint Arnold, a Talbot professor and eminent New Testament scholar. He visited five churches to preach sermons with my interpretation. I trust that his great preaching touched many people.

We visited Han Nam University, where he gave a special lecture for pastors at the Graduate School of Theological Studies. A Pastors' Seminar at Onnuri Church in Seoul gathered 200 pastors, and it was received very well. The Biola Presentation Meeting was also very encouraged by around 70 interested people who wanted to ask individual questions related to coming to Biola. In His grace, we had a profitable and great time during this trip.

11/9/1998. I had been selected for the highest award for faculty in the '98 merit program, so I received a letter from Dr. Gary Miller, Vice Provost.

"Dear Sung,

On behalf of the President, the Board of Trustees, and myself, I would like to thank you for the contributions that you made to Biola University during the past year. Because of God's provision for Biola and the hard work of our many dedicated employees, the last fiscal year ended with a significant operating budget surplus. For the second year the Board has set aside a portion of that surplus to fund End of the Year Bonuses to say "thank you" for all your efforts. - -

Lectures at MGBC

1/18/2000. The wood without the wind, covered with white snow around the school building, was mysteriously beautiful. It was like coming into a fairy land where silence reigned everywhere. How elegant was the beauty of the snowflakes on the tiny branches of the fir trees soaring high into the sky! My eyes usually opened at 3 or 4 a.m. Then, wearing enough clothing with a heavy fur coat, two warm scarves, a wool hat and fur boots, I groped my way to the prayer room in the dawn, trying not to slip on the icy path. Without the wind, it was still bearable in the very low temperature. The woods, with the white snow under the gloomy moonlight and the shining snowflakes on the branches, were enchanting in the silence.

"Lord! Lord!" were the crying sounds from the students' prayers and all I heard, the same every year. I always felt the warm wind of the Holy Spirit when I entered the prayer room, and I was soon able to concentrate on my prayers, which brought abundant blessings to me by receiving many answers from the Lord to my prayers.

Japan and Korea Visit with Dr. Miller

3/13/2000. Dr. Steve Franklin, the president of Tokyo Christian University (TCU), visited Biola, bringing a proposal for a five-year program to combine both the Biola and TCU curricula. Qualified TCU Junior students may come to Biola and study for two more years at Biola and then receive two degrees from both schools.

He dropped by my office, so that I had a chance to discuss with him my Japan trip in October with Dr. Gary Miller, who became the new Biola Provost after Dr. Lingenfelter left for Fuller Theological Seminary. With a warm and innocent smile, that seemed not well fitting with his big stature, Dr. Franklin said to me,

"When you visit to Tokyo, please come to TCU and stay at our guest house."

"Yes, thank you, Dr. Franklin. I had been at your Guest house before which was so nice and comfortable place."

"And... This time when you come, I want you give a chapel message to our students. I'm really asking you."

"Me? No. Since Dr. Miller is going with me, let him speak at Chapel."

"No, I want you do it for us in Korean. Then, it will be more meaningful. We have Korean Language Department in our school, for which Professor Tsutomu Nishioka is the Chair who speaks Korean very well as well as translations. He is one of Korean experts in Japan, so often appeared on TV whenever any national issues occur with Korea."

I promised him that I will speak in their Chapel.

10/14/2000. We spent two nights at Barnabas Hall, the TCU Guest house overlooking a peaceful pond. The school was built on a green belt, so it was as if it was in a forest with beautiful gardens of all kinds of trees and flowers.

Kaori, the President's secretary, came in the morning to take us to the train station to go OCC to meet those pastors who had received their Honorary Degrees from Biola. We went with them to a Chinese Restaurant at Ginza.

We went out with Dr. Akira Izuta and Mr. and Mrs. Watanabe for a Tokyo city tour after lunch. We looked around the shopping streets outside of the Asakusa Temple area, where shopping arcades were lined up by various shops mainly selling Japanese crackers, accessories, and bags. We passed the palace and dropped by the Oriental Bazaar, a souvenir shop. We checked into the Nerima Daiichi Hotel, which seemed at the same level as a Hilton. We dined at an Italian Restaurant near the hotel on a meal that was delicious but not expensive. The salmon asparagus pasta was delicious.

10/15/2000. Mr. and Mrs. Watanabe picked us up in the morning and gave us a ride to Nerima Church, where Dr. Izuta was pastoring. The clean, cute church was packed with around 120 people. Pastor Izuta first introduced me to the congregation, then gave me an opportunity to present the Biola and ELSP program to them before Dr. Miller's sermon.

We had a long drive to TCU in the rain after the worship service. I saw from the car windows that the streets and houses that seemed a lot like in Korea, but they were somewhat motionless and quieter than in Korea.

I met Dr. Nishioka, who spoke Korean so well, at noon. My chapel lecture seemed to receive a good response, especially from the Korean students who heard the message with shining eyes. I told the students that God uses only clean vessels, so they should cleanse themselves to become a clean vessel to be used by God. I hope the message can be applied to their lives.

10/18/2000. We left Japan and arrived at Kimpo Airport in Korea yesterday, and checked into the Onnuri Guest House. We visited Young Shin High School in the morning, and Dr. Miller's chapel message was very good. We ate dinner at the Chinese restaurant in the Hotel Walker Hills, and I greatly enjoyed the amazing taste of the steamed shark fins. We had an evening service at Kwang Sung Church.

10/19/2000. We visited Sook Myung University to set up an MOU between two schools in the morning. Then, we had lunch at Seasons, the French Restaurant in the Hilton, and discussed the summer programs of both schools with Kyung Sook Lee, Sook Myung University's President.

We gave a Biola presentation at Onnuri Church in the evening, for which the church had perfectly prepared everything for the meeting. There were opening praises, a program sheet, buffet style food, presentation materials and even Biola applications. Around 50 prospective students and their parents participated.

Visiting Bethany, the Russian Church

2/25/2001. I made a three-day trip to Bethany Church in Sacramento, CA, to give seminars and a message at their Sunday service. Pastor Soo Bong Lee, a Russian Korean missionary whom I had met at MGBC, arranged the visit, and translated my Korean into Russian. This church had 6,000 first-generation Russian Americans as attending members, the largest church among Russian immigrant churches in the world. The church was truly huge, and their Sunday service was overwhelmed with so many people. It seemed to last more than three hours, and two more preachers preached besides me. It was a wonderful and amazing experience for me.

Hong Kong and Korea Visit with Dr. Norman

4/15/2001. I had just returned home, finishing trips to Hong Kong, Seoul, Pusan, Masan and Taegu.

Holi Chu picked us up at the Hong Kong Airport and took us to Dr. Ho's apartment. Dr. Ho was Dr. Norman's acquaintance and was teaching in the RICE program, where Biola faculty also come to teach during their summer vacations.

4/1/2001. Dr. Ho treated us with a Chinese traditional breakfast this Sunday morning and then gave us a ride to the train station. We met Dr. Pang, one of our Biola friends, at the station, and we went together to his house church, a huge, three-story house where the first floor was used as a church. It was a small gathering, but we had a Sunday service with Dr. Norman's message.

We met Dr. Ho again at the train station in the afternoon, and took an excursion boat to ride to Lantau Island. The lively ocean breeze was cool and fresh and refreshed us in mind and body. As the boat arrived at Lantau, we moved into a small fishing boat and kept sailing to a certain uninhabited island, where there was a rehabilitation school for drug-addicted youngsters. Its facilities seemed in very poor condition. A group of Hong Kong Christian leaders, like Dr. Ho and Dr. Pang, were involved in supporting the school; fortunately, the government eventually decided to give them subsidiary funds to build a new modernized building on that spot next year.

These students were the only people living on this small island, which was covered with trees, shrubs and beautiful spring wild flowers along with the endless sound of waves breaking on the rocks. Until the fishing boat came again in the evening, we had a wonderful time with the youngsters communicating with both our hands and feet, and we explored the whole island with them. The fishing boat came at last and sailed us out on the calm sea to Lantau, where we went to a pizza house and ate a very delicious duck pizza I had never tasted before. We ordered spaghetti dishes with a sauce that had an unbelievably good taste, and the aroma of rose honey tea was also superb with beautiful rose petal decorations. Besides this, the menu had a variety of flower teas. They said that the pizza house was owned and managed by one of the graduates from the island rehab school, and he was planning to open branches in other locations. I was positive that he will be successful in his attempt.

Our tired bodies dozed off on an excursion boat that sailed out on the dark rolling night sea. The forest of buildings beyond the sea was dazzling with brilliant, colorful lights, brighter than even Disneyland, and then we arrived at the main island.

We eventually went near Dr. Ho's apartment, where we were staying, by riding a two-story bus. Dr. Ho took us to a fruit juice shop, where we drank coconut mango and coconut papaya drinks and ate black rice porridges. We had really a busy day but had wonderful, unforgettable experiences.

4/7/2001. In Seoul, I gave a special lecture for students in the Christian Education Department at Seoul Theological Seminary, followed by a Biola presentation in the morning. We had a Biola Night at Onnuri Church in the evening, where the Church had again arranged all the details for the gathering.

When we arrived at Pusan Airport around 11:00 a.m., Pastor Kil Soo Chung from Pusan University of Foreign Studies welcomed us. We checked in to the Cho Sun Beach Hotel, where the rooms had wall-to-wall windows overlooking a wide, peaceful seascape that refreshed our minds. We were planning to set up an MOU with the school tomorrow.

5/26/2001. I left for Buenos Aires for lectures and used Argentina Airlines, which served very excellent meals, but strangely the plane's seats were only 20 percent filled. Pastor Jae Jin Kim, the Director of the Argentina School, welcomed me at the airport, and we went to his house, which they used as the school office. His wife prepared a delicious lunch for me with steamed Kalbi and side dishes of great taste.

We left for the retreat center, built on a huge field, that GMI had rented to use as the seminary. The gardens around the facility were well arranged with many big trees and nice walking tracks.

The May sun light was soft, and the sky was clear, but the smell of burning rubbish, here and there, nauseated me.

My lectures were given each afternoon for the student pastors who had not received regular seminary training, so such a continuing education would be a great help for them. Due to the passionate personality of South Americans, we also had passionate class times. After the final lecture, I received farewell kisses on both cheeks from 80 students in the Argentina style, which completely exhausted me.

That afternoon we visited a church pastored by Pastor Lewis, one of our students, in a remote village that seemed to be a very poor area. Unpaved muddy roads had many holes filled with waters, and dogs were running here and there, and a strong smell of burning rubbish spoiled the air. The church was small and shabby, and the pastor had nine children. Among them, the youngest, his 11-year-old son, beat a drum in the church. The roar of drum along with other instruments was so loud that I was unable to sit inside the church, and I was afraid that the awful sounds might split the boy's eardrums. "Lord, protect the child's ears."

Woman Shined Ewha

7/14/2001. Because of my Argentina teaching, I was unable to participate in the ceremony to celebrate the anniversary of the foundation of Ewha High School on May 30th. Yet I was bestowed the "Woman Shined Ewha" award by the school. What qualifications did I have for such an award! That was only by the grace of God!

I arranged a luncheon for Ewha friends at Biola's Board Dining Room, at which 19 friends participated. Young Ae brought my medallion and the prize, and friends congratulated me by presenting me a bouquet of flowers.

Korea Visit with Dr. Norman

4/4/2002. Although I knew my high school alumni reunion was held in May last year on the day of anniversary of the school, I had been unable to participate because I was on the schedule of lectures for the local pastors in Buenos Aires. Even though I heard that they decided to award me the Ewha Award, it was too sudden to change the schedule.

Oh, how many years had passed by now? The young girls on campus put me in a time machine and brought me back to the old dreamy days. My heart was full of joy. What am I? So, the Lord poured down on me such gracious blessings!

I gave an Easter Chapel message to the young students who filled with the whole amphitheatre as they watched me with their bright, shining eyes. The principal warned me that it would be hard for the students to concentrate on the message because of the wind here, but they all seemed to hear my message with shining eyes. Was it because they were concerned or ashamed about an old senior? Otherwise, did it touch their hearts to hear an old lady's sincere entreaty to meet the Lord Jesus Christ? Wishing it to be the latter, I gave my grateful heart to them.

4/5/2002. Today we visited Seoul Women's University where the President was one of my high school friends. Dr. Norman gave a message with my interpretation at the afternoon chapel service, and I spoke in Korean for the evening chapel service. My message was a plea to meet the Lord and about how much I had been blessed because of my encounter with the Lord. President Lee told me that she was blessed by the message, and we grasped each other's hands firmly with encouragements and promises to pray for each other.

Chapel Lecture at Yonsei

4/10/2002. I was excited to come again to Yonsei University to give chapel messages to the young students at 10 and 11 a.m. The message was about my testimony, about how I have received great blessings since I met the Lord. But I did not see any responses from the students. Two days earlier, Pastor Yong Jo Ha of Onnuri bought breakfast for us at the Hyatt Hotel. At that time when I told him about my chapel lecture at Yonsei, he mentioned the students' attitude, and he said that I had better not have many expectations of it.

I found out the reason today, that it was not caused by the students but from another source. When I finished my 10 o'clock chapel talk, I gave a short prayer to wrap up my message. Then the Chaplain who presided at the service told me, "Don't pray after 11 o'clock Chapel." It was a kind of shock to me.

He seemed proud that he was involved in the Jesus Seminar. I asked him if he knew the book, "Jesus Under Fire," written by Michael Wilkins and J.P. Morland of Talbot. He said, "No." I let him know that this book questions the arguments of the Jesus Seminar, and demonstrates that Jesus and His life in the Bible are true and the same historical Jesus. If you deny Jesus in the Bible, how could you anticipate our students having true faith and giving sincere worship to the Lord?

Mina Graduated College

5/1999. Mina graduated at last from Biola with two majors in Psychology and Sociology this month. I am so grateful and proud of her! We want to give all the glory to our Lord. On commencement day, Kris, Mina's boyfriend, came and stayed by her side to carry her things and bouquets. His eyes were always following Mina, so I could easily see that he was falling in love with her.

"Lord, bless dear children."

New House

8/1999. Due to the grace of God, we were eventually able to move to a new house last month from the old rental home. How grateful we were! It is a two-story house with four bed rooms and three baths, 10 minutes away from the school and from the church. It even has a small park with a playground in the front of the house.

After unpacking I went to the Canadian Rockies with my sister for some rest and relaxation time in nature. We took the same routes that I had on my previous trip. It was a delightful trip to see again the snow-capped mountains, the Banff National Park, the giant glacier behind Lake Louise, and the numerous lakes shining in all different colors of blue and green, plus the European taste of British Columbia and the Butchart Gardens.

My God who loved me as the apple of His eye had poured down abundant blessings upon me for the last 10 years. We had suffered in the gloomy and cold rental house at Gandesa Street starting with the bankruptcy in 1990, yet we have received abundant blessings from God. Upon receiving my degree from Talbot in May 1990, God immediately called me to Biola and made me start the ELI program as the Director and grow it to become ELSP and settle down as International Student Education. God developed the ELSP as a strong program so that we were able to prepare His servants to be used for His Kingdom. We also developed the sister relationship with so many Christian Universities in Korea, Japan and China.

God allowed me to have so many opportunities for worldwide travels and meetings with wonderful, important people. He also enabled me to do simultaneous translations for the Sunday Worship Services at church and gave me thousands of opportunities to translate English into Korean. He had provided me so many chances for teachings and seminars overseas and let me continue to teach at GMU and other schools in the mission fields.

The bankruptcy gave Tom a long and painful period of discipline, during which the Merciful God had still poured His grace on him. Since my God turned on the tap water from above, according to His promise, we always had enough to live on. Then, God gave us a new house to encourage us at the end of 10 years.

"Thank you, Lord. We moved to the new home today. I believe that my God who made things possible from impossible will continue to fulfill His pleasing will for the coming another 10 years for us."

Proposal of Marriage

2/1/2002. Kris visited us wearing in his suit and tie this evening and made an offer of marriage to Mina and gave her a beautiful diamond ring. It took quite a while, so I climbed upstairs to see what was going on, and I saw that they were praying to the Lord, holding each other's hands. That made me feel relief, joy and peace in my mind, since they are standing on faith in the Lord.

I was happy and excited. Why was I so joyful? Kris is not from a great family, nor a medical doctor, nor lawyer nor Ph. D. He is a policeman in his third year of service. His education is just graduating from Biola and the Police Academy. He was tall but skinny, so he did not look that handsome to me. As a Chinese American, his father had died several years ago. My husband and I did not know much about Kris, but strangely he had been attractive to us as Mina's spouse and we liked him very much.

He seemed a good Christian, always gentle and consistent. I have always had a good feeling from him for the last four years during their friendship period. Probably the reason we were so happy about this marriage was that God was pleased about this matrimony, and my heart was pounding as if it were I who was being proposed to. We are happy parents. One thing I was excited and grateful for was that Kris is the fifth generation in his Christian family history.

Mina's Marriage

4/27/2002. Today is the day that my only daughter received her husband, a son for me and my husband. I was grateful for Kris's good personality and his fifth-generation Christian roots. The wedding ceremony was conducted by the senior pastor of the church Kris was attending. The 800 seats in the sanctuary were almost filled with the wedding guests.

The wedding reception was held on the top floor of the Westin Bonaventure Hotel in LA downtown. They set out 45 tables for 10 people at each table and used two halls to make it spacious, so the dance area was huge. A live band continually played cheerful music, and food was served with 11 courses of Chinese cuisine that tasted so good, and the serving waiters were fancy in tuxedoes. The wedding party was fancy and gorgeous, and we were very pleased. They used wedding cakes as center pieces for all the tables, which seemed as an excellent idea, even though the whole cake cost was tremendous. Dr. Norman prayed for the food, and Dr. Cook gave a word of congratulations for Mina and Kris. "Lord, thank you so much. It was truly more than enough."

Mina's Honeymoon

4/29/2002. They told me that their flight to London will leave LAX at 8:00 p.m. today. After six days in England, they will go to Paris and spend another week in Europe, for a total of 17 nights and 18 days.

"Lord, bless the children and be with them wherever they go. Protect them with your angels, so not get into temptation, and deliver them from the evil, nor accidents nor any mistakes."

5/11/2002. Since I received a phone call from the children at the Grand Rochester Hotel in London, one week had already passed, so I was waiting for their phone call. Today is Mother's Day, and Tom asked me to have dinner at the Light House, a seafood buffet restaurant in Santa Monica. The weather was so mild and great in the fresh wind under soft sunlight, which was a perfect day to be out at a beach area. Many shops were crowded with people, so it was really fun to look at around. We had a delicious lunch and walked slowly down on the pier, hearing the waves down below on the rocks. We found an empty bench overlooking the ocean at the end of the pier, so Tom and I sat down to watch the waves on the endless blue sea, but my head was filled with only a thought about Mina and Kris. Then, my cell phone rang. It was Kris.

"Mother, for a while we went out to the Scotland area for sightseeing, and it was hard to find a place to make a phone call. Sorry!"

As I heard his voice, I was relieved. He gave his phone to Mina.

"Mom, here is Paris. Tomorrow we are going to have a Cruise tour on the Seine River from the Eiffel Tower."

"Both of you are all okay?"

"Of course, everything is good, Mom."

"Mina, if you want to have a boat tour, then take a night cruise. It would be a real fun to watch Paris night scenery flowing on the River seeing the Eiffel Tower, Notre-Dame Cathedral and other historic buildings decorated with brilliant lights."

Trip to Alaska

8/13/2002. I left for an Alaska trip with my sister yesterday that refreshed my heart. The air was clean and fresh, and the green environment had an amazing beauty, as I had imagined. In the old days when the United States purchased the land from Russia, everywhere was covered under ice and snow, but now it has become a lot warmer.

They said it was raining every day last week, but the sun was shining today. Due to the white night, it was still quite bright even at 10:00 o'clock at night. The bus was running along the dramatic shorelines of Turnagain Arm, the most beautiful stretches of highway I had ever seen. The basin of the waterway was completely turned to sandbars because of stone crumbs from the surrounding mountains created by the icebergs. Nothing could survive in the water, and even ships were unable to sail, but the scenery had a breathtaking beauty.

We arrived at Whittier, a beautiful hidden harbor, through a newly constructed, 2.5- mile-long tunnel running through the Chugach mountain range. From there we took a cruise boat, the Prince William Sound Glacier Cruise, and had lunch on the deck.

The food was delicious, and it was delightful sailing to look at the grandeur of the Black Stone Glacier, its ice cliffs and thousands of icebergs drifting across the River. It was a beautiful bright day. We saw from time to time those huge snow balls falling from glaciers into the water. Probably it would be the climax of an Alaskan trip!

8/14/2002. Today in the rain we went north to Fairbanks, and on the way we passed Wasila and arrived at Talkeetna, enjoying every second of the picturesque beauty of the ravines. We were continually watching high mountains in the running bus, but the top of Mt. McKinley (20,320ft) was not visible, because it was covered by clouds. The bus stopped and rested for a while at a park, where we saw tombs for those who had died on the way to climb to the mountain. I read several Korean names among the list of the dead.

The flower called Firewood, a bright red color, was very impressive and attractive on the both side of streets. Passing by the Nenana River and some Indian villages, we eventually arrived at Fairbanks, a beautiful city of white night.

8/15/2002. The sun was bright, and the air was clear. We boarded a river boat on the Chena River, one of the branches of Yukon River, in the morning. We sailed along the riverside for four hours, during which we dropped by sled dog headquarters, places to dry salmons in the smoke, and visited the Chena Indian village. We also saw the Trans-Alaska Pipeline that runs for 800 miles and had time to wash for gold at the Eldorado Gold Mine.

Ordained to Pastor

10/3/2002. Two days ago I took a written test, given by the Presbyterian Church International General Assembly (PCIGA), to be ordained as a pastor. The test was mainly based on memorizations of Christian doctrines, so that the result of the test did not seem very meaningful to me. It would be better if they tested about the candidates' quality as a pastor, their Christian philosophy and faith in Jesus Christ rather than memorizing doctrinal answers.

Today, I was ordained to be pastor by PCIGA, which they said was the first time they allowed a woman to be ordained. The reason I wanted to receive ordination was because of the many pastoral students in my ELSP program, my teaching at GMU graduate classes and my ministries in the mission fields.

60th Birthday

10/28/2002. Kris and Mina arranged a surprise party for my 60th birthday, inviting family and close friends to Hilro Hall of the Hilton Hotel in Century City. The menu was my favorite seafood buffet, which had a thousand delicious dishes. I was so grateful to the children, but I knew that this was a gift from my dear God who loves me. His grace and loving kindness are always overflowing me!

In the evening when I opened my iPhone messages, someone was singing the Happy Birthday song to me, and soon I realized that it was Dr. & Mrs. Cook' voices. Oh, what a surprise! Dr. Cook also gave me a surprise at the faculty luncheon given by the President last Monday. Upon finishing the blessing on the meal when everybody was ready to eat, Dr. Cook said,

"Just second... Is there someone whose birthday number ends with 0? It's Sung Lee. Let's sing for her, "Happy Birthday."

I was so grateful to him that I sent an email to him that I want to buy Kalbi dinner at a Korean Restaurant. A voicemail came right away that "the president will pay for the dinner, so you will locate a good restaurant." Dr. & Mrs. Cook and Tom and I had a great dinner at a nice Korean Restaurant newly opened near our home. As a token of my gratitude, I bought three pieces of baby clothing as a gift for his daughter, Laura, who will deliver a baby at Christmas time.

Teaching in Moscow

3/15/2003. As I arrived at the MGBC campus, it was warmer than I had expected, but everything was still covered under snow. The sound of the students' crying out from the prayer room in this frozen early morning was as usual this year, too. I walked carefully on the slippery road covered with icy snow to join them in the prayer room. The snows on the tiny twigs were shining like jewels in the frozen moonlight and looked like downy hairs. The beauty of snow flowers on the branches was so great I hardly knew what to say.

I was concerned, because I had a cold before I left home, but in His grace, as I arrived at Moscow, I was able to get over it. This time, I gave my lectures in English, and Inna, who did a great job of translating, took me to the Bolshoi Theatre to watch the "Nut Cracker" ballet the other evening.

It was a great gift for me when I came to Moscow to teach, that I had a chance to occasionally enjoy opera or ballet at the Bolshoi. I was always amazed by their outstanding music and graceful dances, as well as I lost my mind on the breathtakingly brilliant colors and diverse designs of the performers' clothing. It was true when I watched "Romeo & Juliet" that it was truly extraordinary!

First Benediction

3/22/2003. I gave a message to our students for today's worship service and a benediction for the first time in my life. It was such a touching moment for me, as my heart was so thrilled to be a servant of God that I did not feel even on my ordination day. All the glory, honor and thanksgiving go to my God who chose me and uses me as His servant.

Musical, the Last Empress

4/16/2003. Mina seemed to be doing well now in her four-month of pregnancy, as she suffered greatly from morning sickness in the second and third months. I was glad that she now eats anything well and asked me if she could visit Biola to have lunch with me.

"How do you want to come?"

"I want to see mom. Whenever I feel sick, I want to see mom. But I called you and told you that I am sick, then, you always seemed very upset as if I had done something wrong. Why are you sick?"

"Did I? Sorry! Well, probably my love and concerns for you might bring such reactions."

"Mom, what do you want me to do for you on Mother's Day?"

"Well, nothing."

"Mom, a couple of years ago, a Broadway style musical about Empress Myeongseong of Korea came to L.A. It came again to L.A., so Kris asked me that how about we go together to watch. This was the first Broadway style musical from Korea casted with only oriental performers. We may meet a little bit earlier to have dinner, and then we can go to the Kodak Theatre in Hollywood."

"Okay, great. Thanks. I have wanted to see it very much. I'm sure that Daddy would enjoy it too."

She had recently been sick in bed almost for 10 days because of a cold, so Kris's mom made a special porridge with black chicken and abalones every day. She seemed to receive great love from her mother-in-law. How grateful we are to the Lord!

PCIGA Meeting at Germany

6/7/2003. I was glad that I was able to participate with Tom in the PCIGA meeting held in Germany, where we took a tour that traced the footsteps of Martin Luther, starting from Frankfurt. We followed in the steps of the great reformer for four days, visiting from Eisleben to Worms to Wittenberg and Leipzig.

Nine couples wanted to take a further trip to England, the Netherlands and Belgium, after the PCIGA meeting. The town square in Amsterdam, the capital of the Netherlands, was very crowded with people as usual, but I was unable to see those flower shops and artists drawing portraits of tourists that I had seen in my previous visits.

Many more people were crowded into the Grand Place, the central square of Brussels, where people were fascinated by those amazingly opulent guildhalls, the city's town hall, and the museum buildings. They said that the Grand Place is the most beautiful square in Europe.

We crossed over the Straits of Dover to England from continental Europe, but we were unable to see any of the pastoral scenery that I expected to see in England, probably because it was not the Scotland area. We looked at Buckingham Palace, the Tower of London and Tower Bridge and went to the magnificent, beautiful

Windsor Castle, the queen's official residence and the world's oldest and largest occupied castle. We visited the impressive St. George's Chapel in Windsor Castle, which is the chapel of the noblest Order of the Garter, Britain's highest order of chivalry.

Farewell to 2003

12/2003. I had a two-week teaching trip to Buenos Aires in Argentina at the end of August. The school no longer used a rental facility as they had before, as GMI had purchased an old, five-story building to use as the seminary, which was under renovation. The building was so old and had been deserted for such a long time that twigs and grasses had penetrated the kitchen ceiling from the roof. Pastor Jae Jin Kim and his wife worked very hard on the building, but they seemed to have many difficulties here in their ministry.

In September, I went down to Rosarito, Baja California, Mexico with Tom to participate in a PCIGA meeting for three nights and four days.

In October, I again visited Seoul and Taegu with Dr. Sunukijian. We held a giant Pastors Conference at Duranno in Onnuri in Seoul, and another Pastors Conference that was a combination of 10 churches in the Taegu area. I interpreted for Dr. Sunukijian for the morning conference. The afternoon translation was done by Pastor Sung Soo Kwon of Taegu Dong Shin Church, whose translation was one of the best I had ever heard. He was a professor at Chong Shin Seminary as well as pastoring the Taegu church.

Forever Valuable Things

New House at Hawks Pointe

2/26/2004. I loved the house at Summer Set, which the Lord gave us ten years after we experienced the bankruptcy. Since Mina was married in this house, and I liked the small playground in front of the house so much, I was really against changing houses. If we moved to the new home that Tom wanted, the loan payment will probably be doubled, but still Tom's idea to move was so strong that I was unable to stop him. I decided at last to give up resisting and entrusted everything in the Lord.

> "Lord, I can't fight with Tom. It's impossible for me to change his mind. I really want to live in this house continually. Why does he want to move a better house? Lord, you may change his thought, and lead us to a best way. I have no way but to follow him."

So, according to his wish, we moved into a new house at Hawks Pointe, on a hillside across the street from Summer Set. Once we moved into a new home, it was much more spacious, comfortable and better than the old house in many ways. Once I changed my mind and entrusted everything to the Lord, then I felt peace and joy in my heart.

PCIGA Meeting in Miami

5/2/2004. I had been in Moscow to teach for two weeks since March 20th. Tom and I left for Miami today to be on board a cruise ship to participate in the PCIGA meeting.

The ship was a giant, the Carnival Caribbean Cruise from the port of Miami to Key West Florida and Cozumel, Mexico, for four nights and five days. It had four elevators, and we could hardly see from one end to the other end, with dining halls, a buffet place, cafes, and snack bars where it was all you can eat. It also had a swimming pool with a spa, a gym, a gambling den and a disco place.

Our meeting was held at the disco place, where we had prayer meetings, worship services and seminars during the day. We had a great, luxurious time, looking out over the ocean, resting and eating. It seemed the Lord gave his servants a chance to be renewed in order to better serve His Kingdom in the future.

A great encouragement came to me during the trip when we had a final worship service at Immanuel Church. I had been praying for a long time to receive anointments from the Holy Spirit for the ministry of preaching the Word of God with accompanying signs and wonders. But I had no ideas what to do. The desire for the ministry had occupied my heart for a long time, since I received a dream twice from God.

It happened when the presiding pastor excitedly proclaimed, "The Lord is now here with us." My mouth was crying out, "Lord, anoint me, pour unto me the power of the Words, signs and wonders!" As I was continually crying out for the power of the

Word and his anointing, I began to feel as if I was falling on the ground, because no strength was left in my body. I felt as if all my bones were melted inside of my body, so I was holding the hands of the persons next to me hard to prevent falling, and my body started shaking hard both inside and out.

> "Lord, what is this? Haven't I so much prayed about receiving anointment? Is this your answer? Lord, I don't know what it is. I'm only looking on you and relying on you. My desire is that your will be done in my life and your name alone will be glorified. Lord, lead me in your way."

No Useful Things

6/1/2004. Church held a revival meeting with Pastor Jong Jin Pi, an evangelist guest speaker whose messages were soft and easy to understand during the last week end. Tom participated in all the services from the first hour to the last. Thanks to the Lord, these days, he has changed, since the last PCIGA meeting when he had seemed greatly impressed by those pastors who loved the Lord and hearing their messages. Probably the Lord's time has come for him!

Today, he was continually grumbling to himself while putting new patio furniture and a BBQ grill in the back yard,

"No use! Everything is useless!"

Truly all things are worthless and vanity of vanities! If our house is big with a beautiful garden, even so, what would be that worthwhile? Of course, our new home is spacious, clean, convenient and good. I especially like a nice walking track leading to the top of a hill, which takes around one hour from my home. That is amazingly great, but it does not have any eternal value. We must save our time and money and spend them to invest only for inheriting the Kingdom of God, which will last forever. We must live only for the Lord.

> "Lord, I love you a lot and I want to live only for you. Lord, still thank you for giving us such a nice house. I saw in this morning four blossoms on a pomegranate tree we planted recently. How pretty they were! Also, roses and tiny fruit on a persimmon tree were sweet! Thank you, Lord."

Suddenly in this world of vanity, I was grateful to the Lord for Ecclesiastes 3:13.

> "I know that there is nothing better for them than to rejoice, and to do good in their lives, and also that every man should eat and drink and enjoy the good of all his labor - it is the gift of God."

The 6th Korea trip with Dr. Cook

10/7/2004. I landed at Incheon Airport with Dr. & Mrs. Cook yesterday. Onnuri Church sent a pickup for us and we checked in Cho Sun Hotel.

Dr. Cook gave messages at two worship services at Global Mission Church today. Senior Pastor Lee wanted one of his associate pastors to translate Dr. Cook's message, but Dr. Cook wanted me to translate, so I had to.

We visited the Choong Shin Church in the evening, where I always translated messages whenever we were invited to the church, where I always felt warm and the work of the Holy Spirit.

It was still a megachurch but it gave the impression of the whole congregation being like one big family.

10/14/2004. We went to Taegu by taking the KTX train, which ran like a bullet at 300 km per hour, yet it was smooth and comfortable. I shared a lot with Dr. & Mrs. Cook that it was a delightful train ride.

Many friends, including Pastor Seok Soo Kim and his wife, came out to welcome us at the Taegu Station. A two-day revival Taegu Conference for missions had been arranged by Pastor Kim, and it was so well prepared and became a great success. Pastor Kim is the founder and president of the Light World Mission, an organization training missionary throughout the world with a goal to reach a million local (jagukmin) missionaries. He graduated from Talbot and had been acquainted with me for a long time. I appreciated that he always helped me and other Biola people whenever we visited the Taegu area.

Around 200 college students gathered each evening, and I translated for Dr. Cook and introduced Biola/ELSP by showing Biola videos to the students. Pastor Kim arranged a special breakfast prayer meeting for the pastors, and around 50 pastors gathered for the breakfast in Saturday morning. Dr. Cook spoke about leadership, and it was powerful.

10/15/2004. We held a Biola Night at Sofitel Ambassador Hotel in Seoul this evening, for which we invited Biola alumni and Biola friends. Pastor Chul Shin Lee, Sr. Pastor of Young Nak Presbyterian Church, arranged the meeting in which we shared with the participants what the Lord has done and is doing at Biola. It was a wonderful time of friendship and an opportunity for them to hear and think about Biola. Pastor Jung Hyun Oh of Sarang Church sent over a huge wreath of flowers that was over seven feet high.

Since Pastor Oh had shown his great concern and love for Biola, the school honored him with a special award at the Commencement when Joseph, his son, graduated from Talbot. We hoped that Pastor Oh would continually support Biola.

Teaching at Moscow

4/1/2005. Upon finishing my lecture, I returned to my room on the second floor of the guest dorm by walking up the noisy wooden stairways. Today was April 1, but the temperature was below 15 F.

Two weeks went by quickly, and it became time to return home, so my heart was light and anxious to go home fast. It was the same feeling as when I took the plane to leave L.A. for Moscow, putting off the millions of important daily tasks. My heart was excited with expectation for meeting with new students, but it was also stressful for me to change daily routines to leave for a different world. It had not always been easy to leave for two weeks away from my family, deferring my Biola work and my teaching at GMU. But whenever I arrived at the Moscow Airport, I felt somewhat as if I had returned home because of the airport's familiar smell and their language; that was probably because I had already visited 15 times.

The students sang the song of blessings for me with both their hands held up toward me when I finished the last lecture. I again gave thanks to the Lord for giving me such wonderful opportunities to teach the students in the mission fields.

The students usually stood up when I entered the class room, and they clapped their hands until I said, "Stop, please." Often many students came to me and asked me to sign on the front page of their Bible, as if I were an actress or a very important celebrity, and then I felt a sense of shame and humility for myself.

Tall gray birch trees lined both sides of the highway to the airport. The wide-spread tiny twigs of the trees were still covered with thick white snow. The faces of the departed students and the school staff, for whom I promised to pray, flashed across my eyes. I remembered the girl who always prepared tea and cookies for me and my interpreter for the break time between lectures, who was always polite with a shy facial expression before me. The difference between us was only because we were born in a different world and lived in a different environment.

I think about the Lord's Parable of the Talents (Matt 25:14-30). The Lord said that He will ask for more from the one who has been given more, and someday the person will be held responsible. When I reflected on myself, I have received too much love from too many people throughout my life, so I am "a debtor for love," and "a debtor for the Gospel."

The plane has already taxied down the runway, which meant a safe return home. I gave thanks again to the Lord and felt a relief.

Taiwan and Osaka Visit with Dr. Norman

4/11/2005. The plane landed at the Narita International Airport. In the spring rainfall, full bloomed cherry blossoms over-looking the runway made my heart feel happy and refreshed.

When we transferred to a different plane and arrived at the Taiwan Airport, Prof. Chen from Christ College welcomed us and helped us check in to the Grand Hotel, which felt like we were in a real palace with gorgeous, graceful royal architectural designs with beautiful decorations. The hotel also had clean rooms, and the breakfast buffet was fresh with varieties on the menu that seemed not less than the morning buffet at the Cho Sun Hotel in Seoul.

Morning Worship Service at ORTV

4/14/2005. As we entered the place for the ORTV Morning Worship Service, Dr. Doris Brougham, a 78-year-old missionary who was the founder and CEO of ORTV, was practicing her trumpet in a band at the chorister seat. Her appearance might tell her age, but her actions seemed as if she was in her 30s. I realized one more time that if God is with us, we can be so superb that is nothing to do with age, as the Lord says that the righteous will still bear fruit in old age, they will stay fresh and green (Ps 92:14).

The worship service was beautiful. I had never thought I would have such experiences in Taiwan. The service was completely controlled by the Holy Spirit, and I felt the presence of the Lord.

4/15/2005. For today's morning service at ORTV, Dr. Norman gave a message along with the Biola presentation. As we entered the building, we saw smiling happy faces and felt the strong touch of the Holy Spirit. Throughout the service, my heart was melting in the praises. Tears were running from my eyes and did not stop until the end of the service, and I was so grateful to the Lord that I was able to be in such a beautiful place in Taiwan.

We visited Tamkwang High School with the translator, Mary Ma, and introduced Biola and the ELSP program to 200 students. We dropped by the Wesley Girls High School and visited Taiwan National Museum in the afternoon.

At Osaka

4/16/2005. Pastors Yamamoto and Shintaro welcomed us at Osaka Airport. I was very pleased to see Yamamoto again, for he used to study in our ELSP program. He was always quiet when he attended Biola but, surprisingly, now he talked a lot and spoke Korean so well.

Dr. Norman was planning to give a lecture tomorrow at a pastors' group arranged by Dr. Mitsuhashi. When we checked into the Garden Palace Hotel, a fax message from Mitsuhashi was waiting for Dr. Norman saying that Dr. Norman's draft was not good enough because it was not covering enough about "Evangelicalism." Dr. Norman seemed somewhat irritated.

In addition, I was so upset as I read the last part of the letter that I inadvertently took a hairdryer from the hotel, where I had stayed when I visited Japan the last time, so that the hotel protested to OCC about that incident. Therefore, "please tell Dr. Lee that don't take a hairdryer from the hotel as a souvenir this time," with a memo as "P.S." at the end of the letter.

It must be a lie! I was very upset as I read that part; even if he were next to me, I might want to give him a punch. I was such a helpless human being, even though I was praying every day that I wanted to be like Jesus.

4/17/2005. When I opened my eyes in bed this morning, my heart was refreshed, yesterday's angry feeling was all gone, and I felt so ashamed of the response I had yesterday.

Yes, that was true. However, although I never stole a hairdryer in my life, how many things had I stolen that I could not even remember?

"Lord, forgive me. I am a sinner. Only because of you, I am survived here now."

Because of my Lord, my heart was again filled with joy. Osaka Mikuny Church had reminded me of the old Bethel Korean Church. I saw here and there the congregation members with tears in their eyes while they were singing and hearing the messages. Dr. Norman gave a message for the first Worship Service, and I gave it for the second Service. My message was about "the Spiritual Blessings" in Ephesians Chapter 1. Assistant Pastor Shintaro translated for Dr. Norman, and my Korean message was interpreted by Pastor Yuichiro, who did an excellent job even for the small parts of my emotional expressions.

4/18/2005. The day came at last as Pastor Mitsuhasi arranged the gathering for pastors. I had been prayed a lot for the meeting and Dr. Norman, and the merciful God heard our prayers and worked greatly in his way at the end.

I found a memo from Dr. Norman when I returned to the hotel from a walk later that evening. The memo said that Pastor Mitsuhasi would not be able to participate in tomorrow's meeting. How grateful! Since he will not be there, at least Dr. Norman would not receive any criticism from him. I was relieved and felt peace in my mind.

The meeting was held at the Grace Mission Church, where we were accompanied by Miyamoto and Shintaro. When we arrived at the church, we could see that everything was well arranged. The associate pastor who was in charge of all the meeting details was very kind; surprisingly, everybody who worked there all seemed like angels.

Grace Mission Church

This church was a very famous megachurch in Japan had many branches and thousands of members. The church building was huge and beautiful.

Dr. Norman's lecture mainly covered the interpretation of theological terms, and around 40 pastors in the room paid great attention and seemed very blessed by the Holy Spirit's touch. It was amazing that no one wanted to leave the room, even after finishing the delicious packed lunch prepared by the church. The seminar environment was so great and filled with a loving spirit. My good God answered our prayers for this meeting, for which Dr. Norman and I had been somewhat stressed and concerned.

Dr. Akira-Ken Horiuchi, the Senior Pastor and CEO of Grace Mission Inc., particularly attended the meeting from the beginning, so the environment was even better. After lunch, he guided Dr. Norman and me on a church tour of the sanctuary and the new Education Building up to the sixth floor.

Pastor Horiuchi seemed a very attractive man of God who was always smiling face and kindly greeted anyone encountering him on his way and paid attention to them for a while. We stopped on each floor and reached a huge lounge on the sixth floor, where we chatted for a while on the most comfortable sofa I ever sat on. It took quite a long time until we returned downstairs, but to my surprise, those Associate Pastors and several church members were still waiting for us downstairs. All the members of this church seemed to truly respect their senior pastor and to practice their Christian faith in their daily living.

When we finished our tour and returned downstairs, Pastor Horiuch received a telephone call from Pastor Mitsuhashi. He talked for a while, then, gave the receiver to Dr. Norman, and then Dr. Norman asked me to answer the phone.

I heard an old man's feeble voice through the receiver. His letter was so strong, but his weak phone voice made me sad. He was apologizing to me about the hairdryer part of the letter and told me please disregard the letter, as nothing had happened. He sincerely apologized to me, saying that it had been a mistake and said that he had cancer surgery last year. "Lord, have mercy on him."

4/19/2005. Miyamoto and Shintaro took us to Osaka Castle after breakfast. It was located next to the Osaka Castel Hotel, where Dr. Lingenfeter and I had stayed during our last Osaka trip.

The Osaka Castle was under renovation, but we were able to go inside the Castel Tower (Tensyu Kaku) to see historical exhibitions, and we watched the story of the castle on TV screens on each floor. The history was about the life of Toyotomi Hideyoshi, who invaded Korea to end the Imjin War, but he ultimately ended his life by defeating Korean Admiral Soon Shin Lee. I enjoyed the history of Japan very much as Pastor Miyamoto explained it to me.

TCU Visitation and Chapel

4/20/2005. Yuko Ogawa, the assistant to the TCU President, was waiting for us when we landed on Haneda Airport from Itami. We unpacked our luggage at the TCU Guest House.

As we entered the main gate of the school, a wide road led into the campus, and huge cherry trees lined both sides of the road, but I was sorry to have missed the full blossoms two weeks ago. I slowly strolled down the road covered with white flower petals, enjoying nature.

I was the speaker at today's chapel at 12:30 p.m., and the interpreter was the Korean language professor, Nishioka, as before. The title of my message was "Life of Jesus" from 2Cor 4:10, from which I had been blessed myself.

4/21/2005. We had a corporate meeting today with TCU and Biola on OCC's second floor, where OCC people, TCU and Biola friends and graduates were gathered.

Dr. Ito from TCU took us after the meeting, but he seemed not to know where to go to treat us. He tried several places and eventually came near to TCU and led us to a restaurant called Whagae, which looked like a regular residence but was a traditional Japanese restaurant. The courses came out one by one that I never seen or tasted before. Each dish looked like an art piece with beautiful flower decorations.

Miraculous Seminar

6/3/2005. My God demonstrated His miracles to me one more time. Our International Student Education Department has held the fourth Pastors Conference for Korean pastors, both local and from Korea, for the last two weeks. I had prayed for 40 participants from Korea, but we had received only 12 applications. We needed a good number of participants from Korea, because it would be not enough to cover the seminar expenses only from local pastors. I needed at least $25,000 to cover the costs.

I boldly asked for donations of $10,000 from each senior pastor, including Han of GKC and Senior Pastor Kim of another megachurch in L.A. who was a Talbot graduate. Pastor Kim soon responded that the amount was impossible from his church, and Pastor Han said that he will pray about it. Since the seminar will last for two weeks, GKC will send church workers in two parts for each week. I was grateful to Pastor Han, and he also suggested that our staff may visit the big churches to receive applications from the church members on the spot, but that method did not work, either.

Senior Pastor Kim of Sarang Church tried to help us, too. His church printed out 4000 copies of our seminar flyers and inserted them in their Sunday bulletins. He also announced our seminar from the pulpit. Even so, no one registered for our seminar, and it seemed that God did not work for us. I had been praying so much every morning, so was this not God's will? What was wrong? Should I just rejoice, only trusting in the Lord to do it for us?

In such circumstances, I suddenly received a miraculous answer from the Lord, and the financial problem was beautifully solved. All the departments in the school are supposed to live according to the year's budget and settle accounts at the end of June. In case we have some money left over from the year, it is transferred to the school, so that if we need to purchase anything for the department, we usually buy it before the end of June.

Professor Karen, our Department's Academic Coordinator, came to me several days ago and told me that we need to buy a new movie camera and several software programs for calculating student grades. She requested $800.00. Today, as I dropped by the Dean's Office, I asked Dr. Norman how much money would be left over from our department this year. After checking the papers, he told me that $25,000 seemed to be left over after balancing the accounts from my department's budget for this year. So, this $25,000 will be transferred to the university automatically if our department does not spend any more until June 30th.

I had been so concerning about this conference's expenses, but my God had left over for me the exact amount I needed to use for the seminar. He has been always working for me at the last minute and has tested me in all the incidents to see how much I was relying on Him in faith.

6/5/2005. Now the financial problems were resolved, but the updated registration record showed only two people from Sarang Church and 15 from GKC. The number was very discouraging, but my heart was filled with peace from the Lord, because I believed that my Father who gave me the unexpected $25,000 will accomplish His plan according to His Providence.

6/6/2005. Today I ordered a small banquet for those 10 conference participants from Korea at King's Garden, a Chinese restaurant. I invited Dr. & Mrs. Cook, Dean Norman, the music team, "God's People," volunteer workers and our staff. Subsidiary expenses might surpass the original outlay, but I was happy because all of them seemed to enjoy the meal.

6/7/2005. I was able to see yellow flags far away that our volunteer helpers were waving for parking directions when I drove toward school around 8:30 a.m., entrusting everything in the Lord. At that moment, my heart was trembling with joy and thanksgiving. As I passed the Calvary Chapel building, everybody seemed so busy, some preparing coffee, tea, and muffins, and people from the Finance Department for receiving fees at the tables. I was so grateful to everyone!

People were continually coming, and the praise team, "God's People," directed by Missionary Ung Rae Kim, played graceful praise songs that invoked people's hearts to be filled with the Holy Spirit. From day one, people seemed to love the seminar and showed great responses. I had never experienced such a seminar that went so smoothly. It was the fourth pastors' conference held by our department, and it had always been messy and frustrating on the first day for all the past three seminars and many other international student summer programs we held. Everything went unbelievably smoothly and orderly this time. Pastor Joseph Kim, the Coordinator, Pauline Kim, our staff, volunteer workers and all other helpers had done great job.

Pastor Yong Jo Ha from Onnuri Church in Korea dropped by my office to console me that no one from his church was able to attend our seminar. Pastor Ha helped me and gave me advice about many things while I prepared the seminar, but only one person came from his church. That was because today, Onnuri Church held a Great

New York Conference in New York City, so that all of the Onnuri Church workers had to participate in the conference. Pastor Ha was also on the way to New York, and luckily, as he was able to get some time during his transit at LAX, he managed to drive to Biola to see me this morning. He said with a smile, "Didn't I make you be disappointed?" Then, he prayed for the seminar's success and left for the airport.

What about Pastor Nam from Taegu? He promised me that he will participate with at least 10 of his friends from Korea. I had a good relationship with him for a long time, as he had participated in all our previous seminars with several of his friend pastors from Taegu.

It was true that I relied on both pastors to bring people from Korea. As I reflect on this experience, my God taught me a great lesson that I should not trust in people, because things are only accomplished by God's plan.

> "Trust in the LORD with all your heart and lean not on your own understanding; in all your ways submit to him, and he will make your paths straight (Pro 3:5-6)."

When I climbed up to the platform to say greetings, I felt my heart was choking because of the people who filled the whole auditorium. There were 154 participants in total. By the way, where had they come from? It was the best number among all the four seminars we had previously held. This seminar was done by the Lord, who was pleased with it very much.

> "Thank you, Lord. You are truly the living God who gives signs and wonders to those whom you love. I bless the name of my Lord forever."

Anointment of the Holy Spirit

Instrument of the Holy Spirit

7/26/2005. I felt a hunger that I had never experienced at 5 o'clock in the morning. That was very unusual, because I had eaten a good dinner last evening. Searching for any leftovers in the refrigerator, I found some seaweed soup, so I mixed it with some spoonful of cooked rice in the soup, ate it and went to bed. I fell fast asleep and woke up at 7:30 a.m. as usual with a comfortable stomach. Since I read the Korean Bible on Sunday, I continued to read it until time to leave for church. It was already 2:30 p.m., but still I had no appetite for anything, so actually I had not eaten anything since 5:30 this morning.

Today's sermon at the fourth service was given by Pastor Keith, a missionary from Israel. Upon finishing his preaching, he asked any pastors in the room to come up to the front. He said he was going to lay his hands on those pastors first, then, they would impose their hands on the other people. I saw that Pastor Han, our Senior Pastor, another pastor who had accompanied Pastor Keith from Israel, and Pastor Tae Kim walk to the front.

In such a case, I did not usually walk to the front for laying hands on the people, but today I stepped to the front next to the platform with a blank mind. Four pastors were standing before the platform, and Pastor Keith was laying his hands on the pastors' heads one by one. Upon laying his hand on Pastor Kim, who fell on his back; then, he laid his hand on my head and I was also falling on my back on the floor with a warm sensation, losing all my strength from my body.

As I slowly pulled myself together and stood up, Pastor Keith asked me to step up to the stair in front of platform. Soon people came to the front and Pastor Keith said, "Lay your hands on them." Now a thought passed on me that what if I laid my hands on them but no one would fall, then what shall I do? Immediately I erased such a thought and decided only to look upon Him. No matter what, I would not do anything for myself! I entrusted myself to the Holy Spirit, so that He would take care of it.

When I laid my trembling hand on the head of the first person, nothing happened. Of course, I had such experiences before, praying for people before putting my hands on them, but I never had done it with an anticipation that they might fall. I put my hand very gently on a second person and prayed, repeating "The Holy Spirit, touch her touch her. Holy Spirit touch her," along with speaking in tongues, then she fell down on the floor. I went to the next person, and upon touching her head, she fell, too. This continued happening for so many people, that whenever I touched their heads they fell back on the ground. I was greatly astonished, for I never had such an experience in my life. How I was being used by the Holy Spirit! Truly my heart was filled with joy and happiness because of the thought that I used by the Lord.

I was not hungry at all, even though it had already been 12 hours since I had tasted any kind of food. I suddenly remembered Pastor Han mentioning to the congregation a few minutes ago that Pastor Keith was praying for the people without eating anything since this morning, and neither had Pastor Han himself. I told Deacon Chang next to me,

"I haven't eaten anything today neither, almost for 12 hours, but not hungry at all and having full of energy."

It was really an amazing incident to me. How was it possible that I did not feel hungry at all without eating anything for 12 hours? My God had prepared me for today's ministry without my knowledge, which was truly unbelievable.

Longing for Anointing of the Holy Spirit

7/27/2005. I was unable to stop thinking about the event that happened last week, and my heart was continually trembling in His presence that made me keep praying without ceasing.

I wanted so much for power of God to overflow from me, so that as I give messages and pray with laying my hands-on others for the sick people to be healed, problems solved, signs and wonders manifested (Act 14:3). I longed for the Lord in my prayers without ceasing and entreat Him for an anointing from the Holy Spirit and His touch.

2Corinthians 4:7 says, "We have this treasure in jars of clay to show that this all-surpassing power is from God and not from us." When I accepted Jesus Christ as my personal Savior, the Holy Spirit, the treasure, the Power of God, the life of Jesus, came into my heart. Hence my body became a sanctuary for the Spirit of God and the Power of God (1Cor 3:16). If I am a true Christian, the Power of

God, the life of Jesus, must be revealed in my body and the energy must overflow from me. So that,

> "We are hard pressed on every side, but not crushed; perplexed, but not in despair; persecuted, but not abandoned; struck down, but not destroyed. We always carry around in our body the death of Jesus, so that the life of Jesus may also be revealed in our body (2Cor 4:8-10)."

Since Jesus died on the Cross for me, I died also with Him that I always carry around the death of Jesus in my body. He died not only for my iniquities (Eph1:7), but also for my diseases (1Pe 2:24), curses (Gal 3:13), destructions (Isa 53:5) and poverties (2Co 8:9), so that I became free from all of these. I was fused with His resurrection, and I became a new creature (2Cor 5:17), so the life of Jesus in me would be manifested from my body.

As the life of Jesus is revealed in my body, I am supposed to heal the sick, raise the cripples, open the blinds and raise the dead, only because of the Power of God in me. The Holy Spirit in me is the Power of God and the life of Jesus. The Lord said, "I tell you the truth, anyone who has faith in me will do what I have been doing. He will do even greater things than these, (John 14:12)." What an amazing reality!

Now I am only longing for my God to pour His Spirit like a shower, like wind or fire upon me and anoint me, so that the signs and wonders from God would be manifested through me.

I was not talking here about the Holy Spirit for His saving grace, as in Acts 2:38. I was praying to the Lord for the fulfillment of Acts 10:38, "how God anointed Jesus of Nazareth with the Holy Spirit and power, and how he went around doing good and healing all who were under the power of the devil, because God was with him." I longed for this word of God to be fulfilled in my life, and I had been praying for this anointing of the Holy Spirit to be poured upon me.

Prayer Waiting for Anointing

8/10/2005. Yesterday when I dropped by the GMU Library, a book titled "The Anointing," written by Benny Hinn, caught my eyes, and I started to read. When he went to Evangelist Kathryn Kuhlman's Healing Revival Service, he experienced the anointing of the Holy Spirit. She told Benny that an anointing needs to cost, and her comment touched my heart. The cost meant that you must follow the voice of the Holy Spirit and you must be obedient to His direction in any circumstances.

> "Holy Spirit, your servant is here. I am ready to hear your voice and want to [be] obedient to you. I am praying without ceasing for the anointment of the Holy Spirit in the presence of God."

8/18/2005. I received a confirmation email from Yonsei University to give my chapel message at their chapel on September 26. I had given a chapel talk at the school two years ago, but this upcoming chapel message would be different. The presence of God and the work of the Holy Spirit would be manifested this time, because I have prayed fervently without ceasing for that every day. Maybe my God had been preparing me for the day's ministry, for I was praying that 1,000 students would experience the work of the Holy Spirit through my message. I am now seeing in Jesus Christ that the light of the gospel of the glory of Christ purges the blinded minds of unbelievers, so that it would bring them salvation, heal diseases and solve their problems.

"Lord, I desire only your will be done. Fulfill the dream you gave to me long time ago, that was in a huge auditorium. Was it at Yonsei auditorium? I saw your miracles happening over there. Oh Lord, only if it was your will - - -, fill me with your Spirit and anoint me. Work on the day, September 26."

Saving Message at Yonsei Chapel

8/23/2005. I decided to change the content of my message at Yonsei Chapel. I would deliver the message to 1,000 students, and probably half of them would be unbelievers, so I should proclaim the Gospel of Jesus Christ. If I meet them one by one, then it would be the same as evangelizing 500 people individually. Would not it be an effective way? So, I would like to change my message as if I was proclaiming an evangelical gospel message to an individual. The reason God gave us His power and anointing was to save lost souls! I believe it is most important for them, more than anything else, to hear a saving message. Although the Chapel office criticized me that the message, I delivered two years ago was too evangelical, I still would not lose this opportunity.

I would deliver a powerful message, witnessing the Lord Jesus Christ, such as "Jesus, heaven; no Jesus, then hell." When I proclaim the Gospel and witness Jesus Christ as my Savior, my God will abundantly pour His power and spirit upon me. I would only proclaim the gospel of Jesus, so I changed the content to be a strong saving message.

"Lord, I will pay the price, because you are all meant to me. I will be obedient and do whatever you want me to do, pray without ceasing and continue to praise the Lord. 'I will extol the Lord at all times; his praise will always be on my lips. (Ps 34:1).' I want to die and only life of Jesus and the power of God to be manifested on me."

Both my English Bible class and my GMU students promised to become my prayer partners for this Yonsei chapel ministry. They would pray for me every day from 10 to 11 p.m. until I leave L.A. and, once I left for Seoul, from 7 to 8 p.m.

"Lord, I want to see the glory of God. Make me strong and courageous. If you believe, you will see the glory of God (Jhn 11:40). I pray that this chapel becomes a miracle of God."

9/15/2005. I received an email yesterday from Yonsei Chaplain Dae Sung Lee who had informed me that 45% of their 1,000 students are Christians. Therefore, 55% or 550 students need to accept Jesus Christ as their personal Savior. I prayed that when those 550 students hear my message, God may open their hearts and make them eager to listen, so that all of them are able to receive Jesus Christ as their Savior.

"Therefore, I tell you, whatever you ask for in prayer, believe that you have received it, and it will be yours (Mk 11:24)"

9/24/2005. Onnuri Church sent a car to pick us up from the airport last night, so Dr. Miller, the Provost and I checked into the Tower Hotel. My room was very spacious with beautiful views, overlooking the green forest of Namsan to the left and the brilliant city lights to the right. I saw a huge flower basket on a table from

Pastor Damoi Park, one of the Biola board members who had been a great help for Biola in many ways in the United States and Korea.

9/25/2005. Dr. Miller preached at the College Student Service with my interpretation at Kwang Rim Church at 2:30 p.m. Upon finishing the service, we had a wonderful time together with Senior Pastor Jung Suk Kim, whom I had known from my previous visits. With support from the church, several of the church's associate pastors had attended Talbot for their further studies through our ELSP program. I appreciated his love for Biola. Pastor Kim always had a smile on his face, which probably brings comfort and encouragement to his congregations.

God's Chosen People Believed

9/26/2005. The Yonsei Chapel that I had minded so much was well finished in the presence of the Lord. I had been preparing the message for over a month, even memorizing the manuscripts in prayers. I dreamed that 550 students might stand up to accept Jesus Christ, but only several students raised their hands. Some of them might be unable to raise their hands due to lack of courage; however, the seed of the Gospel was sewn. I believed my job was done, and in His time the seed of the Gospel would be budded and grow up to bloom as flowers in the hearts of those God-chosen people.

> "When the Gentiles heard this, they were glad and honored the word of the Lord; and all who were appointed for eternal life believed." (Act 13:48)

Dr. Jae Yong Lee, Tom's nephew, asked me to excuse him leaving early for another appointment, so he sat down among the students at the auditorium instead of sitting at the faculty seats on the stage. While he was listening my message, he seemed to change his mind and stayed until the end and came back to me up on the stage. We went together to a restaurant we had been invited to by the president, Chang Young Jeoung.

Since he became the president, his manners seemed more stylish. I was grateful to him that he had been always a warm-hearted and trustworthy friend to me. During our conversation he said, "I only rely on the Lord and entrust everything in him," a comment that delighted my heart, as I felt his faith in God.

9/27/2005. After having an MOU ceremony for a Sister Relationship with Shin Hung College, a very fancy luncheon was prepared by the students of the culinary department. The food was extraordinary both visually and for its taste. I was very glad to again see Pastor Shin Kyung Kang, the school's Chairman of the Board of Directors, and his brother, Elder Soon Kun Kang, Tom's good and old friend, for they had graduated from the same high school the same year, as well as the same university. We had a wonderful, beautiful time together.

9/29/2005. We visited and preached at Chun Ahn Galilee Church yesterday evening. I was so delighted to see Pastor Chang Hoon Lee again, as well as the beautiful church members who had visited Biola sometime ago.

Professor Hee Chun Lee from Kim Chun College came to Galilee Church, and after the evening service he drove us to Daejun where we checked into the Yoo Sung Hotel. We will cover many schedules tomorrow, including setting up an MOU between our two schools and giving a chapel message.

God's Tests

Shimei Strategy

10/17/2005. I participated in the PCIGA meeting with Tom held in Washington, D. C. It was at an official PCIGA meeting when one of the meeting's high officials announced the results of the day's Pastoral Ordination Exam. While he was speaking, he mentioned my name and said that sometimes ago, he flunked me out of the pastoral ordination exam because I had not studied the church constitution. Because of that, I had been ignoring him and did not even say hello to him.

I was so surprised to be hear my name unexpectedly in an official meeting, and I felt very insulted by his comment. I do not know him well personally and could not find any reason to greet him; besides, I am not a very social person. However, yesterday evening when he arrived a little before dinner time and my table happened to be near the door, I walked over to greet him.

I went to bed with a heavy heart but had a good night's sleep, and upon waking up I began to pray. Strangely, I had no bad feelings or grudge toward him at all. While I was praying, the Lord told me that "You are going to a tour today, so in the bus tell them you love them." So, upon taking the bus, I requested that the guide pastor give me some time to talk to the people on the bus.

I took the microphone in the moving bus; first, I introduced myself and told them that I love them all. Since my personality is not very outgoing, I usually do not run around greetings and hugging people, so sometimes people might misunderstand me. I told them that please do not misunderstand me, and I truly love them all in Jesus Christ. Even though I do not greet you or hug you whenever I see you, I still love you. I finished talking as we arrived at a stopping place, and I hugged him who sat on a front seat.

> "Lord, forgive me. Lord said that if anyone causes ones who believe in him to sin, it would be better for him to have a large millstone hung around his neck and to be drowned in the depths of the sea (Mt 18:6). Lord, forgive me and help me. Help me that I would not be a stumbling block to anyone. No matter what in the world, no one ever would be stumbled because of me. Make him not to be bothered because of me and rather ignore me."

When I was unfairly treated or criticized on false grounds but overcame it well, then my God remembered it and rewarded me.

> "You prepare a table before me in the presence of my enemies. You anoint my head with oil; my cup over-flows." (Ps 23:5)

I call this the "Shimei Strategy." When King David left Jerusalem fleeing from his son, Absalom, the Benjamite Shimei came out and cursed the king, throwing stones and showering him with dirt. The angry king's general Abishai suggested killing him, but the king did not allow him to kill Shimei.

"Leave him alone; let him curse, for the Lord has told him to. It may be that the Lord will look upon my misery and restore to me his covenant blessing instead of his curse today." (2Sam 16:11b-12)

I like this "Shemei Strategy." Whenever I was tempted, I always wanted to make the situation turn into an opportunity for a blessing. I was praying to God that help me to deal with the Lord only and not to be influenced by any circumstances; then the problems were usually solved themselves. I praised my God that I overcame the temptation this time.

Test on Materials

1/21/2006. Kris and Mina dropped by my house yesterday around 4 p.m., for they had an appointment with their friends near my house. While they were away from their home, robbers broke into their home. They took the safe box from the house in which they had Kris' revolver, a cocktail diamond ring that I gave Mina as a wedding gift, two diamond earrings, a diamond necklace given by her mother-in-law and a platinum necklace from her grandfather-in-law that was too heavy to wear, and other jewels.

The cocktail ring I gave to her was one I bought in Hong Kong 30 years ago. It was a good quality, one caret marquee diamond in the middle with 12 small diamonds around it. When Bethel Korean Church started to build their church building, I donated all my jewels to the church, several rings and necklaces, including this diamond ring. Later one of the church elders tried to sell the ring in Korea, but he was unable to sell it, so I bought the ring back by paying $3,000 to church. Since then I had not worn it, so I gave it to Mina as a wedding gift. Her body was swollen because of her due date for her baby, and she was unable to wear even her wedding ring. The beautiful diamond wedding ring was also stolen, so she might be very sad, but she was rather concerned about me.

> "Mom, I am sorry. We lost the ring you gave to me too. I'm worrying that you may be sad."

> "Then, are you okay?"

> "Of course, I was so shocked and sorry first that I cried. Still Kris and I are okay. Anyway, all the things were belonged to the Lord. We are fine without such things, and just grateful that no one gets hurt. We are concerning more about the stolen revolver that we hope to find soon."

How much she has matured! It would be very hard for most young girls of 29 to bear such a situation. I was grateful to the Lord.

Mina told me last November that she was very much impressed by reading Randy Alcorn's book, "Treasure Principle," and wanted to give the book to daddy as a Christmas gift. The book was about the material things we own and how we should handle them.

> "We are stewards to take care of God's property. My estates would be moved from this earth to the heaven by spending it for poor people and God's work on earth. We should save our things in heaven. It wouldn't be even proper that we leave it for the children."

This incident seemed to me a test from God for them about material things, to give them more abundant blessings. The Lord might want to know that even in such conditions, they considered all things are God's and had an attitude of stewardship.

I believe they passed the test, because I did not hear any complaints or blame of others. We know God controls everything, so if he did not allow something, such things could not happen. When Job passed the test, God blessed him double fold. I believe that God will do the same for my children. I praised Him who causes all things to work together for good to those who love God and those who are called according to his purposes (Ro 8:28).

Opened Door in Taiwan

Taiwan Visit with Dr. Sunukjian

3/27/2006. I was planning to leave for Taiwan with Dr. Sunukjian three days later. I had been praying to the Lord to open a door to Taiwan for a long time, and at last the Lord answered my prayers.

I was able to visit Taipei with Dean Norman last May, as David Rath, an adjunct faculty member of our program, introduced me on the Overseas Radio and Television (ORTV) in Taiwan. Upon returning from the trip, I prepared another Taiwan visit through ORTV, and God allowed me to have a second visit.

Now, God has arranged another meeting for me with a group of Taiwanese people. I heard about Phil Chen, a Taiwanese man who participated in the Tres Dias (TD), a spiritual training program given by GKC some time ago. His mother, Margaret Wang, was an outstanding woman doing business along with mission work. A Christian foundation operated by Margaret and her sister took care of many important ministries in Taiwan and had wonderful connections with many local pastors.

When I heard about Phil and his mother, Margaret came to L.A. along with 30 Chinese pastors from Taiwan to attend GKC TD, so I invited them all to Biola. I arranged a time to introduce them to Biola University, treated them to lunch and invited both Dr. Cook and Dr. Norman to welcome them. I also told them that I would like to see all of them again in Taipei next week.

3/31/2006. When we arrived at the Taipei Airport, a limousine sent by ORTV picked us up and helped us to be checked into the Grand Hotel. Cyndi, the secretary of ORTV's CEO, and her friend Susie came to the hotel in the evening and took us to a very fancy restaurant that had beautiful scenery under Yang Mien Mountain. We ate delicious dishes and enjoyed the meal while appreciating the beauty of the green valley spreading down under thousands of brilliant lights.

Chiang Kai-shek Memorial Hall and 101 Building

4/6/2006. Dr. Sunukjian's seminar, "Biblical Preaching," was well received. Our ELSP introduction materials were distributed to the 150 pastors were participated in it.

I met Mrs. Wang's family at Taipei International Church last Sunday. Phil and his friend Shun picked me up, and we went together to see the Chiang Kai-shek Memorial Hall yesterday. The size of Chiang's statue in the hall and the scale of the memorial building seemed to tell a lot about the Chinese people's taste. I imagined that it would be something like the Lincoln Memorial, but I was so surprised by its size and grandeur, apart from their artistic beauty.

We ate lunch at Din Tai Fung and went to see the 101 building, the highest building in the world. We went up to the building's 91st floor, and it was tremendous that 666 tons of weighted iron hung down from the 2nd floor to protect the building from earthquakes.

Visit to a Possible Prayer Center

4/8/2006. Margaret visited me at my hotel and wanted to discuss about a possible place for TD here in Taipei that she had found that she would like to purchase if the facility seems proper for the TD purpose. The requested price was 4 million dollars, which she was able to pay. The Lord was truly amazing, He was planning another great work in this land by connecting her foundation with GKC. I praised the Lord!

Margaret also promised me that she will help promote our ELSP program in Taiwan. They will first translate our brochures into Taiwanese characters and print out 30,000 sheets to send out to 3,000 churches all over in Taiwan. They will also put full page advertisements about my program in Christian newspapers and magazines in Taiwan.

We decided to see the TD place that she had mentioned. Since it was the season for paying a visit to the ancestors' graves, the traffic was awful. It took us several hours to arrive at the place, which was only an hour away. They said that the place used to be a well-known hotel, but it was presently out of business. The huge rocks in a lake in front of the main building were mysteriously beautiful. Behind the building, many bungalows were lined up according to the mountain ridges; these were able to occupy around 150 people all together. We checked inside the bungalows and looked around the kitchen area, which seemed spacious and good enough.

She kept asking my opinion. Even if it would not be proper for a TD place, she wanted to have a place where pastors and missionaries could come and rest to be refreshed. In her opinion, the price of 4 million dollars seemed reasonable, but it was not easy to decide. We sat down on a bench at the lakeshore and prayed fervently, holding each other's hands, asking to the Lord for His guidance. We had a beautiful time together, chatting about each other's testimonies on the way there and going to see the possible prayer center.

Don and I ate dinner with the ORTV people in the evening, enjoying the night scenes while eating ice cream. On the way back to the hotel, we passed by a huge, bright shrine for Guan Yu, where many people were crowded. I entered the shrine to see what was going on inside, but I went right back out because of the unbearable smell of burning incense. So many people were crowded in several long lines begging for their wishes by offering foods and fruits. That was such a disgusting scene to me, so I prayed that those poor people could meet Jesus Christ soon and get into the way of truth and be saved.

Continued Lectures in the Mission Fields

Argentina Lecture

6/10/2006. I saw my luggage all crushed on the carrousel at Buenos Aires Airport. One side of the bag was completely torn out, and it seemed a miracle that all the contents of the bag remained inside. When I went outside after reporting the bag's condition to the office of American Airlines, Missionary Tae Won Kim and his wife were waiting for me.

My lecture started with an opening worship service at 2:00 p.m., then three sessions on Monday and five sessions for continuing days with each session running for 80 minutes. I did not feel good, as I had caught a cold on Wednesday evening, but I was able to manage to continue teaching five sessions on Thursday.

We went out to see the downtown and had lunch at a Korean restaurant on Friday. The World Cup Game was showing on a giant TV at the mall when Argentina beat Serbia 6 to 0. People were screaming and jumping up and down in their excitement, and confetti was flying everywhere. All the shops and schools were closed until the game was over; it seemed as if the World Cup shakes the whole world as a true world festival. I felt the excitement on my skin.

On the way home, I again experienced God's mercy on me. My reserved seat number was 24C on the aisle side, but as I was boarding, they told me that my seat was changed to 15A on the window side. I usually do not like a window seat, but by then, I had no choice but to take 15A. Today the plane was crowded and fully packed, but strangely the only two seats next to mine were empty. I realized the Lord's angel changed my seat to let me rest for my tired body due to the cold. I praised my God again who always keeps me and protects me.

My God was always traveling with me and took care of me for both important issues and trivial things, so I was not having any troubles. For the broken luggage, American Airlines sent a new Samsonite bag to the seminary on Thursday. Around 130 local pastors, including 40 from Chile, took my class, and through them I would see thousands of souls to be saved in the future. I praised the name of my Lord!

Africa Lecture

7/13/2006. I had to transfer my flight to Brussels at New York Airport. My flight from LA arrived on time in New York, but the Brussels-bound flight was over 4 hours late, so the plane from Brussels to Nairobi had already left. I was so frustrated, because Pastor Won Kun Park planned to drive 10 hours to Nairobi from Malindi to pick me up.

It was not only my problem, most of the passengers also lost their flights, so we all had to get new tickets. The airline workers were ticketing one by one for almost 200 passengers all day long from the morning, so the scene there was one of utter confusion, as people were fighting to get their tickets first. At last a new plane was prepared to leave for Brussels in the evening, but I still could not get a new ticket. Strangely, I was the last passenger, and then eventually an Airline officer came to me and let me board on the plane without a ticket. He told me that he would call Brussels about my situation, so that upon arriving at the airport, they will know how to help me.

When we arrived at the Brussels Airport, everybody's boarding passes were ready except mine. Again, I had to wait until they took care of all other passengers first, then they made new tickets and boarding passes for me. This time I had to use British Airlines to Nairobi via London. The plane was planning to leave for London next day at 5:30 p.m., so until that time, they let me stay at the Sheraton Hotel across the Airport. I called Pastor Park first and explained the situation.

I checked into the hotel and laid my tired body in a clean and comfortable bed and took a good nap. I walked out of the hotel around 3:00 p.m. and went to downstairs in the airport building, from which I took a train going to the Central Station.

I walked slowly from the station toward the Plaza Grande, which was surrounded by beautifully splendid 17th century buildings. Many small cafes and flower markets were lined up on both sides of the narrow streets and running down toward the Grand Place, where people were enjoying mild sunlight and snacks at outdoor tables. A gay marriage for two men was going on at the Grande Square, which was surrounded by magnificent medieval architectures. I felt very filthy, so I just returned to the hotel.

A Trip that Took Four Days

7/16/2006. Even though I left home last Thursday morning, I just arrived in Nairobi today on Sunday morning. As I walked out of the Nairobi Airport, Yoon Sook, Pastor Park's wife, was there waiting for me. We left for Malindi by a school van, and we saw many acacia trees that had beautiful shapes on the way, but because of their big thorns, they were unable to be used even for fire wood.

The car soon started shaking up and down because of the poor road condition with holes both small and large on the unpaved roads. Many huts made of woven palm fronds appeared, as well as some houses roofed with tinplate sheets for those who live well. As we drove for several more hours, we were driving into green fields. We often saw monkeys on the street, and one time we saw a huge one, along with a herd of them. They came up to the street near us looking for something to eat and seemed hungry, so we threw our peanuts to them. Sometimes we saw a herd of cattle appeared on the street, and they were so skinny that their ribs showed through their skins, and their backbones were like a camel's hump. It was a rainy season, so all the grasses and trees were green, but from November to January, all the plants were dried up, and animals fell on the streets due to water shortages.

It was a pitch-dark night when we arrived at Malindi via Mombasa after a 10-hour trip. They said the road we drove on was the national main highway, but there were no street signs or lights on it, so I wondered how they could drive without seeing street center lines or exit signs.

The whole area became pitch black without electricity after sunset, but fortunately the seminary had electricity. For it was winter and the rainy season, so it was the best weather now, but it was still very warm and humid. Even with fans and all the windows open, my clothes were soaked with sweat after lectures.

7/18/2006. I had to sleep inside a mosquito net and took malaria pills, but it was a great reward and an awesome feeling to walk on Malindi Beach, walking in the warm waters. Many fancy hotels were lined up along the beach, whose customers were mainly vacationers from Italy and Europe. Thousands of palm trees were also lined up on the beach around the hotels, their round fruit clusters hanging high up. We ate lunch at an Italian restaurant looking over the ocean.

100 Local Pastoral Students

7/19/2006. All of the pastoral students were from local churches, and most had no seminary training, so this kind of continuing education would be a golden opportunity for them. They were anxious to learn, and to see such students made me feel it was worthwhile to come such a long distance. I praised my God again for giving me such a privilege and wonderful opportunity and good health.

Even I did not feel good at home, but strangely once I boarded a plane, all went well and it was easy to nap and rest. This time, it was also great, even with the long trip that was 72 hours of flight and 10 hours of driving on unpaved, rough roads. I feel God's special grace and his anointing for my teaching ministry in the mission fields. I again promised the Lord that I would be obedient to Him, going anywhere He sends me to be used to teach His servants.

Steve, my interpreter for Swahili, did an excellent job, even though he only had a high school education. They said that those educated people in Africa understand English well, but the less educated prefer Swahili, the most spoken language in Africa. This language sounded to me very gentle and beautiful like a melody of their music.

7/23/2006. We continued praising and worshiping the Lord for almost two hours. They sang the praise songs while moving their bodies and dancing according to African rhythm and beats. I was already very exhausted and sweated a lot as I started my sermon; even so, I was able to give a good message in the power of the Holy Spirit. Praise the Lord!

Silver Malindi Beach

7/29/2006. Usually I missed home in the second week on a mission field, but the two weeks here went very fast. Yoon took care of me so well that I often felt I was on a vacation. In addition, it was a bonus from the Lord that I enjoyed walking on silver sands on the Malindi Beach in a mild ocean breeze overlooking the lined-up palm trees. I also would not forget the pastoral students who wanted to learn so much and their passionate praise and worship services. I experienced a really precious and wonderful group of servants of God at the seminary. I eventually returned home on another long flight.

Meeting President Young Sam Kim

10/11/2006. I visited Korea again with Dr. Cook and his wife. Pastor Billy Kim (Chairman of the Broad of Far East Broadcasting) helped us to set up our schedules in Korea, which turned out to be excellent. He invited us for dinner at his home, and he arranged a time for dinner with the previous Korea President, Young Sam

Kim on Thursday the 19th. We were led to a Korean barbeque restaurant, Bamboo House, where the President dines often. We saw some security officers around the building who seemed to guard the President. We ate a very delicious bulgogi barbeque there. The President looked healthy and young for his age and ate better than any of us. I prayed that although he is retired, as a Christian, he would continually have a positive Christian influence on the country.

Taiwan Visit with President Cook

1/4/2007. It was 11:30 p.m. when I arrived at Taipei Airport with Dr. and Mrs. Cook. As we checked into the Grand Hotel, my room number was 520, which was not the room I had reserved in L.A. Through a window in the room, I was able to see the hotel entrance under brilliant lights on the midway and shining on a river on the left side, and a highway with endless lines of bright red lights. It was a wonderful room with a great view. Thanks to Margaret paying extra money, she made the room change for me, so that I could stay next to Dr. Cook's room.

1/7/2007. I liked the fresh and neat breakfast buffet at the hotel. Yesterday evening, Dr. Cook gave a message for the worship service at Bread of Life Church in Shilin, which Margaret attended, where around 800 young people were gathered. Her translation was powerful.

Margaret and Phil returned again this morning and drove us to the Bread of Life Church, where we had another three services, and 1,000 members were gathered for each service. I heard that this church has 100 branches all over the world. Each service was filled with the Holy Spirit, and it seemed all the people were blessed. The continuing three services seemed a bit too much for Dr. Cook, but his messages were great with Phil's interpretation.

Phil took us to a night market after dinner, which looked like the South Gate Market in Seoul. So many things to see and to eat, but we just watched them all for fun. When we went into an alley selling chou tofu made from fermented tofu, the smells were unbearable. Phil repeatedly said that the smell was disgusting, but its taste is unbelievably special and good.

1/12/2007. When we entered the ORTV Worship room, Dr. Doris Brougham was playing her trumpet, as she had before. She welcomed me with a big hug and gave me an opportunity to introduce myself to the congregation, who were all so beautiful in the fragrance of Jesus.

I went to the Friday Bible Study at ORTV in the evening, where 600 people were gathered together; in contrast, at the last April meeting when I visited there were only 350. Probably half of the 600 were unbelievers; however, I was hopeful, because at least they had put one foot in the Christian world. Jason in our group was an unbeliever, but it seemed he would meet the Lord soon, so I gave him a booklet, "the Four Spiritual Laws," that I carried all the time.

PART 4:

Glorious God, My God

Resist the Devil

1/25/2007. I saw a devil in between sleeping and waking, as I was lying on a recliner in my room, around 3:00 a.m. in the morning. The devil flew from top of the TV set in the room to the opposite wall; it looked like a very small ape but pulpy like a jellyfish, disgusting and gruesome in dark color. I was so frightened out of my senses, but I started speaking in tongues and also yelled out, "blood of Jesus, go away devil, go away in the name of Jesus, go away." I resisted the devil in the name of Jesus and sang praise songs about the blood of Jesus. Soon it disappeared, and I had never seen such a creature so clearly in my life.

Several years ago, when I had a chance to travel to Germany to trace Martin Luther's footsteps, I was able to look inside the room where Luther had seen a devil. I remember a drawing of a tiny ape on the ceiling of the room, on the spot where Luther saw a devil. What I had seen in my room was the same ape shape ape I saw in Luther's room.

The devil is a reality, looking for any chance and seeking whom he may devour, as a roaring lion (1Pet 5:8). The Bible tells us, "Resist the devil, and he will flee from you (James 4:7)." "And these signs will accompany those who believe: In my name they will drive out demons (Mk 16:17)." We must cast out devils in the name of Jesus.

Evil Spirits in Satan's Church

It was several years ago, when we still owned a shopping center in Bakersfield. We often liked to leave for Bakersfield on Friday afternoon to look after the shopping center and stayed at a good hotel near it to rest and then returned home the next day. Tom usually liked to dine out and enjoyed staying in a good hotel to swim and eat delicious food.

One day on the way to Bakersfield, we passed by a small art school that had a beautiful campus with a green field. No one was seen, and the green grasses and trees looked so fresh and peaceful that we wanted to stop there for a rest. We decided to park the car over there and planned to eat Kimbap I had prepared at home for the day's special lunch. We carried with us Mina's pet, Pipi, a bright yellow with blue and light green-colored canary. He was also excited and happy to be out, even inside of a cage, flying up and down, enjoying the fresh fragrance of green grasses.

While having lunch, we saw a funny peculiar-looking, round-shaped small barn that had a sharp point on its top in the field around 50 meters away from us. Out of curiosity, the three of us walked toward the barn after lunch. It had no door, only a big door-sized hole in the wall as an entrance. Tom suggested that we better not go inside, but I wanted to see what was in there. I slowly advanced inside the barn, looking around, and I saw here and there the traces of people who had made fires, and there were many burned candles on the shelves around the wall. I realized instantly the place was a Satanic Church worshipping Satan. Now, I could clearly feel the devils were attacking me, since my hairs were standing on the left side of my head with a numbing sensation, the same experience I had before when evil spirits attacked me. I was running fast out of the place and crying out, "Jesus! Jesus! Blood of Jesus!"

I knew that the devil was still in me because my head was still numb. I pretended nothing had happened and evaded the situation adroitly when Mina asked me what was inside the place. We checked into the hotel where we used to go and hung Pipi's cage on the balcony. I suggested to Mina and Tom that they go to the pool and start swimming, and that I would join them soon. I became continually upsetting and excited in numbing head. I locked the door and started speaking in tongues, the evil spirits straight on, constantly crying out to the blood of Jesus, the blood of the Lamb. "In the mighty name of Jesus and the power of the Cross," I ordered the demons, "I am binding you in the name of Jesus, go away from me. Go away." As I shouted and struggled for almost one hour, the numbness in my head disappeared, and peace came into my heart. I realized that the evil spirits had left me, and I was lying on the bed, exhausted.

Soon Tom and Mina returned from the pool, and they asked me why I had not joined them. I told them that I was tired and had rested, and acted as if nothing had happened. I was grateful to the Lord that He prevented Tom and Mina from coming inside the place.

Soon after that, Mina, who was looking inside of the bird cage, was screaming out of horror and shock,

"Mom and Dad, Pipi. . . Pipi."

"Why, what's the matter with Pipi??"

"Pipi is dead!"

My heart was pounding. It reminded me of the event in the Bible when the demons got into a herd of many swine, then all of them were killed (Mt 8:31-32). It must be that the evil spirit that was in me had gone into poor Pipi. It was truly an extra ordinary experience!

Korea Visit with Biola Faculty

10/12/2007. I visited Korea along with Dr. Li-Shan Hung, the Chair of Piano Department at Biola, and Dr. Kangwon Kim, a violin professor. We visited Seoul Women's University (SWU), and two professors gave performances for their three chapel services, and I gave them messages.

Since we arrived in Seoul, we had stayed at the guest house of Youngrak Presbyterian Church, but today, the two professors moved to Kangwon's parents' house. Dr. and Mrs. Cook arrived in Seoul to be at his retirement reception arranged by Dr. John Oh, the Senior Pastor of Sarang Church in Seoul, so I moved into the Ritz Carton with Dr. and Mrs. Cook.

The two professors performed to celebrate Biola's centennial at Sejong Chamber Hall on the 16th. It was sponsored by the Provost's office, the Alumni Office, and the Conservatory of Music Dept. of Biola. Around 300 people came to the concert, and after the centennial concert, Dr. Cook's retirement reception was held at the hall.

Preaching at Yonsei University Church

I gave a message for the Sunday Service at Yonsei University Church today. Jae Sook, Tom's niece, came to my place to pick me up to go to the University Church early in the morning. The quiet Sunday morning Yonsei campus and green gardens with trees and well-arranged shrubs made me feel relaxed and happy in such a peaceful surrounding.

The Ruth Chapel was under renovation, so today's worship service was held at the Theology Hall, which was an emotionally touching service for me. Upon ending the service, people came and lined up to greet the Senior Pastor and today's guest speaker. Surprisingly, the first couple to come to us was Dr. Jung Hoon Choi, my beloved Yonsei professor from whom I had taken many classes. It was a real surprise that he came to me with his wife and greeted me with delight. How could I ever imagine that such an event would occur in my life?

Dr. Choi was one of the candidates for the Yonsei President election, and recently he had served as president of a university in Kangwon province. He received his degree from Stanford and returned to Yonsei. Several years ago, when I visited Korea, he took me to a Korean barbeque house at University Road in Seoul and ordered five serving of Kalbi for the two of us. The Senior Pastor Han boasted about him that he was serving the president of the church's Men's Group.

The University Church members were mainly Yonsei faculty and their family members. All church members went together for lunch to a buffet restaurant in a nearby hotel to treat me, the guest speaker.

I met many good people, and usually the church pays, but Jae Yong, who came with his wife, paid for everybody's lunch, which must be expensive for a hotel buffet. Jae Yong is also Tom's nephew, Jae Sook's younger brother who was the professor of Yonsei School of Engineering as well as the Director of Admissions of the University (later he became the 1st Vice President of Yonsei). They are Tom's oldest brother's children, and his brother was a professor of Kaist in Korea.

Lecture at GMI Missionary Training Center

10/17/2007. We had lunch with Pastor Chul Shin Lee and his wife of Youngrak Presbyterian Church at Chee Hong at the Chinese restaurant at Hotel Liz Carton yesterday, and we had a great time. Dr. and Mrs. Cook left Korea today, and I moved to GMI Missionary Training Center at Yangju city, where I taught Christian Education to missionary trainers for three days.

President Cook Returned to the Lord

4/2008. Dr. Cook returned to the Lord on the afternoon of the 11th of this month. It was an unexpected and sudden happening to all of us. He had given a message at a college in Texas on Thursday evening and returned home on Friday morning, and that afternoon, he returned to the eternal home to be with the Father. They had known since last Christmas time that his heart condition was not good at all, so the family members were somewhat prepared for his passing.

A Memorial Service was held at Fullerton EV Free Church on Saturday, the 19th. It was a huge assembly: the main sanctuary, which holds 5000 occupancies was packed, and the Chapel and other church halls were also crowded with callers for condolence. I served as an usher on that day. He had arranged for his own memorial service in advance himself.

The memorial service was very touching. I saw him as a giant of a man and felt proud of him and grateful that I had known and had a close fellowship with such a man. I visited Korea with him eight times and went with him on other, numerous international trips.

The last program of the service was his video presentation in which he spoke to us as though from heaven about what he was seeing over there. His message was powerful, touching and emotional in grace of God. He was telling us the view of heaven which is full of glory in brightness and shining golden jewels and flowers everywhere, and all kinds of inexpressible beauty. He ardently appealed to us to proclaim the Gospel to those unbelievers. His sudden absence was such a shock and so hard to overcome for many students, faculty and staff, that the school had to set up a consolation room to comfort them. He left for home to be with the Lord, loved by so many people who had been influenced by him. He will be remembered by all for a long time as Biola's forever president, mentor and teacher.

Lectures in Chile and Argentina

At Chile

7/25/2008. I left by Lan Airlines to teach at Santiago, Chile, and Buenos Aires, Argentina. The plane stopped in Lima, Peru, for around one hour, then left for Santiago. Missionary Hyo Seoung Kwak and his wife gave me a cheerful welcome at the airport around 5:30 a.m. I was checked into Hotel Kernel, owned by a Korean, which was clean and good, including breakfast.

We had a beautiful spirit-filled worship service at church on Sunday morning, pastured by Pastor Guillermo, one of the participants of the seminar. We left for La Aurora Retreat Center in the afternoon, where the classes will be held, but it is located at a remote place, so we arrived late, in the dark. The place was freezing cold because of cold winds smearing into the rooms through the brick walls. It was almost midnight when the car carrying electric blankets and portable heaters arrived at the center. My lectures were on schedule according to the plan, a total of six hours of lectures per day; even with an interpreter, it wasn't easy.

7/29/2008. After I finished the three hours morning class, I was led to a beach with Missionary Eun Hee and her parents. The beach had clusters of black rocks here and there, but it was calm and beautiful under gentle sun lights in a mild weather. Eun Hee's father was a very healthy and energetic man in his 70s who prepared a special breakfast for us this morning with fish, abalones and sea urchins he had bought at a local market last night.

Pastureland Owned by Mr. Jorge

7/31/2008. All the students left for their home church for Sunday services after finishing one session this morning. They will be back on Sunday night, for all of them are presently working for the church. With Pastor Kwak's family, I left for a pastureland owned by Mr. Jorge, one of Pastor Guillermo's uncles, for the weekend. We arrived at his house in the rain, which was very huge inside with many guest rooms. He was raising around 600 animals, including sheep, llamas, goats, chicken and turkeys, and they said 200 new lambs were born over the last three months.

8/2/2008. It was still raining on Saturday morning, but we decided to go out to see the animals after breakfast. A herd of sheep and llamas were grazing here and there, and lambs were skipping about in the rainy field. When they saw Mr. Jorge's truck approaching, they were running toward the car, and they seemed very happy and excited as Mr. Jorge called them with a loud voice in a peculiar tone, "wha cha!" We walked under umbrellas enjoying nature on the endless pasture field.

To Buenos Aires

8/3/2008. We had a wonderful Sunday Service at Guillermo's church, and we went to a restaurant to eat asado (a meat dish); after that, they dropped me at the airport. I arrived at Buenos Aires Airport around 10 p.m., where I met Pastor Seung Kun Han, his wife and Jihe, their daughter. It was so great that GMI owned their own building for the seminary in Buenos Aires, but the number of students was not as many for this time than I expected.

I heard the interpreter had a sudden problem and was unable to make it, but the gracious Lord sent another interpreter, Pastor Ed Kim, whom I had met during my first Argentina teaching trip. He was an outstanding translator, and God prepared him for me this time. However, because of his schedule, we had to reduce the total teaching hour to four and a half hours per day instead of six. That became a great relief for me, since I was very tired and in a bad condition due to the Chile teaching. Probably the Lord knew already the six hours would be too much for me, so he reduced the hours for me. I had nothing but praise to my God.

The Lord's Time

9/2/2008. In reading up to seven books out of the 15 books of "Romans Story" written by Nanami Shiono, my heart was filled with just one fact: that human beings are such weak and helpless creatures. No matter how glorious and superb man could be, even like Julius Caesar, he had no choice but to die from a knife. Man's glory is like a flower or weed and a leaf of grass which will be withered in the evening, and even a vapor that appears for a little time and then vanishes away (Jm 4:14). No matter how much you boast about your greatness and outstanding, you are nothing but an ordinary helpless man.

Throughout world history, both east and west, people are anxious to be successful and famous in a short period of time. Consequently, some have experienced untimely death or ruined themselves. True wisdom is to wait for the time of the Lord according to His will, in patience without rushing, for only His will will be done.

When I am ready and waiting, God will let me know in His time, as I am speaking with someone, reading the Bible, or even shopping in a market. I receive the Lord's answers when it is His time for me.

Korea Visit with President Barry Corey

10/14/2008. I had my first trip with Dr. Corey, the new Biola President, to Korea, and it was also his first Korea visit. When we checked into the Hilton Hotel, Nam San, we found fruit baskets in our rooms from Pastor Billy Kim.

Dr. Corey gave a Leadership Seminar for students at Torch Trinity University in the morning, and appeared at the Biola Gathering for alumni and friends at the Renaissance Hotel in the evening. All the arrangements for the Biola night were prepared this time by Sarang Church, so I was greatly appreciative of the church and Senior Pastor Oh.

10/19/2008. We made another MOU with Calvin University (President Ja Yeon Kil) yesterday. President Corey gave a message with my interpretation for their chapel after the ceremony. We had a Biola Presentation Night at the Torch Mission Center of Onnri Church at 7 p.m., so it was a very busy day.

After Dr. Corey gave a message with my translation at Wang Sung Church this morning, then, Calvin gave Dr. Corey a ride to the airport, and took me to the Torch Center, where I was planning to stay five days more.

The room space was small, but I could have my three meals in a downstairs restaurant if I wanted to. My room was on the fourth floor, and the Sanctuary was on the first floor and open from early in the morning, so I would go and pray. A book store was nearby, and there was a track leading to a mountain starting from behind the building. I would enjoy all of these: eating, walking, praying, resting, napping, and reading, so I liked staying here.

10/23/2008. I gave a message about prayer at a Wednesday worship service at Wang Sung Church yesterday morning. The sanctuary was small, but it was completely packed with people both upstairs and downstairs.

I visited An Yang University this morning, which reminded me of visiting with Dr. Cook a couple years ago. At that time, Dr. Young Shil Kim was the school's president and father of the current president. Upon arriving there, they treated me with a fancy lunch. I gave two chapel messages at 1:30 p.m. and 3 p.m.

10/26/2008. A car came from Calvin Church this morning and picked me up to the university campus. Calvin Church was a university church, where I gave a message; after that, I moved to Sung Do Church to give another message in the afternoon.

Loves from Pastors

Pastor Yong Jo Ha, Senior Pastor of Onnuri Church

Whenever I went to Korea with Biola people, we had always received tremendous help from Onnuri Church pastored by Yong Jo Ha. They helped us, in most cases, for all our necessities starting from the airport pickups. They always perfectly prepared for Biola presentation meetings with a praise team, a program sheet, a buffet style dinner, handouts, and even Biola brochures. I am always deeply appreciative to Pastor Ha and Onnuri Church. Pastor Ha had kept a special relationship with Biola by supporting some of Biola's library funds. He had also received an Honorary Doctor's Degree from Biola for his Durano Ministry.

Love of Pastor Ja Yeon Kil

I visited Wang Sung Church many times during my Korea trips. Ja Yeon Kil, Senior Pastor of the church, had been a great friend to Biola, and was one of the most respected Christian leaders in Korea. He had always positively supported my ministry with a warm and gentle spirit. After worship services, we always ate a delicious lunch prepared for us at the church. I want to give once more thanks to Pastor Kil for his love and generous support.

Love of Pastor Billy Kim

Upon finishing the two o'clock service at Onnuri, we left for Soo Won City in car that Pastor Billy Kim, the Chairman of the Board of the Far East Broadcasting, sent for us. We planned to have dinner with Pastor Kim's family at his house, and we were scheduled after that meal to go to Soo Won Baptist Church where Dr. Corey will give a message. I had known Pastor Kim through Dr. Cook, because I was invited for dinner at his house along with Dr. Cook some time ago, but Dr. Corey met Pastor Kim for the first time today. It was the same with Pastor Joseph Kim, Billy Kim's son, but they had a delightful time as if they had been good friends for a long time.

When I looked around the living room, I saw an unfamiliar small picture on a wall in which Billy Kim was cutting his birthday cake. Besides him, the picture showed his wife, Korean President Myung Park Lee and his wife, and Pastor David Cho and his wife. He proudly told me that the cake was backed by the First lady, and he had a close relationship with the president's family. I felt good that respected pastors have close relationships with the president of Korea, so that they may give him good advice and prayers. I gave thanks to the Lord for that.

The food was delicious, and we had a wonderful time in a warm atmosphere. Since Dr. Corey and Pastor Joseph were the same age, they seemed to be enjoying their conversation and understanding each other's sentiments well; they were especially excited that Aaron, Pastor Joseph's son, was planning to come to Biola next year.

For the evening service, Pastor Billy Kim led the service and interpreted Dr. Corey's message. Before the start of Dr. Corey's sermon, they presented beautiful bouquets to Dr. Corey and me. He also arranged a Biola presentation time for which he invited the congregation to come to a room next to the sanctuary after the service. He was quite a man of passion and strength by whom I was always challenged.

Lecture in Shanghai

11/28/2008. I left for Shanghai via Incheon by Korean Airlines. I felt some tension about this trip because it was my first trip to a communist country, especially to teach underground church workers. It would be simpler for me if I was be caught; I would be expelled from the country, but our students might suffer bitterly. I had requested prayers for this trip from my English Bible Class and GMU students and trusted in the Lord that this trip would be as safe and successful as other travels.

Upon arriving at Pudong Airport, I saw a giant wall along the way to the emigration entrance. This airport huge and magnificent was built recently, and Pastor Park (called Mr. Ha here) was waiting for me.

11/30/2008. It was Sunday, so we used the first session as the Sunday Service and continued for four sessions. I lectured for seven sessions every day: three sessions from 8:30 a.m. to noon, one session after lunch, and another two from 2:30 p.m. to 5:30 p.m. Two students came from the hill country of Western China, but they had received a phone call from their home upon arriving here. The police had gone to their home to inquire about their whereabouts, so they had to leave right way to return home, spending another 18 hours in travel. I had only seven students, but they were all ministers of the church who had graduated from a four-year China Seminary.

They came from all over China. The students who came the shortest distance spent two days by train, and some took four days by train. Pastor Park had taken care of these students with compassion from those days when they attended the China Seminary. He wanted them to be filled with the Holy Spirit and become faithful servants of the Lord. He spoke Chinese so well that he was translated my lectures.

12/2/2008. Pastor Park's apartment was our gathering place, and students were not allowed to go outside of the apartment during the two-week stay. The apartment had three rooms and a huge hall between the two rooms in upstairs, so no one could know what was going on inside of the apartment from the outside.

One afternoon, we suddenly heard a bell sound while lecturing. We immediately stopped our class and started to clean up the place, putting away a cross on the wall, and the Bibles, books and posters showing Christianity. The students quickly hid in a room and I was in another room, but fortunately, it turned out that a guard had come to deliver something to Pastor Park.

12/3/2008. Since the students were all involved in church ministries, they had to go back home before Sunday to lead their own church services. When they left the place, they had to leave one by one in 10- or 20-minute intervals.

Six students were Chinese, and one was a Korean Chinese, Mr. Chung, who came from Shenyang with his wife, who helped Pastor Park's wife while she prepared every day's meals for the two weeks. We ate Korean food every day, which was delicious, and the kimchi taste was the best.

After all the students left safely, Pastor Park gave me a Shanghai City tour. We went out to the public square by subway;

the subway station was huge and complicated, so we had to walk a lot where it was crowded with people and dusty. I saw so many new, high modern buildings under construction, next to extremely poor homes.

12/4/2008. I visited two cities, Suzhou and Zhouzhuang, with Pastor Park and his wife, and Mr. and Mrs. Chung. I had greatly anticipated Suzhou, because the city was known for its famous sightseeing spots, such as Hanshan Temple, Yu Garden and cruises on the ancient canal. The city had a profound cultural background and well-preserved, ancient residences. On the way to Zhouzhuang we saw many new towns with nice scenery, clean houses and new apartments under construction.

Zhouzhuang was a clean and beautiful ancient water village town. Roads went in the front of houses, and a canal was behind the houses where the ferry boats were running. One of the sightseeing courses was riding a ferry boat on the canal, but it was not much fun to watch the houses on the water. The water was just behind those homes, so when they open their back doors, they could fall right into the water. Some of the old back walls of the houses were covered with moss in a disgusting state. As we passed the water way, we saw a man sweeping his yard and throwing his trash into the water. Meanwhile on the opposite side, a lady appeared at her back door and washing her clothes with the water. Our guide told us that the government provided a campaign through TV to educate people during the Olympiad, but those programs were all gone after the Olympiad.

Jesus is the Life

8/1/2009. The best-known Korean poet was visiting here in the L.A. area, so his high school and college alumni had arranged special welcome meetings. A writing club in Garden Grove was planning to have a meeting to hear his lecture, so Tom and I decided to go to the meeting there. In fact, he was a friend of Tom's from both high school and college in Korea, and also, from a long time ago when we lived in L.A., he had visited our home and stayed with us several days.

He has become the most famous modern poet in Korea, and he was receiving tremendous love and respect from the public. How famous he is! We are all so proud of him.

However, I became sad when I was listening to his lecture, for he seemed to have not met the Lord yet. He mentioned that he would not be afraid of death, but he did not seem to overcome death. He was a very humanistic poet who was all about being human. He did not seem to know about the spiritual world, the grace of God, salvation by Jesus Christ or the power of the cross. He considered believing in Jesus Christ as just one of many religious activities.

I want to say to him that believing in Jesus Christ is not a religion but life. I love my life, so I believe in Jesus Christ who said, "I am the way, the truth and life."

If you die and see heaven and hell in front of you, but you did not believe in the blood of Jesus, you must go to hell, then what shall you do? The reason you do not know this fact right now is only because you have never been dead.

If you receive the Holy Spirit, the Spirit of God would let you know this secret, because the Holy Spirit is able to know God's deepest things (2Cor 2:10). I know about the existence of heaven and hell, because the Holy Spirit let me know about the secrets. Just as I know about myself by my own spirit, God's things are also comprehended by the Spirit of God that is the Holy Spirit. When we receive this Holy Spirit, He lets us know about God's secret, the secret of heaven (1Co 2:11-12).

When I believed in what I did not know, it became known to me by itself without my efforts. Because the Spirit of God came into me and let me know all the spiritual things, which are impossible to know with earthly wisdom. That knowledge is unable to be comprehended by any kind of worldly studies or academic degrees, so the Bible says,

> "For since in the wisdom of God the world through its wisdom did not know him, God was pleased through the foolishness of what was preached to save those who believe (1Co 1:21)"

God Causes All Things

Things Done According to His Will

9/23/2009. I am so happy remembering all of God's benefits (Ps 103:1-5) given to me. He forgave all my sins, healed all my diseases, redeemed my life from the pit, crowned me with love and compassion, and satisfied my desires with good things, so that my youth is renewed like the eagle's.

He has taken care of me throughout my life and truly worked diligently from the beginning to the end to make me what I am today. He forced me to study the English language, even though I hated to learn it; eventually he made me able to simultaneously translate Korean Worship Services into English for English-speaking audiences for 15 years. Without such training, I would probably be unable to handle the job for my position in an American university.

It also seemed possible that I was able to get my doctor's degree because of my husband's frequent outside activities. If he was always around me at home, then how would I have time to study? He spent so much time outside, that I had nothing to do but study.

I visited six countries last year, due to teaching in the mission fields and other tasks for Biola. No matter the reason I had to be away from home, in such a situation, if Tom had not allowed me to go out, I would not be able to go. If he did not like to meet friends outside and dine out with them, then how could I visit so many countries so often?

It was only possible that my dear God caused all things to work together for good to me (Rom 8:28), according to His plan and His will. Everything for me has been done in His grace, so I praise His name and give Him all the glory and honor. I will continue to pray with delight in Him that only His will be done in my life.

Second Korea Visit with Dr. Corey

10/14/2009. We had a very tight schedule for this trip and met myriads of influential people in Korea. Dr. Billy Kim helped us a lot, and President Corey seemed content with all the schedules.

Dr. Corey left for L.A. on Wednesday, the 21st, and I kept my luggage at the hotel and went to Moonja's house with a small pack for a two night/three-day trip. Fourteen of our college friends were gathered together the next day early in the morning, and we went down south to Ha Hoe Village in Andong, a historic traditional place.

Even though all of us had changed and grown old, we were delighted as if we were back in the old days. Everyone's faces were shining with smiles, and we had endless happy talks. I was also excited and happy to see those beautifully changed mountains and green fields with trees and woods. I loved the huge rice pads, vegetable fields, and many apple tree orchards in Andong that made me feel rich.

Our time was getting shorter daily, and I wondered if our friends are all preparing well for their eternity? Such a thought popped into my heart as I was watching the burning red autumn leaves all over the mountains. I returned to Moonja's home on Friday and spent one more day at her house.

A fruit package was delivered to me from Dr. Corey soon after the trip, and I found a pretty Thank You card praising my spirituality and compassion.

20th Moscow Teaching

2/13/2010. I flew on Aeroflot to Moscow for my twentieth visit to teach at MGBS. My lectures started on Monday morning for three hours, and another three hours after lunch; even with a translator, it was hard work. There were six hours on Tuesday, three hours on Wednesday, six hours on Thursday, and I returned to America on Saturday morning.

I had some free time on Wednesday afternoon, so I wanted to go out to see the Kremlin Palace once more, because I had come to Moscow every year but had not been out at that area for the last few years. I went out with Missionary Young Yu in a car driven by a Korean-Russian driver. The city was changed so much with new buildings, and it was cleaner, so that I felt as if I were in a different world, one like certain busy European cities. The streets became bright and brilliant with a thousand lights after sunset, but they were packed with so many cars that seemed they were not moving at all, just like a huge parking lot.

Our driver seemed frustrated and began to try to pass other cars on the way home, and then soon he was involved in a small collision with a car front of us. It was a very minor accident, but it seemed to be our driver's fault, because he had attempted to make a lane change to pass the car.

The other driver immediately called the police, and we had to wait until the situation was settled. I urgently needed to go to the bathroom, since I took my blood pressure medicine after dinner that dehydrated the water from my body. The street we had the accident on was a beautiful, huge road with six lanes on either side of the street and in between, there was another space for three or four cars to be able to park that was used by police cars. It was Kutusovsky, the famous street in Moscow. My situation was becoming urgent, and a police officer told us that a public toilet was located at the subway station across another street, and it seemed impossible to get there.

Then, I saw a very huge gate in the darkness around 50 meters away from us on the street. It was the 28-meter-high Arc of Triumph, a famous historical monument built to celebrate the victory in the Napoleonic War in 1812. Young Yu and I decided to go see if there were any place that could solve our problem near the gate. We saw stairways leading to the underground from the gate, but we were so urgent that we gave up going down to the basement and just looked for a corner place behind a snow pile.

How feeble a human being is! We have no way but to die if one of our lowest basic needs is not met, just as Maslow's hierarchy of needs indicates! How ironic a situation at the front of the famous Arc of Triumph, the human victory! It was an amazing experience at an amazing place on a Moscow night.

Korea Trip

3/31/2010. I was checked into a guest room at the Torch Mission Center for this trip. I was invited yesterday as a guest speaker for a teachers' seminar for students at the Teachers' College at Young

Rak Presbyterian Church, and today, for students of the Teachers' College at Yoido Full Gospel Church. My topic was "How to teach students to be changed?" Around 150 teacher candidates attended at Young Rak Church and 400 were gathered at Yoido Full Gospel Church. I was grateful to the Lord for giving me such opportunities and privileges.

When we teach the Bible to students, it's crucial that their lives be changed, besides learning the contents of God's Word. The key to a Bible study is to make the Word of God melt into the students' daily lives. How can they remember for a long time the Words of God they learned and live by acting upon them? It's a big challenge for Bible teachers and pastors, because the Lord said that in James 1:22, "But be doers of the word, and not hearers only, deceiving you."

I gave lectures on "Christian Education" at An Yang University on the 6th and at Seoul Women's University on the 8th.

Longing for the Lord

4/28/2010. These days, Tom has been suffering from his stuffy nose and dryness in his mouth, but doctors could not find anything wrong in his body through many kinds of tests. They said that it may be an allergic reaction but they do not know.

He has been looking for the Lord and longing for God for the last two years, since his body has been losing strength and weakening. Our church held special early prayer meetings at the beginning of this year, in which he participated without skipping a single day, even when I was unable to accompany him.

His pronunciation has become less clear, and it became hard for him to pray, but he was anxious to become nearer to God these days! I have been praying throughout my life so hard to see what I am seeing now. I give glory and honor to my gracious God who answers my prayers.

Diagnosed with Parkinson's and Dementia

1/28/2011. We have visited several neurologists since last November, and most of them thought that he might have Parkinson's and a vascular dementia, because of his walking patterns and his difficulty finding the right words as he communicates with people. He had been taking prescribed medicines for a while, but they gave him side effects of loose bowels and dizziness, so he has been continually changing medicines and seeing different doctors for second opinions. I also tried to get all kinds of brain foods and supplements for activating the brain and prayed fervently for his health, relying on His Words. I am now praying his brain is clear enough to understand the Gospel of the Lord well, so he can have a deep relationship with the Lord.

> "Therefore, I tell you, whatever you ask for in prayer, believe that you have received it, and it will be yours (Mk 11:24)"

> "Lord, heal him. We are only looking on you, because there are no other ways but you. Only by His stripes we are healed (1 Pet 2:24)."

His heart seems now all in to the Lord, and he attends the Early Prayer Meeting every day without missing a single day. Even though he has difficulty distinguishing between people and remembering names, along with losing his ability to talk, he was anxious to come nearer to God, which makes me cry.

Faith in Waiting

3/1/2011. How fast the time goes by! It is not an easy task going through the mighty breakers crashing over me. Even the great Apostle Paul was grieved for his weakness, but God responded to him as "My grace is sufficient for you, for my power is made perfect in weakness." So, Paul boasted gladly about his weaknesses, so that Christ's power may rest upon him (2Cor 12:9).

Every morning when I opened my eyes, I found myself praying, for my soul was so anxious to seek Him and longing for the Lord as a thirsty deer pants for water brooks. As I started crying out to the Lord, the words of promises smeared into my heart and brought peace in my soul, and I felt that all the problems are fading away.

I am praying every morning that Tom's memory ability will be damaged no more. I do not know when my dear Lord will answer this request, but I am sure that He will answer according to His will that causes all things to work together for our good. Therefore, if the Lord does not give me an answer immediately to what I want, I can still always rejoice, pray without ceasing and give Him thanks. I do not know what the best for us would be, but I know that my God will give us the best thing for us in His time. Is it not our faith? I should just wait for Him who has promised that "whatever you ask for in prayer, believe that you have received it, and it will be yours (Mk 11:24)" and "if you believe you will see the glory of God (Jn 11:40)."

Joshua, My Fourth Grandchild

6/9/2010. Mina delivered a baby at 7 a.m. this morning, and I was able to hold him in my arms around 10 a.m. Joshua was only 7 pounds, a small baby, but very cute and handsome. How could such a baby like him be inside of his mom's stomach? Truly amazing with tiny fingers and toes! "Thank you, Lord." My mouth automatically opened itself with praises and blessings.

> "Josh be strong and courageous! God will be with you and He will fight for you wherever you go. You will always live a victorious life in the name of Jesus."

When I entered the hospital room today, the newborn baby's eyes were fixed on the letters "BIOLA UNIVERSITY" printed on the red t-shirt I wear. At that moment I said to him without thinking, "Josh, you will love Biola and become a president of Biola someday." Now, I felt I had received a mission to pray for him throughout my life for this. A future president of Biola must be born today, since the Lord said that if you believe you will see the glory of God. Praise the Lord!

Time to Retire

5/24/2011. I believe a great leader is the one who helps his followers to fully fulfill their potentialities. The leader himself cannot do it all; rather, he helps the followers do it themselves by giving them strength and encouragements. Provost Sherwood Lingenfelter and Dean Ed Norman were such leaders, so under their leadership I was always happy, and I was able to do my best, because they always trusted in me and supported me. Dr. Norman often mentioned to me that the reason he was in his office was just to help me be successful at what I was doing. When he was the dean, our department flourished the most, developing new exciting programs and recruiting a great number of international students. Consequently, my department was able to contribute to the school by bringing in an awesome amount of extra funds. After Dr. Norman retired, a new dean came, and she started to cut off my wings. I was unable to fly freely, and the program began to go down.

Replacing her, the new Dean Pennoyer visited my office today, and he said that if my department continues in this state, probably it must be closed within two years. Enrollments had been tremendously reduced for recent semesters. I told him then that I will also retire in two years.

I could tell that the situation was under God's plan, because the U.S. Government no longer issues student visas for international students who want to enter our program. The ELSP program is a unique program for international students to study the English language along with their academic courses, according to their English proficiency level. However, from now on, the government will issue student visas only to those students who want to study the English language only, or who are otherwise fully prepared to study academic courses without ESL training. My God who called me and used me for the program for the generations according to His plans, now wants to close the program along with my retirement. I have nothing to say or complain about closing the program, because everything is in His hands.

Kiev Lectures

6/3/2011. When I arrived at Kiev airport, I was surprised to see Ira, who used to work at MGBC as a staff member from Sakhalin Island. I praised the Lord that God had made her a pastor during the years, and she became the translator for my lectures this time, and it was great that the school had its own building.

As I opened my eyes in the morning, the beautiful early summer scenery came into my view through the windows. The gentle breeze under a clear blue sky with mild sunlight was blowing on the endless green fields, and roosters were crowing leisurely. I heard, far away, some noises by children who were playing ball games on a playground.

6/6/2011. I gave a message at their Sunday worship service yesterday, and rested in the afternoon. The congregations were composed of our students and neighbors in the village in a quiet and remote countryside. I went out to see their vegetable garden in the afternoon, where the students cultivated lettuce, potatoes and other greens. The students were taking turns watering and taking care of the garden, so they would save on some food costs. Pastor Kim and his wife are also directing a middle and high school in the city of Kiev, besides this Bible college. They are planning to start an elementary school this September, too, in a building given by the government.

I did not feel any tiredness, by His grace, and I was able to give four 90-minute lectures today. Before I left L.A, I had pains in the back of my neck and shoulders, but now all the pains were gone. I was praising the Lord for His glory and honor.

Filled with the Holy Spirit

6/8/2011. It was a hard day, but I was happy today. All day long, I gave four lecture sessions of 90 minutes each and gave a message at the Wednesday night service. Upon finishing the service, I continued to pray for around 40 people, one by one, laying my hands on them. Starting with several of them, I began to feel some person's hearts and their burdens which were delivering into me, and I could not stop crying from inside of me for those people. Pastor Ira held a tissue box and kept pulling out tissues to give to me. I was supposed to be very exhausted because of crying in prayers for more than hours, but I was not tired at all. Rather, strangely, I felt a sort of smearing, quiet joy and strength flowing from inside of me. Again, I praised the Lord for His glory and honor.

Pastor Kim arranged today's schedule for me so I could rest all day long, because yesterday was a heavy day for me. I rested in my room in the morning, and after lunch I went out with Sergei, a student who was able to speak English, to walk along a mountain road leading into a pine wood. It took around one hour, and it was the best weather for a walk under tender breezes in gentle sunlight.

All around were green pastures where fat cows were grazing on the green grasses, boasting their giant breasts as huge as a football. The country path was very silent with no one except passing cars from time to time. We saw clusters of small houses far away across the fields, which had a variety of wild flowers blooming with bright colors in white, yellow, and pink. I took many pictures on my phone.

6/9/2011. I went out with Missionary Joo Soon, wife of Pastor Kim, and Pastor Ira to see the high school building located in the city, which was granted to them without cost by the government. Then we went to Khreschatyk, the main street of the city, and to Andriyivski Uzviz for shopping. Kiev was the first capital of the Soviet Union, where the Yalta Agreement was signed; then the capital was moved to St. Petersburg, and from there to Moscow. We visited the Metro, a huge market, to buy some groceries.

6/10/2011. We went out to the harbor at the Dnieper River, which was a long river flowing from the Volga River into the Black Sea. The scenery on the barge was quite different from the scene I remembered on the La Plata River in Buenos Aires, where I saw many fancy summer houses and expensive structures along the shore, but here I saw woods and nature itself with its undeveloped grandeur. I was able to see through the shrubs and trees in the woods, and occasionally far away the city buildings and the golden domes of the Orthodox churches. This river was longer and wider than the La Plata, so the tour time was doubled.

20 Years Ministry

7/1/2011. Tom wants me to stay with him these days, so I was unable to visit to Korea this year, the first time since I had been working for Biola for the past 20 years. God enabled me to travel to so many places in the world during those 20 years, and soon after my last 20th teaching trip to Moscow, the MGBC was closed under the present system. The school will be changed in the future, so that all the lectures will be given in the Russian language by local Russian teachers under a Russian Director. I was praising the Lord for the wonderful consequences that seemed to be done in God's timing according to His plan, because we had raised thousands of young Russian Christians to be evangelical Christian leaders for the last 20 years.

12/1/2011. I received an award from Biola, where I had worked for 20 years, which gave me a great feeling. My God had poured down unspeakably abundant blessings upon me during those years. The Lord led me to go to so many countries from 1991 to this year, often three to five times per year, to teach in the mission fields, giving the Biola University presentation and recruiting students for our ELSP program. I was never tired and was always happy and delighted, because the Lord was with me, and they had been the best days of my life.

When I look back at those 20 years, I wonder how many people in the world could have enjoyed such a gracious and blessed life. Because of Tom's health condition, I traveled only once this year, to Kiev. I had always been happy both in the past and in the present, because God's love and His tender mercies have been always overflowing on me.

Happy Days

Lovely Man

Since Tom started to lose his memory power and his body became weaker, he wants to rely on me and has seemed nearer to God as I pulled him there, and those things brought us the happiest times in our lives. In those days when he was still healthy and strong, he seemed to sometimes easily hurt himself and blow out his temper without any understandable reason, at least in my opinion. But those parts of his character seemed to be crumbling away and disappeared little by little, and he has been a changed and lovely man, so that my heart is deeply aching and sad as I looked at him. The side effects of the medicines brought him constantly bad constipation and/or vomiting, but he was not complaining and just accepted them quietly, which made my heart break.

These days, I must help him take care of all the medicines he is taking, put on his clothes, and wash his face and bathe, but those tasks make me grateful that I can help him. Every day and all their moments are precious to us, and we really appreciate our lives and are trying to accept life itself as joy. We are now truly happier than ever before. He seems like a disappearing sun in a glorious sunset in the sky, quietly shining its last beauty that I love greatly.

Our Worship Time

2/2012. This month Tom wanted to stop receiving the acupuncture treatments he has received since last December, for he seemed to realize they do not help him much. He prayed for all our meal prayers these days, and we had a simple worship time after dinner by memorizing the Apostles Creed, reading a chapter from the Bible with loud voices, verse by verse in turn, and closed it by praying the Lord's Prayer together. Before we went to bed, I prayed fervently for him to be healed in the name of Jesus by laying my hands on his shoulders, since the Lord said, "these signs will accompany those who believe: in my name they will drive out demons; they will place their hands on sick people, and they will get well (Mk 16:17-18)." Also, I was claiming to the Lord that Tom has a right to be healed, because the Bible said "by His stripes you have been healed (2Pe 2:24)" So, I prayed every day for Tom, relying on the Word.

3/2012. Mina suggested that dad's condition seemed to be worsening, and it would be good to have a family trip together before it was too late. Kris had already made a reservation for a 10-day Alaska cruise for eight people leaving on August 20th. I prayed that Tom's condition would be improved for the trip, so that all our children would cherish the memory with their grandpa for a long time.

5/14/2012. Because of my sick husband, I began practicing love with my hands and feet, when I used to only talk, washing his face and hair, putting his clothes on him, giving him his medicines on time. I began to love him even more.

I really want to be a woman of love for the rest of my life like Jesus. Yet, no matter how much I have tried, I could not do it, because no matter how much I love Tom, I would never lay down my life for him. But love covers a multitude of sins (1Pe 4:8) – although you have done many kinds of mistakes and many wrong doings, still love can say, "Well, it happened. I can forgive you." 1st Corinthian 13:7 says about love, "It always protects, always trusts, always hopes, and always perseveres."

Woman of Faith

7/27/2012. I truly want to be a woman of faith. Then what is faith? In one word to me, it is becoming a happy person without worrying about anything. My dad, the Mighty God, loves me as the apple of his eye, so I have nothing to worry about and always have a peaceful mind. What kind of worries would a baby have on his mother's bosom? The Lord said, perhaps the mom may forget her own baby, but He never forgets me and has inscribed me on the palms of His hands (Is 49:15-16) and always keeps me and watches over me, so I have nothing to worry about.

The faith God wants from us is not only that we believe in His mighty power, but that we also believe He is my dad who loves me dearly and wants to give me the best. He anticipates from us a level of faith that we can trust in him 100%, so that I rejoice and give thanks even when my prayer requests have not been answered or never will be answered.

Our prayers should request His will be done, rather than requesting something to be done for my will in worldly desires. However, still, because of my dear husband, my heart is heavy as I open my eyes every morning!

Casting Out the Demons

8/15/2012. It has already been two years since I suffered some severe pains from the disks in my back on the right side of my neck. I have been praying for this every day for healing and overcoming the pains with joy and peace. Because of my busy daily schedules with work, keeping doctors' appointments for Tom and taking care of him, I have been unable to get much time to take care of myself.

Today as I had a worship time with Tom, I prayed fervently, casting out demons in believing his Words.

"And these signs will accompany those who believe: in my name they will drive out demons; (Mk 16:17a)"

I was repeating this verse in a loud voice and rebuking the demons in the name of Jesus to leave my body; then, I suddenly felt stiffness in the back of my head. I felt the demons that were annoying my body were leaving it, and my voice was getting louder and louder, and eventually I clearly sensed the evils were leaving my body. At the same time, I experienced an extremely light feeling like a feather on my shoulders. The pain was gone in a second, gone completely and instantly, not little by little or a little bit better. Hallelujah! I clearly found out that the devils who brought the pain on my back neck had run away in the name of Jesus, by the blood of the lamb. Praise the name of our Lord Jesus Christ!

> "Resist the devil, and he will flee from you. (James 4:7b)"

It is necessary that we use not only medicines and doctors (Jerem 8:22) as well as praying for healing, but we must also cast out demons in the name of Jesus. When we cast out the demons in the name of Jesus, who had already defeated the devil, the evil spirits have no other choices but to flee from us. I was continually casting out the demons that brought on Tom's dementia and Parkinson's. "Lord, help me put on the full armor of God." We must always remember that our struggle is not against flesh and blood, but against the evils (Eph 6:12).

Alaska Cruise

8/31/2012. We returned safely from the Alaska Cruise for which we had prayed for a long time. The room in the ship was comfortable, like in a good hotel, and the food was excellent, but it seemed too much for Tom that we might not have the trip. I checked with both Dr. Bahadory, his primary physician, and Dr. Neff, the neurologist, to make sure for him before we left for the trip. They told me that the cruise would be fine, but he suffered greatly during the trip and had to stay lying in bed the whole time. The ship was floating somewhere in the Pacific Ocean, and we had no way to return home sooner than the tour schedule. I hoped and prayed that he would recover upon returning home.

9/4/2012. Tom did not show any recovery at all, and I greatly regretted the cruise. Before the trip, he was able to manage taking his medicines himself when I reminded him, and we could go to church together on Sunday, but now he was unable to do these things. He had no strength and only wanted to lie down on the bed and seemed to lose more memory power and become more confused.

Love in Patience

10/12/2012. These days, I felt that I lived two lives, because I had to take care of Tom for everything. But I was so grateful that he could move and walk, and more, that he is alive and stays next to me!

His left hand has been swollen during the past five days, so we visited the doctor's office to take an X-ray and MRI to see if any blood clusters blocked the vein. It took us all day long and was so stressful. Love must be able to endure with patience, gently and humbly!

> "Oh Lord help me. It's too hard for me. I felt so much exhausted this evening. Truly love is patient, believes all, hopes for all and endures all. Yes, I know well, help me Lord."

These days, my brother Ed and his wife drop by my house after the church service every Sunday to bring food and help me with any chores. I am grateful to them, as it becomes a great encouragement and strength for me.

11/5/2012. Tom took long naps during the day and looked sick. Because of the Megace hormone pills, his appetite seemed to return and helped him not lose too much weight. He became unable to control his urination any longer, and strangely he was afraid to sit on the toilet, or sit anywhere. He seemed to forget to sit on the toilet, because he could not figure out the distance from him to the toilet seat, and even as he sat on it, he was unable to start voiding soon. He seemed blank, and I had to wait until I could smell that he had relieved himself.

11/16/2012. We had to change his medicines many times because of side effects. Although he was taking eight Kabadopas pills per day, his condition showed no improvement. Dr. Neff prescribed a different medication, but it made him keep falling. He was so vulnerable that he fell without warning even while standing up from a chair or when holding on to something. The problem was that once he had fallen on the floor, I was unable to put him back on a chair alone. Many times, I had to run to the next-door neighbors to ask for help. So, we stopped that medicine for him and used a dementia patch called Youpro, which was so strong that he was able to stand up by himself from the bed and walk alone, but then his blood pressure went up so high, and he behaved strangely. Suddenly he did not follow my instructions and rushed with full energy, so I took away the patch. I was continually monitoring and sending emails to follow Dr. Neff's directions.

Thanksgiving season has come already, but it seemed to have nothing to do with us. My daily life is under a heavy yoke and burden. My wish was only that Tom was not too hard and was able to stand well another day. I pray all the time that only God's will be done in our lives, so that My God will only be glorified and exalted under any circumstances.

Going to the Emergency Room

12/21/2012. Strangely, Tom did not want to move his body since yesterday. He used to open his eyes every morning around six o'clock, and we would go together to the bathroom to shower, but today, he did not want to move and showed no responses. I called Kaiser and discussed his condition with an emergency nurse.

I called 911 according to the nurse's advice, and we went to the ER. They found the trace of a stroke at the bottom left side of his brain on the CT scan results. They moved him into the Intensive Care Unit and planned to take another CT tomorrow morning to compare the two pictures. I was shocked and remembered that he fell the other day, but it was a light fall. He often fell because of the medications he took, but I did not doubt that this stroke was due to the fall. They took another CT of his brain this morning, and the picture did not show any changes. They said that he needs to stay at the hospital for several more days.

12/24/2012. Since Mina delivered Isabelle three weeks ago, she was not in a condition to visit dad at the hospital, but the whole family, all seven of them, came to the hospital and brought meals yesterday and ate with me. I indeed appreciate such amazing children. Today is Christmas Eve, and they again brought dinner for me, and we ate it in a hospital lounge together. Tom was getting better, and they planned to move him to a regular hospital room.

To a Nursing Hospital

12/29/2012. They admitted him to a nursing hospital yesterday near our home, where he will receive physical therapy to recover his walking ability. They said that if he shows any progress in the treatments he can continue to stay there until he is completely recovered, but if he shows no progress, he will be discharged. The trainers told me that Tom does not show any responses, so that it seems hard for them to expect any progress.

1/5/2013. Dr. Ford was a Kaiser doctor assigned to take care of Kaiser's patients at the nursing hospital. Tom was getting slower, and it was harder for him to swallow foods, so they changed all his meals to liquid form, because the hard food gets into his pores, and then it may develop into pneumonia. They told me that many dementia patients are eventually forgetting how to swallow food and are unable to swallow; instead, they must be fed through a tube connected to their stomach or neck. I was so frustrated.

1/15/2013. Upon Tom being discharged from the nursing hospital, I needed a professionally trained caregiver to stay for 24 hours/day with Tom. Fortunately, I was introduced to a caregiver through an agency, someone who was a good Christian and had much care giving experience. She came to the nursing hospital to receive an orientation to take care of Tom, and we made a contract to pay her $100 per day. She is scheduled to move into my house on Wednesday, since Tom will be home on Thursday.

1/19/2013. I had completely prepared everything for his home-coming on the 16th, but I suddenly received an unexpected phone call from the nursing hospital. Tom had a high temperature, so Dr. Ford cancelled his discharge from the facility.

He had high temperatures going up over 100 degrees for unknown reasons for the last three days. The doctor said Tom's chest X-rays and blood tests are normal, so he wondered if the high temperatures might be caused by a certain virus. Since the patient refused to swallow anything, they planned to stop feeding anything through his mouth and instead provide food and medications through an IV.

A surgical procedure to put a tube into his stomach was scheduled at Kaiser for next Tuesday. When the tube is inserted into his body, he will be moved to stay at a nursing hospital for up to 100 days according to the insurance contract.

I arrived at the nursing hospital around 9:30 a.m. today. Soon a nurse came into the room and measured Tom's blood pressure, which was 238/125. We thought something was wrong with the blood pressure machine, so another nurse came in and she measured it manually and that showed 190/100. It seemed to me that happened as they started the IV and stopped all the medicines, including the blood pressure medicines he took. Since it was Saturday, Dr. Ford was not at the hospital, so the nurses called him and waited for more than an hour, but they received no response from the doctor.

The frustrated nurses called 911, and paramedics came and gave a shot to lower his blood pressure temporarily, and they moved him to an emergency room at a regular hospital near the nursing hospital. The ER doctor ordered a CT to make sure of any strokes and gave him an IV providing the blood pressure medicine Tom had previously been taking. They contacted Kaiser and Tom was transferred to the Irvine Kaiser Facility to be hospitalized.

1/20/2013. The five-year-old new Irvine Kaiser building was very clean, and the nurses at the ward were all kind. Tom's blood pressure was controlled, and his operation to insert the tube was scheduled for tomorrow. They only gave him an IV today, and it was annoying to hear him continually groaning due to the sputum boils in his chest. The nurses tried to get the sputum out of his airway, but they continually boiled. He seemed so sick, and today is the fourth day they gave him only water. I was very frustrated.

1/21/2013. The operation putting the tube into his stomach was done well, and they were planning to move him back to the nursing hospital. I realized that I was not yet ready to send him to the Lord. Whenever anything happened to him, my heart trembled hard and I shed tears uncontrollably.

1/22/2013. An ambulance came and delivered Tom to the nursing hospital. The boils of phlegm in his chest seemed severe, and the noises became louder. It was no use that the nurses and even I tried to take the boiling sputum out of his throat. Dr. Ford told me that he will prescribe stronger medicines to reduce the phlegm and pain.

Cost of Life

2/4/2013. I had a meeting with the medical teams to discuss Tom's situation this morning. They reviewed his condition and made a strong opinion that Tom's dementia and Parkinson's are hopeless, so in case he gets pneumonia, the way would be to let him go with less pain by taking the tube out of his body. Their thought was that eventually they would have to use stronger antibiotics in case of pneumonia; then he would start having diarrhea that results in severe pain, and probably his life would be meaningless in a continuation of torments.

However, my thought was different. In any circumstances, human life is so precious and valuable, that to keep the life, we must pay the price, so Tom also might pay the cost to keep his life. Besides, Tom's life belongs to God who gave it to him, so God will take it from him in His time. We can hardly make any decisions for another person's life, and what we must do is only to help them to live.

2/20/2013. An interview was requested by a woman doctor who came from Kaiser instead of Dr. Ford, who had gone on vacation. After reviewing Tom's chart, she told me that I should be next to him with a ready mind. It would happen today or tomorrow and would not take more than a week.

Kris and Mina decided to move into my house to stay with me for a while. Fortunately, Kris was able to get off from work until the end of March because of Isabelle's birth. The seven people who filled my empty upstairs rooms became a great relief and comfort for me. I really appreciated Kris and Mina.

2/22/2013. Dr. Ford mentioned to me this morning that they will give him only water and will stop feeding him for 48 hours, as food was too stressful on his body. If we continue feeding more liquids into his lungs, that would result in more phlegm, which will bring him more pain.

2/24/2013. He has had high temperatures since yesterday afternoon and was not even breathing from time to time. His blood pressure came down, and his oxygen level went to 71, so we thought he was coming to the end. So, I called a pastor, and we had a kind of farewell service with the children. However, his blood pressure went up at night, and his oxygen level also went up to normal.

Dr. Ford came in the morning and heard Tom's chest sound and told me that the tube should not be reinserted. His body has no strength to digest food, which may bring more phlegm, and it might cause him to choke.

"In such a condition, if we feed him, he might go sooner. We should let him go in peace. We should give him stronger medicines to release him from pains. It will be maximum 3 or 4 days."

See You in Heaven

2/27/2013. Today, Tom left for Heaven to be with the Lord. He went to his Father's house since he had received Jesus Christ as his

Savior, and there was no other place to go except Heaven for him. "Thank you, Jesus." How happy are those who have a heavenly place to go after their life on earth!

I tried so much to be with him at his bedside, but I was so sad when I found that I missed the time to bid farewell to him. I had stayed all day long at his bedside, then his temperature went down, his blood pressure was up to 91, and his breathing had returned to normal, so I left him for a few hours to get something from home. It was the same as yesterday and the day before yesterday, so I thought today would be okay, too. I was greatly frustrated and felt panic when I received a phone call from the nursing hospital.

My heart was sinking as I was running to him, but Mina would not let me drive myself to the hospital. Also, Mina could not leave the baby and the other children at home without an adult, as Kris had gone to their home to pick up something earlier. So, we had to wait for around 30 minutes for Kris to return home, so we called other relatives and friends. When we arrived, Pastor Aaron Oh and his friend were there. I really appreciated Pastor Oh, who had always been a great help when Tom was still at home. Whenever I was in trouble, he ran to our home like a bullet to help us.

Tom's face was completely white, without expression, and it seemed like it was carved in a piece of marble. His mouth was open as before, but his nose line was handsome, and I remembered the old dream that I had before our marriage. I whispered to him in tears, "I love you. I love you. I am sorry I couldn't give you a farewell kiss."

"Dear Lord, thank you that you called him and received him where you are. Thank you that you delivered him out of the jail, his painful body to you. Lord, I entrust him in your hands. Please take care of him. For the

last 40 years without missing a single day, have not
I prayed that just today he should go back to your
bosom! 'If you believe, you will see the glory of God'
so that I have confidence in you. Now I see he is seeing
your face next to you."

The Happy Three Years

3/6/2013. Looking back on our 46 years of married life, the last
three years have been the happiest time for me. As Tom became
sick, he completely started relying on me. We prayed together
every day several times, we read the Bible, the Apostle's Creed
and Lord's Prayer. Little by little, he was forgetting words and was
unable to pronounce the words, so it became increasingly difficult, and eventually the moment came that we had to stop these
worship activities.

I was happy during those days and grateful that I was able to
give my love to him. However, my love could not help him much,
so I cried a lot. My heart is now at peace, because he is enjoying
freedom in Heaven with the Lord; he has flown out of the painful
jail of the mortal body.

Goodbye, My Love

3/8/2013. Paul, my nephew, drove me to Loma Vista Chapel this morning. The place was cozy and filled with sweet aromas from myriads of flowers, which gave me a quite different impression from when I was there yesterday. Wreaths surrounded all the chairs in back, and roses and lilies were beautifully arranged on the shining wooden coffin. Next to the coffin, his gentle, smiling face in a black picture frame was amazingly handsome. It seemed a good idea that I did not allow them to open his coffin, so that people could continually remember his healthy and handsome young face.

3/9/2013. More people gathered for his memorial service this morning, held at the Miracle Center of Grace Korean Church, where they arranged a simultaneous interpretation system for our American friends, including Mina and Kris's Chinese friends from their church. Caleb recited Palm 23 and Abigail read from John 11, verses 25 and 26, when Jesus says to Martha, if you believe in Him, you will live even in death. Mina's memorial speech was moving, and I felt proud of her. The message given by Pastor Suh Lee was comforting to all of us, and the audio about Tom prepared by Pastor Oh was also great.

While I was listening to his short bio read by Jae Jung, his nephew, my life memories with him were running through my mind. When he came to America, he wanted to quickly stand up financially, so he left Utah, left the studying to me, and he was all in to make money. He worked hard and earned plenty of money and also spent it freely. He was involved in many social and community activities and their organizations and made many donations to them that could contribute to the development of the Korean American Community in the Orange County area. He served as the President of the Korean American Association of Orange County, was President of the Han Woo Assoc. in OC, President of the Seniors' Association in OC, Chairman of the Board of Korean Schools in OC, President of the Youth Sponsorship Group in OC, Vice President of the Korean Lions Club in OC, and was a member of the National Unification Advisory Council.

Mina's Memorial Speech for Dad

Sharing at My Father's Memorial

During the difficult weeks leading up to my father's passing, I spent some time thinking about life and the many blessings in his life. One of the blessings I considered was that my father had a full life. He graduated from the most prestigious university in Korea, he was able to immigrate to the United States and he became a successful businessman. My father also really enjoyed people and being around people, so he had many friends and was involved in several different organizations. And he was blessed with five grandchildren.

Another blessing was that my father had a wife that loved him. My mom told me once that when she met my dad, she fell in love with him because he was so handsome. And even though my parents were different and had separate interests, she made many attempts to share in his interests. She even tried to take up golf. And for decades, my mother prayed fervently for my father. She prayed that my father would come to know and love the Lord. The Lord answered her prayers. Then later in his life, my mother took great care of him as he became more and more debilitated and more and more dependent on her. And in his last days, she sat all day and most of the nights by his side in the hospital.

But the greatest blessing is that my father was chosen by God to be His for eternity. Even though my father was blessed in this life, it was short. And it's not just his life; it's all our lives.

The Bible describes our lives as a vapor. Here, then gone. When my father left us, he went to be home with his Father in Heaven; to begin his life in eternity. He is finally free. Free of his deteriorating body, free from the worries of this world and free from sin and the effects of sin. He is infinitely happier now than his happiest day on earth.

> In Psalm 16:11, it says: "You make known to me the path of life; In Your presence there is fullness of joy; At your right hand are pleasures forevermore."

I respected and treasured my father the most during the latter years of his life. At that time, my father was retired so he was no longer the primary provider and his declining health meant he wasn't the strongest. He wasn't bringing home any more awards and he wasn't the president of anything anymore, but he was humble, so I respected him. He was gentle and that was his strength. My children felt warm and comfortable with their sweet grandfather and I loved him for that. That is how I want to remember him. I am thankful to the Lord for giving us these last sweet years with him. They were a gift, a treasure. And treasures like that only come from the Lord. And when my children ask about their grandfather, I will tell them about these latter years and that he was blessed by the Lord.

My Husband, My God

3/16/2013. One-week has already passed, but still flowers from the wreaths covered his tomb, where I felt peace, not like at the hospital, where he was groaning out of suffering and agony. Since he has been released from his prison and was now with the Lord, this tomb is only for the old house his soul used to live in, but still I like to be at his tomb as if I was at the hospital bed next to him.

3/19/2013. It is so strange and hard to comprehend. Why has nothing changed, but Tom isn't next to me? Why is yesterday's sun rising this morning, all the signal lights on the familiar streets are working as usual, and all the people we know are all healthy and live busy lives just same as yesterday, but why isn't Tom next to me? Why did God take him so early? It is hard to adjust to understand the situation that he isn't next to me, and I have become a woman without a husband.

3/20/2013. Today I had an 11 o'clock dentist appointment. When the dentist asked me casually how Tom is doing these days, suddenly my eyes started pouring out tears like a waterfall without any warning; I never had such an experience before. As if his asking about him was a signal, my heart was so sad and so broken that I wept bitterly. I was on the dentist chair with my mouth open, and my tears were continually running down both cheeks like rain. The dentist was so embarrassed and seemed not to know what to say to comfort me and could not continue to be scaling as well. It was so strange a phenomenon that I was unable to control the tears running down on my cheeks all day long.

The children came down to buy me dinner in the evening, and on the way to the restaurant my tears still did not stop. I have been in a blank state for the last two weeks, so that sometimes I felt he was still in the nursing hospital, but now I was starting to feel his empty place, which made me lonely and sad. He was unable to speak or move his body, but his presence was still next to me, which was becoming a great comfort and strength to me.

5/28/2013. I was like a person who has lost her home, for my husband was my home. Wherever I was, my heart was always hurrying to return home where he was waiting for me. But I do not need to be hurrying these days, for I have lost my home, so I wanted to cry, and was too lonely. Even my Lord is whispering to me that I am with you and the One who made you is your husband (Is 54:5).

From time to time when his senses came to him, he looked at me with pitiful eyes. He could not move his lips, but his eyes were telling me, "I love you. Thank you." His twinkling whispers pierced into my heart and became twinkling stars that will shine warmly and beautifully in my heart until the day I will see him again in the presence of my God.

My Love, My Lord

8/14/2014. For the last year, there have been many changes around me, among which the biggest was that I moved to a small, one-bedroom house not far from beach. Tom would not have liked it, but I love the house, because it was small and open as if I came for a vacation.

During this move, I lost my wedding ring that I had put on for 40 years. I lost it on moving day, dropped it some place on the way to move. I tried very hard to locate it, but I could not find it, so I decided to stop trying to find it, because it sounds a bit absurd, but I felt that the Lord may allow me to lose it. I was sorry and sad but decided only to look upon the Lord, and I told myself, "Well, I am happy without the ring. I am only living in His grace, and no matter what is happening to me, I can satisfy, I adore Him and love Him."

Several days ago, I walked to a small shopping area near the South Gate of our complex to do some errands at the bank, where I saw a jewelry store next to the bank. These days, I occasionally felt the emptiness of my ring finger, and I missed the ring, so I entered the store to see if there would be a ring like mine.

I saw, in a front showcase, a diamond ring with a marquise shape the same as my lost wedding ring. I tried it on my finger, and it fit perfectly on me. The actual cost was $7,500, but they would give it to me at $4,200 with a discount. That seemed to me a good price for a one karat diamond. However, $4,200 seemed too much for me to spend for a ring.

Then, a shop keeper who heard my lost wedding ring story said to me, "Did you check with your insurance company?" With a light mind without any expectation, I just wanted to check with the Insurance company for my old home owner insurance, which had ended two months ago when the house escrow was closed.

I was unable to find any record of my old home owner's insurance except the name of the company, no agent name, no phone number or policy number. I went to Google on the Internet and picked up any contact number of the insurance company and called, giving them my name and old home address and asked them to find my policy record if they could. Soon the person on the other side of the phone said that he found my policy record and inquired information about the ring. I told him that we bought the ring more than 40 years ago, and I have not kept any certificate for the ring, but I could send a picture showing that I wore the ring on my finger, if they needed.

I received a phone call from the insurance company a few days later, from which I received an unbelievable report. The appraisal price of the ring was around $7,500 (I could not understand how they knew the price without not even seeing the ring), but usually the company pays $1,000 maximum, in case you have a special coverage for jewelry in your home owner insurance package. The insurance man told me that in my case, however, someone had recently upgraded my insurance coverage, so that even with $1,000 deductible, they could pay me $3,000 in cash, and they had already mailed a check to me.

I was so startled. How could such a thing happen! Who has upgraded the coverage and how did the insurance company know the ring cost would be around $7,500 without seeing the ring, which was, strangely, the same amount as the original cost of the ring I wanted to buy? I had not yet sent any picture of my lost wedding ring to them. We also had purchased the minimal coverage to meet the bank requirements for home owners when we bought our home owner insurance. Because we did not need any special coverage for jewelry, I did not have any jewelry, except the wedding ring I always wore. The most amazing thing was that someone had recently upgraded my coverage. Who did this? I saw again my Lord's miracle. My God probably exchanged the wedding ring from my husband to a new ring from my Lord.

Another unbelievable thing that happened on that day was that I received a check from the escrow company that was leftover from the escrow that ended two months ago, which I did not expect at all. I realized that the Lord really wanted to give the ring to me, so I would get the new marquise diamond ring that I wanted.

This ring was from my God as a wedding ring with the Lord. From now on, forget Tom, and always remember the Lord is my true husband. This ring will remind me always that my God is the living God who manifest signs and wonders at any time, whenever He wants. Through this ring incident, my God gave me positive confidence that He is always caring for me and guides me and leads me in His way. He inscribed me on the palms of His hands, and my walls are continuously before Him (Is 49:16).

I will always kiss His Son (Ps 2:12), so I will be forever rejoicing and in peace, and forever happy.

"Dear Lord, I promise you that I will love you forever"

Epilogue

I had spent six months in emptiness and confusion following Tom's departure from me, and then I started to read my old diary to fill my empty heart. It gave me a great comfort and encouragement, and made me happy, because I realized God's amazing love had poured upon me throughout my life. This thought inspired me to publish a book from the diary, and since last September, I slowly started to gather episodes together. I truly appreciated my God and praised Him when I realized everything the Lord had caused everything to work together for good to me in His grace.

This book is a recording about how God has worked in my life and led me throughout my life. The Lord has been my Shepherd and led me beside quiet waters; He guides me along the right paths for His name's sake. He prepares a table before me in the presence of my enemies and anoints my head with oil. His goodness and love will follow me all the days of my life (Ps 23) until I see His face.

Everything in this book is true, because the book was written based on my diary. Also, any part of the information in this book cannot be from my pride, for I am only His masterpiece. The Lord is my husband, my life, and everything to me. Truly all the praise, glory and honor be to my God!